East Fife On This Day

An East Fife crowd in the 1930s. Almost everyone is wearing a bonnet

East Fife
On This Day

David W. Potter

Kennedy & Boyd,
an imprint of
Zeticula Ltd,
Unit 13,
196 Rose Street,
Edinburgh,
EH2 4AT,
Scotland.

http://www.kennedyandboyd.co.uk
admin@kennedyandboyd.co.uk

First published in 2019
Copyright © David W. Potter 2019
Cover design © Zeticula Ltd 2019
Cover photograph: An East Fife crowd in the 1930s. They are all quite well dressed but there is a total absence of women.

Every effort has been made to trace copyright holders of images. Any omissions will be corrected in future editions.

Paperback ISBN 978-1-84921-178-9
Hardback ISBN 978-1-84921-188-8

All rights reserved. No part of this publication may be reproduced, stored in a retrieval system, or transmitted in any form or by any means, electronic, mechanical, photocopying, recording or otherwise, without the prior permission of the publishers.

Acknowledgements

I am indebted to quite a few people who have helped and encouraged me in this book, in particular Jim Corstorphine, the author of that fine book "On That Windswept Plain" — the history of the first 100 years of the club.

Jim has also been the club photographer and he has supplied the photos, and I thank him very much.

The club in general has been very supportive.

My old friend Alan Guild who played for the club in the 1960s when a student at St Andrews University also gave me a few stories, as did a lifelong supporter, the late Willie Warrender.

To those whom I have omitted, my apologies, but I hope I can make it up to you by your enjoyment of the book.

David Potter
Kirkcaldy, June 2019

A lovely view of old Bayview

Contents

Acknowledgements v
Illustrations ix

Introduction 1
July 5
August 51
September 107
October 149
November 197
December 239
January 277
February 319
March 359
April 397
May 445
June 489

Index 523

A view of old Bayview from the Aberhill end of the ground

Illustrations

An East Fife crowd in the 1930s.	ii
A lovely view of old Bayview	vi
A view of old Bayview from the Aberhill end of the ground	viii
The Wellesley Road turnstiles	xii
East Fife 1907.	6
A rare trip to Spartans	11
New Bayview being constructed in July 1998	20-22
Kyle Wilkie in action against Dundee	27
More than a wee shower of rain	28
Laying the astroturf in July 2017	30
Kyle Wilson shoots in a game against the Pars	32
A young Henry McLeish in 1968	38
Nathan Austin and Peter Grant jr (Falkirk) at the Falkirk Stadium	41
Tommy Adams	45
Lloyd Young in action at Stark's Park	49
East Fife 1920	52
The Menu For the Centenary Dinner	54
Nathan Flanagan is surrounded by Stranraer players	59
Action in a game against Albion Rovers.	61
David Muir at Ibrox	63
Programme cover: EF v Rangers Gorman Testimonial 1984	64
Scot Symon on the left with his men, 1947/48	67
Bayview at East Fife v Clydebank on August 10 1968	69
A good view of the old Bayview stand in that game v Clydebank	70
Programme cover: Rangers v EF 11 August 1956	72
Programme cover: EF v Manchester Utd 13th August 1995	74
Programme cover: EF v Raith Rovers 13 August 1975	76
Craig Johnstone scores at Recreation Park, Alloa	78
Charlie Fleming in action against Aberdeen in 1953	79
John Nangle, scorer of East Fife's first goal	81
Programme cover: EF v St Mirren 17 August 1996	83
Dom Currie	88
Charlie Fleming	90

Jimmy Bonthrone	94
Programme cover: St Johnstone v EF 27 August 1983	99
Willie Telfer challenges Davie Duncan on 28 August 1948	101
East Fife supporters at Ibrox in 2013	104
East Fife with the Second Division trophy and the Fife Cup.	106
East Fife in 1927.	108
Programme cover: Gretna v EF 7 September 2002	114
Derek O'Connor scores for East Fife against Raith Rovers	116
Programme cover: EF v Stranraer 10 September 2016	119
Programme cover: EF v Hibernian 11 September 1968	122
Lloyd Young in action at Station Park, Forfar in 2010	124
The first ever photograph, taken on September 12 1903	125
Dene Shields and Andrew Cook in the Fife derby in 2008	128
Paul McManus and Kevin Twaddle of Ayr United	137
Paul McManus has just scored	145
East Fife in 1927.	151
Henry Morris in his Scotland colours	151
Scotland, October 1 1949 with two East Fife players	153
George "Dod" Aitken	154
John McArthur, Chairman	163
Hearts v East Fife at Tynecastle in 1948.	164
Alan Guild	172
Programme cover: EF v Clydebank 17 October 1970	174
Programme cover: Forfar v EF 23 October 1982	179
East Fife have just won the League Cup on October 24 1953	183
East Fife with the League Cup won in 1953.	184
Liam Buchanan v Rangers.	187
Davie Duncan scores for East Fife against Dunfermline in 1949	191
Old Bayview's last match v Livingston on Hallowe'en 1998	194
East Fife in 1971.	198
Davie Duncan scores in the Scottish League Cup final of 1947	200
Programme cover: Celtic v EF 3 November 1973	202
Programme cover: Montrose v EF 9 November 2002	209
Programme cover: Partick Thistle v EF 15 November 1975	216
The stand at new Bayview filled to capacity in November 2008	218
Jonny Page has just scored against Clyde at Broadwood.	223
Steve Hislop scores against Forfar	226
Craig Johnstone in action against Arbroath	232
East Fife with the huge Scottish Qualifying Cup	240

Programme cover: Stirling Albion v EF 3 December 1960	244
Phil Weir	251
Scot Symon, Manager	261
Chris Duggan in action at Gayfield, fending off Scott Martin	274
East Fife v Meadowbank on December 31 1994	276
East Fife in 1981	278
Ian Gardiner challenges at Bayview on January 5 1952	284
Ross Brown and Willis Furtado	287
Action at Pittodrie against Aberdeen	289
Tommy Adams	299
Chris Kane heads for goal against Brora Rangers	302
The East Fife team that beat Raith Rovers 3-0 in 1970	308
A great view of Bayview on January 26 1991.	310
Cartoon of East Fife v Kilmarnock on 31 January 1923	317-318
Team photo taken at Christmas 1960 at Station Park.	320
Dalymount Park, Dublin and the game is off!	323
Kyle Wilkie scores against Montrose	328
The East Fife team that put Aberdeen out of the Scottish Cup	341
Kenny Dalglish of Celtic tries to beat Ernie McGarr	342
Chris Duggan at Somerset Park, Ayr.	344
Ian Gardiner scores v Partick Thistle in February 1953.	357
Taken on 18th January 1964 at Glebe Park.	360
An odd incident on March 5 1938.	365
"We've won the League!"	377
A section of the crowd on March 19 1938	382
Henry Morris	385
A "near thing" from Stark's Park in 1938	388
Team Photo 1967.	398
Action from the Scottish Cup semi-final against St Bernards	400
Gary Naysmith in action at Gayfield	402
Charlie Fleming	408
Dan McKerrel scores the winner against St Bernards	414
Celebrations at Broadwood in 2016	418
More celebrations in 2016	420
Programme cover: Hibernian v EF 18 April 1958	423
Adult Ticket for 19 April, 2018, against Arbroath.	425
Showing off the Division Three trophy in 2008	426
Programme cover: EF v Kilmarnock, 23 April 1938	431
Bobby Linn in action against Albion Rovers at Cliftonhill	435

The crowd await the return of their Cup heroes, April 27 1938	437
East Fife's Scottish Cup winners	438
A somewhat primitive colour postcard	439
Jamie Insall shoots in a game against East Stirlingshire	443
East Fife season 1974 75	446
Action from East Fife and Edinburgh City	449
Stranraer is the venue for this action.	453
Kenny Deuchar is chaired high after promotion is clinched	459
Programme cover: EF v Queen's Park 10 May 2003	461
Stevie Nicholas is on the ball here in the game	462
Mascots!	469
David Muir scores at Peterhead	471
The Menu Card for the 110th Anniversary	478
Methil residents admire the Scottish Cup in 1938	479
Scottish Cup on display in 1938	480
East Fife July 2009.	490
The Bayview Pie Hut	521

Introduction

The name "East Fife" is very much interwoven into the fabric of Scottish football. As the name suggests, this club represents not so much a town as an area. Slightly to the west is Kirkcaldy and Raith Rovers, and further west still are Dunfermline and Cowdenbeath, while to the North is the now ageing "new" town called Glenrothes, a hybrid and multi-cultural area, to which East Fife once came dangerously close to migrating.

But apart from these three industrialised areas, East Fife can draw support from more or less the rest of the Kingdom of Fife, an interesting balance between the heartland of the Levenmouth area — the slightly bourgeois Leven, and the undeniably working class Buckhaven and Methil. They were once heavily industrialised but are now sadly run-down. But loads (I should perhaps say "shoals"!) of East Fife supporters dwell in the lovely rural fishing villages like Crail, Pittenweem, Elie and the larger University town of St Andrews.

Until 1998 East Fife played in Methil at Bayview, from which one presumably got a good view of the bay at one point although latterly the houses and shops rendered difficult any such opportunity. It was called in 1903 "that windswept plain" as the excellent East Fife author Jim Corstorphine tells us.

In 1998 they moved to a new ground much closer to the sea which is sometimes called New Bayview. It is as yet incomplete with only one side furnished with a stand — and on the other three ... well nothing, actually ... although there have been temporary stands erected there on the occasion that Rangers came calling, for example.

Match day at New Bayview can be a desolate experience sometimes. Sitting in the stand (and you can't go anywhere else, for there is no other place) means you are protected from the prevailing west wind, but totally exposed to the other three directions. Ironically there is a solar power farm next door (some hope, one might think on a miserable November day!) and there is now an all-weather pitch in place.

One wet day last October the fire alarm went off at half-time and everyone standing in the queue for the pies was advised by the tannoy

The Wellesley Road turnstiles

to leave at once and not use the lift. It was cheerfully ignored by everyone, and the irony did not go unnoticed. The dangers of anyone being burned to death in the cold, wet, open ambience of New Bayview are not high!

Little remains of the old Bayview, and that is a shame, for the place positively reeked of the atmosphere of Scottish football. An old, unattractive but functional stand, a separate building for the dressing room, terracings on the other three sides, only one of them covered, and a half-time scoreboard to tell everyone, in a pre-electronic age, how the other teams were doing.

It was from that cradle that came the great East Fife teams of bygone days! The late 1940s and early 1950s saw three Scottish League Cups, all before teams like Celtic and Hearts had even appeared in a final! Do not disturb our dreams of Adams and Fleming of long ago!

Bayview is in Methil. Methil's motto is *Carbone Carbasoque* — "by coal and canvass" a clear indication of how East Fife supporters would tend to earn their living, by either working down the mines of by fishing. "Never grudge what you have to pay for coal or fish" my grandfather used to say on the grounds that men's lives were at stake getting them for you — and certainly the mineral wealth of the land and the harvest of the sea did not yield themselves lightly, for the area is rich (if that is an appropriate word) in tragic stories about pit accidents and sea drownings.

Methil, apparently, has no heraldic coat of arms, and the reason is quite obvious, in that the place did not really exist in medieval times. Similar to places like Coatbridge in Lanarkshire, Methil is a child of the Industrial Revolution, born more or less to churn out coal for the greedy demands of the industries that put the Great in Great Britain. Or to export coal to bring in even more money!

One must always make a major effort not to get too carried away with a cosy, idyllic picture of a mining community peopled by decent, hard-working honest men and sonsie faced, cheerful ladies with about eight children, constantly happy and supportive to everyone else; both parents forever telling their children about the value of education and insisting on Church attendance on a Sunday; everyone "looking out for each other" in times of strife and industrial tension.

That is the picture of romance and the deliberate whitewashing of reality, but yet there is an element of truth in the stereotype as well.

The other side of the coin contains the crime, the violence, the jealousy, the hatred, the poverty, the alcoholism, the teenage pregnancies, the inbreeding and the incest — such things did exist as well. And one would be a fool to deny it.

But a football team is a great unifier. East Fife are a great community team. The love of the team gives everyone something in common to get upset about, to cheer about and to get involved in. There is nothing wrong or unusual in a football team representing its community and its geographical area. Indeed it is healthy and necessary.

There have been times when the Levenmouth community has been at the sharp end of things. It was arguably the pointless Thatcher v Scargill civil war of the mid-eighties which ended the concept of "community" in that area, but the earlier strike of 1926 saw general and widespread suffering of the Fife miners at the hands of the brutal and vindictive coal owners.

There is little point in denying that, but what better way was there to hit back than through the football team? In 1927, little more than six months after the final surrender in the Miners' Strike (the General Strike had been a 10-day fiasco), East Fife gave everyone a boost by reaching the Scottish Cup final — while still in the Second Division!

Eleven years later, with war clouds looming and with many Fife miners fighting in Spain in the struggle against Fascism that everyone would eventually have to face, East Fife went one better — and actually won the trophy, also while in the Second Division!

The historian cannot fail to write about these days, any more than he/she can avoid the three great League Cup triumphs of 1947/48, 1949/50 and 1953/54. This time it was different, although there is still a sociological link. By now, the miners were in the ascendancy. Coal mining had been nationalised and the slavery to the hated dynastic families with their low wages and scant regard for safety while all the time professing some bogus interest in the welfare of the miners was over. Everyone now worked for the National Coal Board. "We are the masters now," said a Labour politician in 1945. East Fife similarly now realised that there was no need to be afraid of Rangers and Celtic. They too could win trophies.

And there is the story of the great Henry Morris. It is a story that proves that fact is stranger than fiction. Henry played one game for Scotland, against Ireland in 1949, scored a hat-trick in an 8-2 victory — and never played for Scotland again! You could not really make that one up, could you?

Similarly far-fetched was the International career of Charlie Fleming, a man who had nicknames like "Legs" and "Cannonball". He actually only scored two in his one and only game for Scotland! And he is one of the very few men to have played for a team called Great Britain!

There are still those who recall these far-off days. Every East Fife supporter would love to see the great days come back. It does not look, at the moment, all that likely, it has to be said, but then who am I to say that? The story of East Fife Football Club is a great one, and really needs to be told.

East Fife are, by some standards, a very young team, founded some 20 years after Raith Rovers, and a good 30 years after the time when senior football began to take off. The first Scotland International was played in 1872, the first Scottish Cup final took place in 1874, and East Fife kicked their first football in 1903. The others therefore got off to a good start, but East Fife caught up.

This book does not claim to be anything like a history of the club. A "day-by-day" historical diary of the club cannot, by its very nature, claim to be that. In addition, there have been certain eras of the club where it is perhaps wise not to say very much; conversely, the author will make no apology for a heavy emphasis on 1938, and the great years immediately after the Second World War. The achievements of that era speak for themselves. He will similarly make no apology for relating football to other things going on in the world. The best football books are, paradoxically, not entirely about football.

Never is this more apparent than in the summer months. Not a lot of football has been played by East Fife in the month of June, for example. The author however has taken advantage of these lacunae or gaps to indulge his passion in other aspects of the very rich cultural and social history of Fife and Scotland.

The author is not, by birth, an East Fife supporter. This does not mean that he cannot look upon them and admire all that they have achieved. And it's a lot!

July

East Fife 1907. Observe the goalkeeper wears the same jersey as everyone else but is distinguished from the others by a bonnet.

July 1 1916

This was the day of the big push. The idea was that it would take everyone to Berlin in about a month's time. It was in fact the carnage which is now referred to as the Battle of the Somme.

Never was there a better example of the "lions led by donkeys" statement about the British Army, as the whistles blew early in the morning and an hour and a half later, about 20,000 casualties were sustained! While no-one doubts the heroism of the men concerned, the judgement of those who led them into it is deservedly lampooned in TV series like "Blackadder" for example. Indeed, there would have been a strong case for describing Douglas Haig as a "war criminal".

Many East Fife supporters were among the dead and wounded, and at least one ex-player was badly wounded — a man called Private Ralph Skene, who now lived in Kirkcaldy, but who had played in goal for East Fife before the war, as well as playing for Kirkcaldy United and Dunfermline Athletic for a spell.

On the same day, James Logan of Raith Rovers was also badly affected by shellshock. German artillery did not discriminate between Fife football teams! Such however was the effectiveness of British propaganda that it would be several years after the war before people began to realise what a shocking defeat the Battle of the Somme had been with the Generals, Douglas Haig in particular, guilty of callous disregard for the lives of their soldiers.

Newspapers of the time were still talking about an "advance" and a "success" and "hitting Huns all round" — but the casualty lists told a different story.

July 2 1921

Football was taking a back seat at the moment, although everyone was looking forward to seeing East Fife in the Scottish League for the first time in August.

But the weather was good and there was now a temporary lull in the miners' dispute after several months of the pits being idle. Fortunately there seemed to be no lasting damage to the pits, and the Government had lowered the tension a little by standing down the detachment of the Black Watch which had been assigned to guard the collieries in the East of Fife, but only a fool would think that the problem was solved.

Meanwhile East Fife were taking steps to ensure that their good players were being re-engaged, for not only was there a great deal of interest in the Scottish League, there was also a desire to have another attempt on the Scottish Qualifying Cup.

Other sporting interests going on at the moment included Warwick Armstrong's Australians on tour in Great Britain — a team that was already clearly far too strong for JWHT Douglas's England.

Today there was much excitement about the Heavyweight Championship of the World between Jack Dempsey and Georges Carpentier at the Boyle's Thirty Acres, Jersey City, New Jersey. There was great support for the "Manassa Mauler" as Dempsey was called, but Carpentier (commonly called "gorgeous Georges" and pronounced Carpenteer by those who were not very good at French!) but it was the defending champion Dempsey who won, knocking out his opponent in the fourth round. It was the world's first million-dollar fight.

July 3 1960

One of the clearest signs that the bad days of poverty and unemployment were passing (even though they had not entirely disappeared) was seen in the way that television was now an increasingly important part of working class life.

More and more households now possessed one with local firms showing some enterprise in allowing the renting of television sets with names like Ekco, Pye and Defiant.

It took football a long time to waken up to the potential of television, which it persisted in seeing as some kind of a threat, with only the very occasional game, often the Scotland v England International allowed on TV. (The last three Scotland v England Internationals at Hampden had been televised in 1956, 1958 and 1960.)

However, teams like East Fife were not as quick as they might have been in realising that TV offered an alternative to football on a Saturday afternoon, and that if facilities were not quickly improved, people might choose to spend a Saturday afternoon watching Horse Racing, Rugby League or even Wrestling on TV in the comfort of their house rather than standing in the cold and the rain to watch East Fife at Bayview.

Sport on TV was generally good — recently, for example, the nation had been able to see most of an England v South Africa Test Match and the Men's Singles final at Wimbledon in which Neale Fraser had defeated Rod Laver. And yet, football was still Scotland's number one sport. The challenge was whether football, particularly at the level of East Fife, could adapt to the new age. Sometimes one wondered if it ever would.

July 4 2017

This evening at a dreich Ainslie Park (not the sort of weather that one associates with July!) East Fife played Spartans in a pre-season friendly and lost 0-1 in front of a crowd that one would have to describe as minuscule, albeit voluble and encouraging.

Ross Allum scored the only goal of the game for the Edinburgh side, but the game was not really taken very seriously with both sides making substitutions more or less at will.

The idea was that everyone in both squads could get a game so that the management could make informed judgements about their players for the important tasks that lay ahead.

There was a lot to admire about the Spartans. Founded in 1951 by Edinburgh University graduates, some of whom presumably being Classics men, who admired the mighty deeds of Leonidas and company at Thermopylae in 480 BC, and called their team "Spartans" whose motto was to be "live together, play together, win together".

They used to play in the East of Scotland League but now play in the Lowland League, and have had several successful forays into the Scottish Cup, their key ingredient being enthusiasm. At the end of this season, they would reach the play-offs for the Scottish League. They would have to be called a football success story.

East Fife? Well, tonight proved nothing, but it was clear that hard work would be required to maintain the progress made in last season's promotion from Division Two. And the League Cup fixtures were fast approaching, for there was not really a great deal of a "close season" these days!

July 4 2017

A rare trip to Spartans for Manager Darren Young and his Assistant Tony McMinn

July 5 1948

No-one really realised it at the time, but today was the most revolutionary day in the history of the United Kingdom.

It was the launching of the National Health Service pushed through with commendable urgency and determination by the Labour Government and in particular Aneurin Bevan, the occasionally controversial Health Minister with a wife from Cowdenbeath.

Today at the Park Hospital, Davyhulme near Manchester, Mr Bevan officially started this new venture, losing no opportunity as he did so to blast the Conservatives for their perceived neglect of the nation's health in the past.

Generally speaking, the new scheme was welcomed locally (they had all voted for it overwhelmingly in 1945) and it did herald a new era of healthy children — (have you ever wondered how your writer and so many others like him have survived these past 70 years?) but locally the conversation tended to centre on the concern about whether East Fife had enough good players to survive in the First Division.

Winning the Second Division was one thing, but surviving in the First was another thing altogether. Certainly much needed ground improvements and extensions were being carried out so that the capacity would be in excess of 20,000 by the opening of the season on August 14.

In the meantime, was there anyone who could stop those invincible Australians? Today they hit 774 for 7 against Gloucestershire, and that was without Don Bradman who wasn't playing! Arthur Morris hit 290, and Sam Loxton hit 159 not out. The weather too was glorious this summer.

The war was now definitely over, restrictions were gradually being eased and rebuilding was in full swing. Life was good. And East Fife were doing well!

July 6 1918

Bayview Park was the scene of a gala day held in glorious unbroken sunshine this Saturday afternoon.

It was the Buckhaven Co-operative Society's annual event and over 2,000 children were marshalled in Randolph Street to march to the ground to the music of the Town Band.

War or no war, it was felt that this sort of thing had to continue for propaganda reasons, and the children were all given juice and scones, in spite of the shortages of all sorts of ingredients. East Fife's officials were there to welcome the children, and hopes were expressed that some sort of football might be able to be played at Bayview this coming season, although it was becoming harder and harder to arrange a team, and travel of any distance was now more or less impossible.

The crowds watching the gala were noticeably short of young men, apart from a few with still blackened faces who had been working their Saturday morning shift at the coal face.

As to what was happening in France, the position was unclear — there had been so much over-optimistic rubbish in the newspapers in the past — although confidence was expressed that with the help of the Americans, the slaughter might soon be ended.

At home, concern was expressed about the prolonged drought and the effect that this might have on the growing of crops, something that was becoming more and more vital every year, and there was a bizarre report or two in the local papers about Fife miners threatening to down tools (something that would have had serious consequences for the war effort) over the rise in "car fares". (In 1918 a "car" was a tramcar, as distinct from a "motor car", and a vital way of travelling to and from Kirkcaldy).

July 7 1949

Convalescent after a recent heart attack and still in what was described as "indifferent health", East Fife's Chairman John McArthur was seen to be out and about today at Elie watching a couple of games between the Perth Battalion of the Boys Brigade at their summer camp, and a team from the Danish Boys Brigade who were staying in Dundee.

Sociable and kindly as always, McArthur made himself known to everyone including the Danish boys who possibly did not have any detailed knowledge of East Fife FC!

The two games, one senior and one junior, were won by the Danish boys, but a good time was had by all in fine weather, even though the pitch was not all that great!

Mr McArthur had been Chairman of East Fife for some time and had served in various posts over the years on the SFA. He would have cause to be happy about his team in recent years. This year, not only had East Fife survived their first season in the First Division, confounding those who had predicted a quick return to "the vile dust from whence they sprung" (as Sir Walter Scott would have put it), but they had actually finished fourth!

And there was still, of course, the Scottish League Cup of season 1947/48 to recall. And of course, the new season started in a month's time, but Mr McArthur was confident that Manager Scot Symon would have his plans for another good season. In the meantime, it was good for Mr McArthur to enjoy the good weather and to try to build up his strength for the coming winter.

July 8 1952

East Fife players returned for training today, but the first thing they did was congratulate their trainer, Johnny Gear, who won the 80 Yards Veterans Handicap at Powderhall in Edinburgh last Saturday. His prize was a Gold Medal and £25.00, and he had beaten a field of 68!

He was no stranger to the winners' rostrum for in 1936 he had won the Marathon at Powderhall. Johnny Gear was a man who was underestimated in the success of East Fife in this era, but no team can win things unless they are 100% fit, and clearly Gear played a large part in that.

Not all the players were there that day as some were still on holiday, but the stress in any case was on laps and short sprints. Ball practice would be delayed until later, the idea being to make every player "hungry" to get a kick of the ball!

We are told that Henry Morris did not turn up until evening because he was working as a lumberjack during the day! We are also informed that (a comment on the times they lived in) Davie Duncan and Willie Finlay arrived for training in recently acquired cars, such was the new found wealth of the professional footballer!

This was only a pre-training session as it were, and training would begin in earnest after the Fife Holiday week. Work had also begun on the building of new turnstiles, which everyone hoped would be ready for the start of the new season in a month's time.

July 9 1946

Much discussion and argument took place today concerning the legal case raised by James Grieve Morgan of Freuchie, a former employee of Dundee United who was suing the club for compensation for injuries received.

The injuries had been sustained in September 1943 in a game against East Fife as a result of which he had been permanently incapacitated as a football player. Dundee United admitted that compensation was due to their former player. It was simply a question of how much.

Morgan claimed £2 per week, but Sheriff JW More at Kirkcaldy Sheriff Court granted him £1 7 shillings and 5 pence compensation instead, saying that although Mr Morgan was finished as a football player, he was still a fit young man, aged 31, and able to lead a full active life otherwise.

Indeed, his former employers Messrs Low were willing to take him back as a machine tool operator at a reasonable wage of £4 3 shillings and 6 pence, and therefore Sheriff Low felt that £2 would have been excessive.

Most football fans had little sympathy with Morgan, and felt that he should be grateful for what he had. It was not after all, the fault of Dundee United or East Fife that he had been injured. It was all simply part of the game. There would of course be many more cases in the future where players would sue their clubs, sometimes justifiably, sometimes not, but it was generally agreed that football and litigation did not really go well together.

July 10 1903

Normally football took a back seat at this time of year, but this year in the Levenmouth area, there was much excitement and animation about the new team which had already been formed called "East of Fife", but already being shortened to simply "East Fife".

There were those who doubted the wisdom of this move. Did the area have enough supporters to make a viable senior team? Might it not be better to stay at Junior level? The new club had already received a bad blow when they had been turned down for the Northern League, but perhaps a more serious problem was that they did not yet have a ground to play on.

If they could not acquire a piece of land for their own exclusive use, it was difficult to see how they could be taken seriously, for they would have to rely on borrowing a piece of land from someone else, or playing fixtures away from home. Like the Jews of the Old Testament, they badly needed a "home of their own".

On the other hand, they had signed another player, a centre forward called Robert Houston who had played for both Hearts and Tottenham Hotspur. They were certainly determined to give it a go and had even decided that their strips would be green and white hoops.

Rumour had it that the famous Celtic team of Glasgow were going to wear a similar strip in place of their green and white vertical stripes, and rumour also had it that negotiations were going on with Mr Campbell on behalf of the club, trying to acquire, either by rent or purchase, the ground called Town Hall Park and currently used by the junior team Leven Thistle. It was a reasonable piece of grass, but was it suitable for senior football?

July 11 1930

The weather was hot, and in other circumstances everyone would have been happy, but the country was in the throes of the ever deepening economic depression, which had begun in New York the previous autumn — with what was called the Wall Street Crash — and was now sweeping Europe with resultant bankruptcies, unemployment and short time working. In the East Fife area, there was also the added complication of the aftermath of the Miners' Strike of 1926.

But there was still the football season to savour with East Fife looking forward to the new season in the First Division following their promotion in April.

A new player called David Moyes, a left back from Kingseat, had joined the club, but apart from that, the squad was still more or less the same — something that the supporters were not all that happy about because it was one thing to win promotion from Division Two and another to be competitive in Division One.

It remained to be seen how stalwarts like Casciani, Gowdy, Weir and McGachie, who had served East Fife so well, would do in the new circumstances of Division One. But money was tight in football as well as in everywhere else.

In the meantime, a certain interest was being expressed in the fortunes of the Ashes series between England and Australia. Each side had won one Test Match each, but today at Headingley Donald "Boy" Bradman scored 309 not out in a devastating display of batting, leading people to wonder whether, already at this stage of his career, he was the greatest batsman of all time.

July 12 1927

Today in Blairhall was born the man who is regarded by quite a few supporters as East Fife's best player of all time — Charlie Fleming.

Yet he was a humble man. He was born at a bad time, less than a year after the final defeat of the miners in the strike of 1926, and by the time he was in his teens, war had come back to Europe once again.

He was probably just too young for World War II, but he certainly would have been deployed as a "Bevin Boy" — one of the young men employed in digging up the coal so necessary for Britain's war effort.

He was certainly playing football for Blairhall Colliery when he was signed by East Fife in 1947. He played 173 games for the club and scored 117 goals (a high proportion for a man who was not an out-and-out striker) and little wonder that he earned the two very complimentary nicknames of "Legs" and "Cannonball".

It is less easy to explain why he earned only one Scottish cap, particularly as he scored twice on that occasion! His transfer to Sunderland in early 1955 was a source of great grief to supporters of East Fife, but his career at Sunderland is still talked about in reverential terms by the lovers of the Wearside club.

Sadly, he won nothing of note with Sunderland, a great team who by the 1950s had peaked. After his career was over, he was Manager of Bath City and later Trowbridge Town. He died in August 1997.

July 1998

New Bayview being constructed in July 1998

July 1998

July 1998

New Bayview being constructed in July 1998

July 13 1915

East Fife, who — to their intense disappointment — were not elected to the Scottish League last year, were offered an opportunity of getting in this year! And all, in a funny sort of a way because of the war! The war was clearly already having an effect on players and it was only likely to get worse if and when conscription was brought in.

This now seemed inevitable because the amount of casualties was a lot more than anyone expected and the war now gave every sign of not being settled any time soon. The problem of transport for away games was a pressing one, and with this end in view the Second Division clubs petitioned the Scottish League to ask if they could reform into two sections — Eastern and Western.

This would clearly leave both sections short of numbers so East Fife had already been canvassed to ask if they would wish to consider joining the Eastern section before tomorrow's meeting. There could be 11 teams in that Division — four from Fife, two from Edinburgh, two from Angus, East Stirlingshire, St Johnstone and Dundee Hibs.

In England, all competitions had now been regionalised, and in Ireland, football had been suspended altogether, so this idea clearly made sense. Football had now won the argument that it should continue, but there were still questions to be answered about whether the idea was practicable or not.

As it happened, the Scottish League simply decided to abolish the Second Division for the duration of the war, but East Fife played in an unofficial Eastern League of 12 teams in season 1915/16.

July 14 2018

"Walk on, walk on with hope in your hearts ..." says the supporters' song, and once more East Fife began a new season, the 116th of their existence.

It was a League Cup fixture (oh, the memories of long ago!) as a few intrepid supporters started off for McDiarmid Park to play Premier League St Johnstone.

But it was still too early. Today was Bastille Day in Paris, it was the start of the Glasgow Fair and various Fife holidays, the weather was glorious and basically it was too early for football!

But it was what it was, and 1687 people turned up to McDiarmid Park, with possibly about 100 from Fife. St Johnstone were in many ways an example to many of the smaller teams, and they had been in the Premier League for some time. Well led by Tommy Wright, they had even won the Scottish Cup in 2014 and continued to have aspirations away above their station in life in a city which was not really as obsessed with football as other cities were.

East Fife's Manager Darren Young opted for a sensible defensive policy, but it was not a "parking the team bus in the penalty box" sort of job, and there were a couple of times when East Fife came close to taking the lead. But a 0-0 draw it was. However under the rules of the competition, the teams went straight to a penalty shoot-out for an extra point. East Fife went first and everyone scored their penalty until the luckless Craig Thomson had his shot saved by the goalkeeper, and then Drey Wright scored for St Johnstone, so only one point for the Fifers rather than two!

July 15 1925

It is always a shame when someone decides to spoil a lovely beautiful summer with a piece of pettifogging legal bureaucracy! In this case, it was an attempt by Fife County Council to extort money from East Fife!

What it seems to be all about is the new grandstand built on the ground which had been "feued" to East Fife. This seemed to make Mr JM Mitchell, the County Clerk and Mr RR Purdon, the County Assessor, think that Fife County Council were entitled to rates from the building of property on "feued" ground.

Naturally East Fife were less than totally keen to pay more money, and the phrase "ye canna tak the breeks aff a Hieland man" comes to mind, for there was a great deal less than the riches of Croesus in the Methil coffers. But at a meeting in Cupar of the Finance and Property Committee of Fife County Council, it was agreed to test this matter in court.

East Fife themselves however were now looking forward with optimism to the new season. Players had been signed, the fixtures were out with a trip to newly relegated Third Lanark on August 15 the first game, followed by Stenhousemuir at home a week later.

Meanwhile the mining dispute continued with the coal owners apparently determined to force an issue, but the Executive Committee of the Miners' Federation meeting at Blackpool issued a statement saying that they were equally determined not to accept anything that involved a worsening of their conditions, and influential members of the Labour movement like ex-Prime Minister Ramsay MacDonald, James Maxton and Arthur Henderson were expressing their support for the miners.

July 16 2016

The season opened with the new Scottish League Cup format which included a penalty shoot-out if the game was a draw.

The opponents at Bayview today were Dundee, a club whose recent history had been fitful, to put it mildly. Nevertheless, they were still looked upon as a "big" team and the crowd of 1407 was well above the average.

It was hard to imagine, however, Alan Gilzean and Ian Ure in the ranks of this Dundee team! It was even harder to come to terms with the fact that both clubs had won the League Cup three times each. The decline had been steep in both cases.

Today Dundee went ahead with a volley from Kane Hemmings from the edge of the penalty box. That was in 35 minutes, and for a long time, it looked as if the Dens Park men would hold out against the increasingly frantic attacks of East Fife, and indeed it would have been no great injustice if Dundee had scored again.

But East Fife kept going and the rescuer was, not for the first nor last time, Kevin Smith, who took a free kick from 25 yards and curled it over the defensive wall. This success seemed to spur on the home side and they finished well on top, but without being able to add to their score.

And so to penalties. The hero was goalkeeper East Fife goalkeeper Willie Muir who saved twice from Rory Loy and James Vincent, and although Paul McManus missed for East Fife, the penalties ended 4-2, and thus East Fife started their campaign with 2 points and Dundee 1. But it was a result which didn't really help anyone.

July 16 2016

Kyle Wilkie in action against Dundee

July 17 2017

More than a wee shower of rain at Tynecastle today for Ben Gordon

July 17 1956

Fraserburgh of the Highland League announced that they had secured for the post of player-manager the services of Don Emery, until recently the right back of East Fife, although he had been comfortable enough in both full back positions.

Emery was now 36 and it was the right time for him to move on. He was one of the few Welshmen who played in Scottish football. He had been on the ground staff of Cardiff City for a spell, but then had joined Swindon Town just before the Second World War.

He went to Aberdeen in 1948. He joined East Fife in 1952 and won a Scottish League Cup medal on the day that East Fife beat Partick Thistle in 1953. He was never a flamboyant, personality player in the sense that Tommy Adams or Charlie Fleming were, but his no-nonsense tackling and grim determination to do well earned him the love of the Methil faithful.

His "day job" was as a representative of the Webster Tyre Company in the Aberdeen area, and Fraserburgh seemed to be a good place for him to move to. He indicated that he desired to bring with him his friend Tony Harris, a dentist in Aberdeen, to play for "the Broch", and he was also determined to put an end to the practice of players training with other clubs and only appearing at Bellslea Park on a Saturday.

For Fraserburgh, his greatest moment came on January 31 1959 when Fraserburgh, under his leadership, managed to put Dundee out of the Scottish Cup by winning 1-0 at Bellslea Park.

July 2017

Laying the astroturf in July 2017

July 18 2017

Not everyone was in favour of the new format of the Scottish League Cup, but it could not be denied that in tonight's Fife derby against Dunfermline Athletic, it produced an exciting finish in the penalty shoot-out for the extra point, even though the shoot-out itself lacked the tension that it normally would have if it were to decide who goes through to the next round of a Cup, for example.

As it was it was only one point at stake here, but as East Fife had already lost their first game at Peterhead on Saturday, every point was vital. A sizeable Pars support brought the crowd up to 1094, but those supporters with a passion for history would recall that these two teams played each other in the final of this very competitions in 1949/50.

"Alas! Alas! A devilish change indeed," Robert Burns might have said, but the two teams put up a reasonable performance for the spectators this warm July night, East Fife wearing a new strip of red and white vertical stripes which made them look like Sunderland or Sheffield United.

It was also the first night of the controversial astro-turf, but that did not prevent some fast open football being played. Chances at both ends, but none of them were converted, even when Manager Darren Young (himself a Dunfermline old boy) came on, and so we moved to penalty shoot-out time, down at the sea end where it had suddenly become a little colder as the sun began to disappear.

It was exciting as well with everyone netting accurately. 5-5, and so we moved on to sudden death with even both goalkeepers bracing themselves to take one, until with the score at 9-8, poor Ben Gordon hit the post and the Pars had the extra point.

July 18 2017

Kyle Wilson shoots in a game against the Pars

July 19 1956

Willie Finlay, the centre half of Philp, Finlay and Aitken fame, today signed for Clyde in the Station Hotel, Kirkcaldy.

The fee was not disclosed at the time but was later admitted to be £3,000. There was not a great deal of doubt that the main problem for Willie Finlay was not so much a dissatisfaction with the club itself as an inability to get on with Jerry Dawson, the Manager who had taken over from Scot Symon after he had left for Preston North End.

Finlay had got very well with Symon, although it had not been Symon who brought him to the club. Willie had been with the club since 1946, having been born in Auchterderran in 1926 and joining the club from Bowhill Rovers. Indeed all three of the famous half back line, Philp, Finlay and Aitken were Fifers.

Clyde were perhaps an odd club to go to, for they had just been relegated, but Finlay was very much involved in their successful promotion chase in 1957, and then in 1958 he reached the peak of his career when he won a Scottish Cup medal as Clyde beat Hibs 1-0 in the final. He played on for Clyde for a few years after that, finishing off his career with, of all people, Raith Rovers.

He died in 2014 at the age of 88. His departure in 1956 however was looked upon with disquiet by the supporters of East Fife, for it seemed another nail on the coffin. Quite clearly the good days had gone, and a major effort would be required if the Second Division was to be avoided.

July 20 1951

Those who felt that East Fife had made a mistake by letting goalkeeper John Niven go on a free transfer would have cause to feel doubly unhappy today with the news that Niven had signed for Kilmarnock.

The six foot tall Niven had played for East Fife since 1943, having been signed from Renfrew Juniors and he had been a regular and reliable goalkeeper until relatively recently. He had also played briefly for both Hibs and Dundee in the war year.

The highlight of his career with East Fife had clearly been season 1947/48 in which he had played consistently well in the team which gained promotion, and in which he had won his one and only honour, a Scottish League Cup winner's medal when East Fife had beaten Falkirk in a replay.

The replay had been a one-sided affair, but that could not have been said of the first game, and East Fife supporters recalled with gratitude the times that John was called upon to save the day. Injury prevented him playing in the successful 1949/50 League Cup final against Dunfermline Athletic and also the Scottish Cup final of that year when East Fife lost to Rangers.

When he was freed by East Fife a few months ago, several English clubs expressed interest, notably Blackburn Rovers, but John always said that he wanted to remain part-time with a Scottish club, and now Kilmarnock had stepped in and offered him terms.

He went on to play in another League Cup final for Kilmarnock in 1952/53, this time in a losing cause to Dundee. He is generally regarded as one of East Fife's best ever goalkeepers.

July 21 1999

Tonight the New Bayview was declared officially open.

The ground had been used for some time but this was an official ceremony with diverse characters like Henry McLeish and Tom "Tiny" Wharton on hand, then there was a friendly game against Kilmarnock which the Premier League side won without very much bother.

A large crowd was present, and there was no doubt that the new stand looked good. There was of course nothing on the other three sides — there still isn't — but this was tactfully described as having "scope for future development".

The two guests of honour were well known to the public. Henry McLeish was of course a former player of East Fife from the 1960s, and in 1999 was MSP for Labour for Central Fife. The following year he would became Scotland's First Minister, but would have to resign after a scandal in 2001 involving the use of one of his offices in Glenrothes.

Tom "Tiny" Wharton from Clarkston in Glasgow was now President of the Football Trust, but had been a famous referee. He was called "Tiny" because he was anything but. His huge bulk often gave him a great psychological advantage over the players whom he dominated.

He was also famous for calling the players "Mr Johnstone" and "Mr Baxter" when admonishing them.

Hopes were expressed that this new ground would serve East Fife well for many years, but there were many supporters who missed the character of the Old Bayview, where so many great players had once played, and which had such a large part in the rich tapestry of Scottish football.

July 22 2018

It came true at last — at least in a penalty shoot-out, for Forfar beat East Fife 5-4 at New Bayview after a 1-1 draw.

At least it earned East Fife and Forfar Athletic a place in the national spotlight for a while, but supporters of both clubs were entitled to feel a little underwhelmed about it all, because in neither Fife nor Forfar does it work.

In both robust Scottish dialects, the sounds are quite different! It does work in England though and it was attributed to the late Eric Morecambe who always tried to get his friend, James Alexander Gordon, the reader of the results, to say it. It would also have worked with David Coleman and it was attributed to him as well. Sadly in Scotland, and in Methil in particular, it simply did not work! Nor did it ever happen until today, in a sort of a way, for the real score was 1-1.

The down side of all this nonsense was that it happened on a Sunday in midsummer before a crowd that numbered a few hundreds, and the result did no good at all to East Fife's chances of qualification for what, a long time ago, was their favourite competition — the Scottish League Cup.

The weather was beautiful, but about 10 miles away in Falkland, a Village Cup cricket match was going on. Falkland were playing a Yorkshire team in the quarter final of the tournament with a trip to Lord's appearing on the horizon. Sadly, Falkland lost, but the crowd at the cricket outnumbered that at the football, something that says a great deal about the advisability or otherwise of summer football in Scotland.

July 23 1945

This was the day that applications closed for the job of Manager of East Fife.

John McArthur, who would of course go on to be Chairman, but is described in 1945 as being the Secretary, is quoted as saying that there had been many applications for the job on both a full-time or a part-time basis.

The applications had not yet been sifted because some of the Directors had been on holiday (first things first!), but a short leet would be drawn up in about a week's time.

McArthur himself had been doing the job during the war years, and would continue to do the job (which in spite of all his protests, he rather enjoyed!) until such time as an appointment was made. 16 players had been signed for next season, and season tickets would be on sale from Monday as the football season approached.

The country in the meantime was awaiting the results of the General Election. The Election had been held on July 5, but the ballot boxes had been locked away until such time as the "soldiers' vote" was brought home from the far flung parts of the world and added to each individual constituency. The results would be declared on Thursday but those who claimed to know about such things expected it to be a foregone conclusion in the return of Winston Churchill and the Conservatives.

But people had long memories of the depression and unemployment, and the "soldiers' vote" was very significant in that those still in uniform had cause to nourish a strong hatred of the Officer classes. Labour won by a landslide!

July 23 1968

A young Henry McLeish in 1968

July 24 1912

The first ever balance sheet of the East Fife Limited Liability Company appeared and it showed a loss.

The club had gone "limited" a year ago as an alternative to closing down altogether. What it actually signified to the average spectator was very little, but it did mean that everything now had to be more publicly accountable and above board.

The loss this year was put down to several factors. One was that the enclosure encircling the ground was not secure, and there were several places at which unscrupulous people could come in without paying their six pence to do so.

But the main factor this year had been the national coal strike in the spring which had imposed severe restrictions on travelling and had caused the cancellation of three games against Cowdenbeath, games which would in normal circumstances have yielded a large "gate" money.

The biggest source of expenditure had been on players' wages — £280 and another £70 on top of that to include expenses, while the takings at the gate came to £310, something that might have been a great deal higher but for the unfortunate circumstances in the coalmining industry.

A very large percentage of East Fife's supporters were miners, and a strike often meant less money to be spent on football matches. In addition, referees, policemen and gate checkers all had to be paid.

Nevertheless the "tact" of the Directors was praised, particularly Chairman Rolland for keeping things under control. What would make a huge amount of difference would be a good run by the team in the Scottish Qualifying Cup, and then perhaps a visit from or to one of the Glasgow or Edinburgh teams in the Scottish Cup itself.

July 25 2015

East Fife had never done well in the League Challenge Cup (the trophy for all Scottish teams other than those in the Scottish Premier League) and today was no exception.

It was generally agreed, though, by all in the 1175 crowd that East Fife had done well against a team from a higher Division, and that they possibly deserved at least extra time rather than the two painful late blows that they suffered.

The crowd at the Falkirk Stadium (like New Bayview not yet totally complete, although at a slightly more advanced stage of development in that it had three sides developed) was surprisingly large for the time of year, and they saw a good game of football.

Falkirk were of course the beaten finalists of last year's Scottish Cup (and many people felt they were a better side than Inverness Caledonian Thistle in that game) and were still on a high from last year's campaign, and Peter Grant (son of a more famous Peter Grant who played for Celtic) scored a good early header.

But then Kevin Smith equalised for the Fifers on the 15th minute mark, and that was the way that things stayed until the last fatal three minutes of "added on" time. First Bob McHugh scored with a rebound, and then with East Fife still reeling, John Baird got a late clincher.

It had been a good game of football, nevertheless, and East Fife supporters felt that their side had been a little ill-done-by by Lady Luck. Nevertheless it was an unpleasant feeling to go home, still a week short of August, and already out of a Cup!

July 25 2015

Nathan Austin and Peter Grant jr (Falkirk) in a game at the Falkirk Stadium

July 26 2016

565 people (Aye! Aye! Summer football fair brings the crowds in, doesn't it?) were at Station Park this Tuesday night to see what was effectively East Fife's exit from their favourite trophy, the Scottish League Cup.

In theory they could still qualify from their section, but in fact it was Peterhead (whom East Fife had beaten on Saturday) who went through.

Tonight it was Forfar who were the victors, and most East Fife supporters agreed that they were the better team, but what stuck in the craw a little, as they munched their obligatory Forfar bridie — a glorious delicacy, incidentally, and something that makes a visit to Station Park an absolute necessity for any football fan — was the thought that one of Forfar's goals (they were winning 1-0 at the time) looked very much like handball on the part of Jim Lister to everyone apart from referee Mike Northcroft.

Lister seemed to use a hand to bring it down before rifling it a good left foot shot. Forfar fans, a decent bunch, tacitly agreed with the prevailing opinion, but the only man whose opinion really matters is the referee and he said it was a goal.

There was no doubt, however, about the other goal scored by Andy Munro in the early stages of the second half, and from then on Forfar took control of the game and saw it out.

Forfar themselves now felt that they had a chance of qualification as well, but a 0-7 hammering from Dundee on Saturday saw to that, whereas Peterhead's 6-5 win on a penalty shoot-out against Dumbarton was enough to earn them qualification. Painful!

July 27 1950

The attendance at the East Fife FC AGM was one of the largest ever seen in the history of the club, but it ended not so much in uproar as in confusion about what it was all about! The financial statement was read out, and it revealed that East Fife were happily in the black to the tune of £9,000.

This was an astonishing amount for a provincial club, and everyone expressed satisfaction in that it showed just exactly what having a good team on the park could do, for of course that team had not only won the Scottish League Cup in 1949/50, but had also reached the Scottish Cup final where they had been beaten by Rangers in front of a six figure crowd of 118,000.

But then three Directors who had to retire indicated that they wished to stand again and they were joined by another two, so that there were five candidates for three vacancies. No vote, however, was taken for an amendment was passed to have an extraordinary general meeting to "consider amendments to the articles of association of the company".

The present company had been formed in 1911 when there were six Directors, but as many as nine could now be appointed, whereas at the moment there were seven.

What all this was about was a matter of little concern to the punters, but they were delighted to hear about the healthy financial position of the club as they looked forward to the new season which opened in a fortnight's time with a trip to Celtic Park.

July 28 1936

Clear signs that the new football season was upon us came in the advertisement in *The Leven Mail* this morning for the public trial match to be held this Saturday between East Fife against a Select, or as it tended to be put (in rugby terms) "Probables v Possibles".

Admission would be a nominal charge and proceeds would go to the Wemyss Memorial Hospital. In the event 2,000 appeared to see East Fife win 5-2.

Manager Dave McLean expressed satisfaction with his squad of 15 players which included three new arrivals — Willie Carver from Arbroath, who had also played for Broughty Anchorage and Forthill Athletic, and who had taken part in Arbroath's promotion winning season of 1934/35; an unknown character from Glasgow Perthshire called Joe Rodi; and a dainty winger "in the Tommy Adams mould" from Motherwell called George Winning.

McLean said "If we can avoid our usual bad start to the League, we should do well". Excitement as always at the start of the season was in the air, and it was obvious that the worst of the depression and unemployment had passed with factories and mines all working well.

The only problem seemed to be foreign relations with Hitler a somewhat sinister character, although he might have been temporarily assuaged by being allowed to host the Olympic Games in Berlin, which were to be opening shortly.

And there seemed to be serious trouble in Spain. Something more than a military coup was going on with the Army and the Roman Catholic Church in rebellion against the legitimate Government with Hitler and Mussolini showing ominous signs of wanting to join in.

Tommy Adams

July 29 1921

The area may have been bedevilled by industrial problems but things were buzzing on the football front.

East Fife were preparing to play in the Second Division of the Scottish League for the first time, and the first game of the season was at Bayview against Bathgate on August 20. Pre-season training had started with runs along Leven beach to the amusement of the Glasgow tourists, and it was hoped to add another few players to the squad.

There was also this season to be an East Fife Juniors team playing in the projected Fife County League, an amalgamation of the Fifeshire Junior League and the West Fife League. East Fife Juniors would be playing in the East Division along with Denbeath Star, Dunnikier Colliery, Leslie Hearts, Michael Colliery, Rosslyn Juniors and Wellesley.

The slightly larger Western section would contain Bowhill Juniors, Broomhall, Dunfermline Athletic Juniors, Glencraig Celtic, Hearts of Beath, Inverkeithing Juniors, Kelty Rangers, Kingseat Juniors, Lochore and Crosshill United and Rosyth Recreation.

Clearly football was back with a vengeance after the Great War, with a new young generation of players coming forward to take the place of those who had not returned from the conflict, and interest in the game was higher than ever.

It was often felt that football was now required more than ever to take people's minds off the horrors of poverty and exploitation. Earlier this year in a by-election, Kirkcaldy constituency (which included large swathes of East Fife supporters) had shocked the nation by voting Labour. Maybe the message was that enough was enough.

July 30 1966

No, this was not one of the highlights of most East Fife supporters' lives!

It was the day that England won the World Cup by beating West Germany 4-2 in extra time at Wembley, and unless you had gone to Mars or some island in the Pacific Ocean, there was no avoiding it!

So how many people supported England in Levenmouth? Well, there were a few English people, normally nice and decent folk, and I suppose one could permit oneself a little happiness for them.

It was also undeniably true that Scottish people tended to support the English cricket team (they were currently in 1966 playing the West Indies, but without any great success) and on the far more important and serious occasions of 1914 and 1939 there was absolutely no doubt about whose side we were on when England took on Germany!

But supporting England at football? No, a step too far, that one! Yet, they did have some good players and they played well together as a team ... but it was the boasting and crowing BBC that one found hard to handle!

Nevertheless, Levenmouth and all of Fife, like everyone else in Scotland, came to a halt to watch the game. Denis Law, famously, played golf that day and maybe there were some who could genuinely ignore it, but most of us joined in the national anthem of "Deutschland Uber Alles" (a few ex-servicemen were appalled at that!) and booed "God Save The Queen", then watched the tragedy as it unfolded.

"They think it's all over...." Some hope that! They are still on about it yet! 1967 was a better year, though!

July 31 2010

It was a sad thought for East Fife supporters this afternoon as they made their way back to their cars. We had not yet reached August and yet we were comprehensively out of the Scottish League Cup, the tournament which was so much associated with East Fife in the long distant days of the late 1940s and early 1950s.

It was all the worse to be knocked out by rivals Raith Rovers at Stark's Park before a paltry crowd of 2,187, when these two used to attract almost 10 times that! The small crowd was due to several things, not least that July is far too early for football with people involved in other things. It was also a sad reflection on the last few seasons of both clubs, and the extent to which they had alienated their supporters — with several East Fife supporters at least talking nostalgically about the old Bayview and what a mistake it was to leave it.

But it was that other gracious old lady of a stadium called Stark's Park that was the scene of the action today. It was Frenchman Gregory Tade who scored twice in the first ten minutes before John Baird added another to impose a deep cloud of depression over the small gallant band of East Fife supporters.

Things took a slight turn for the better after half-time when Bobby Linn, that man of many clubs, scored with a free-kick for East Fife, but any hopes of a revival came to naught and Jamie Mole's header effectively killed the game and triggered an early departure for the lovers of East Fife.

July 31 2010

Lloyd Young in action at Stark's Park

August

East Fife 1920

August 1 1914

The weather was lovely this Saturday, and most East Fife supporters and some of their players were at Leven Links today to see the final of the Scottish Amateur Golf Championship.

About 2,000 were there, and in theory one had to pay to get in, but it has always been very difficult to keep people out of a golf course! The crowd who came to see the game saw a rather one sided final in which James Mason of Carnoustie beat George Myles of Monifieth by six holes and only four left to play.

Many problems had been caused by the crowd who kept encroaching on the fairways and the wish was expressed that the football season would soon start to keep "them" occupied.

Indeed the conversation was much about football and East Fife. Could they win the Central League this season? And what about Raith Rovers, cup finalists of 1913? Wouldn't it be great to see East Fife one day in the same League as Raith Rovers as well as Kirkcaldy United? And what about Glasgow Celtic? Could anyone catch them?

It now being August, training for the football season had already started. No doubt about it — golf and cricket were fine, but football was the real thing.

Unfortunately this beautiful, almost idyllic summer Saturday, there was another topic of conversation, however ... something about the Kaiser of Germany and the Czar of Russia wanting a war with each other, with talk about embargoes at Methil Docks on German trade, and fleet mobilisation etc. What on earth was all that about?

The Menu For the Centenary Dinner

August 2 2014

Not for the first nor last time in their history, East Fife returned on the long journey from Stranraer with a broken heart, and in this case with their League Cup dreams in tatters.

The great days of this tournament were now a distant memory — indeed some young supporters did not believe that they could have happened — but it had been hoped for a decent Cup run to bring in some money.

True, they had beaten Forfar last week in the League Challenge Cup, but that was not the trophy that was likely to produce the financial goods.

Today at Stair Park, it was an even game, and the bus load of East Fife supporters in the 275 crowd had reason to be optimistic at half time. The game however hinged on a decision by referee Andrew Dallas in the 58th minute when the influential Kevin Smith was shown the red card for a rather crude foul on Scott Robertson of Stranraer.

I suppose it all depends on who you support whether you considered it a red card offence or not, but neutral Press opinion tended to think that a yellow would have sufficed. It meant however that in the heat of August, eleven men now played ten.

East Fife seemed to be holding out heroically for extra time and then possibly the lottery of a penalty shoot-out, until Anthony Merenghi of Stranraer passed the ball to Craig Malcolm and he shot for the top left hand corner. It was a good goal, and good enough to win the game for the men of the south-west, for it was scored in the 90th minute and the four minutes of added on time were not enough for East Fife to get an equaliser which, in truth, would not have been undeserved.

August 3 1993

Not many East Fife supporters look back on season 1993/94 with tears in their eyes recalling great players, great games and fine performances.

The tears were more likely to have been those of anguish and frustration, never more so than on the first day of the season. The pre-season had been vaguely encouraging, in so far as it told anyone anything at all, but Manager Alex Totten, a man of many clubs in a long and varied career, did seem to have a certain "go" about him.

The season was given a certain boost with the news that the Scottish League was going to move to four divisions instead of three, and that if you ended up sixth in Division Two, you would go into the new Division Two for 1994/95 whereas the others would join two new clubs in Division Three.

It would turn out to be a season in which East Fife just made it, but it was also a depressing season. It began when East Fife exited their favourite tournament, the Scottish League Cup, at the first time of asking to Albion Rovers at Bayview.

The score was 2-1 to the Rovers, and the 873 crowd were far from happy. It is not often that boos are heard at the first game of the season, but this was the case here, and already a good money-spinner of a tournament had gone on the Tuesday night before the first Saturday!

To their credit the players rallied when the League season started by winning the first four games — but then they lost the next four, and people started scratching their heads again.

August 4 1956

Following the euphoria of Jim Laker taking all 10 wickets in the Old Trafford Test Match on Tuesday, it was time to start thinking about football again.

The international situation was showing signs of deterioration, though, as British Prime Minister Anthony Eden and Egyptian President Nasser were beginning to act like two dogs over a bone, or two spoiled brats in a nursery.

It was all about the Suez canal, but for East Fife supporters, it was the trial match today between the Black and Golds versus the Whites, the Black and Golds being the "probables" and the Whites the "possibles".

Sammy Cox, one time of Rangers and Scotland, had now joined the club as had goalkeeper Jimmy Watters of Hearts, but Willie Finlay, the centre half and the last part of the great half back line of Philp, Finlay and Aitken had now gone to Clyde.

His place was now taken by Harold Davis, who would later make his name for Rangers, but significantly, not at centre-half. And it was nice to see the old warhorse Sammy Stewart still there and now about to start his 18th season with the club. The game was entertaining enough, ending up 4-3 for the Black and Golds, but that was not necessarily what the management wanted, for it raised the obvious question of how the reserves were able to score three goals against the first team. It would obviously be a difficult start to the season next week because

East Fife had been drawn alongside Aberdeen, Rangers and Celtic in their League Cup section — last season's League Cup winners, League winners and Scottish Cup finalists! Nothing easy there, but on the other hand, three clubs with big supports who would bring loads of money.

August 5 2017

Following the abysmal collapse of the Scottish League Cup campaign, the League Division One (the third tier) began to-day with East Fife having the long trek to Stair Park, Stranraer to kick things off.

As always, it was a long way, but then again there were worse times to do the long trek than on August 5. (The next time would be February 3!)

409 people turned up to see the game, and they saw a rather disappointing game enlightened only (for Stranraer fans) by a good goal taken from the 18 yard line by Jamie Hamill. This happened about half way through the second half, and hard though East Fife tried, they could not get back into the game.

It was really rather difficult to become optimistic about the coming season, even though there were derby games to look forward to against Raith Rovers and games against near neighbours in Forfar, Arbroath and Alloa.

Indeed Alloa were the first home game, then Arbroath and finally before August was out, the derby game against Raith Rovers. The Manager did his best to cheer everyone up (well, that is his job, isn't it?) by saying that no-one gets promotion or relegation in August, and that a League campaign of 36 games was a long one.

And there was some hard luck today at Stranraer — chances might have been taken, and the weather was warm when most games in Scotland are played in conditions which were a great deal worse than that!

August 5 2017

Nathan Flanagan is surrounded by Stranraer players

August 6 2016

East Fife opened their Division One campaign with a 2-2 draw against Albion Rovers at New Bayview.

On a dullish day, a crowd of 682 appeared including a fair smattering of the supporters who are often considered to be the bravest in the United Kingdom, those of Albion Rovers whose survival against the odds is often a subject of wonder and awe, and a tremendous example of the triumph of determination.

This was, of course, flag-day for East Fife and the Second Division flag was duly unfurled before the start. Things started with a bang with a goal from Kevin Smith. This was in the fourth minute, but then the wee Rovers equalised through Calum Ferguson, a man who had been signed in the summer by Rovers manager, Darren Young.

That was the score until the stroke of half-time when the luckless Ross Dunlop managed to get in the way of a Jason Kerr shot at goal. Hopes were high of a home win, but then Ryan Wallace equalised for the Coatbridge men.

The jury was still out on East Fife's chances in the First Division, for everyone was aware that with teams like Livingston and Airdrie in the Division, things would not be easy for Gary Naysmith and his men.

The League Cup campaign had not been encouraging, but there was still the League Challenge Cup, a trophy in which East Fife had yet to star. Next week's game involved a long trip to Peterhead, but quite a few supporters had signed up for the trip. It was the start of the season, and excitement was still in the air.

August 6 2016

Action in a game against Albion Rovers. Mark Lamont and Mark Ferry feature.

August 7 2012

It was East Fife's fortune to be the first team to play against the new Rangers.

Rangers had gone bust in February and one of their punishments was being demoted to the bottom tier of Scottish football, and having to play in the early rounds of the Scottish League Cup. By chance East Fife were drawn there, and a crowd of over 38,000 were at Ibrox to greet the new Rangers.

It was an impressive show of defiance on the part of Rangers supporters who had not deserted their club, although some of their players did, disappearing like snow off a dyke whenever the money ran out, and this was after all the insincere displays of jersey kissing and inane statements about how much they loved the club!

As for East Fife, this might have been an opportunity to make a statement, but clearly the occasion was too much for them. They subsided without much fight to a 0-4 defeat with two goals from Lee McCulloch and one from Lee Wallace and Dene Shields as Gordon Durie's team were played off the park.

At one point an urban fox made an appearance, but that was about the only relief that East Fife had all night. It may even have been that Gordon Durie was himself affected by the raw emotion of it all, for he was, after all, an ex-Rangers player, but that is little excuse for an appalling performance which dispirited the small band of East Fife supporters.

But even the hardest of hearts in the ranks of Rangers' many enemies could not really have grudged a moment of lightness in the apparently never-ending gloom of Rangers supporters.

August 7 2012

David Muir at Ibrox

DAVIE GORMAN
BENEFIT MATCH

30p

Moment of joy for East Fife keeper Dave Gorman... oblivious to the Bayview mud he hugs the ball thankfully after saving a penalty kick from Rangers' sharp shooter Willie Johnston (right).

Souvenir Programme

EAST FIFE v RANGERS XI

7th August, 1984.

August 8 1964

The weather was glorious for the start of the season, and the result was glorious for East Fife as well.

A crowd of 4,000 at Stark's Park saw East Fife win 4-1 over Raith Rovers to set them on the way to qualification from the League Cup section. In the other game in the section, Queen of the South beat Montrose 2-0.

There had been some questioning of whether the fans would turn up given the increase in prices, but the fans answered that question and the East Fife section of the crowd certainly enjoyed themselves. This was the height of the Beatles culture, and incredibly, Beatles songs were sung as the crowd queued to get through the painfully slow turnstiles.

In footballing terms, there was now the genuine belief that promotion for Jimmy Bonthrone's side was a possibility. George Christie scored before half-time then added another two in the second half while Morris Aitken scored the other with Rovers' only counter coming from the a man with the unlikely name of Felix McGrogan.

The sight of the Raith fans heading for the exits throughout the second half told its own story. It was the first game of George Farm as Manager at Stark's Park, and although Raith Rovers would fight back, it was a bad start.

In the cars and the buses back to Methil that night, there was euphoria and the relishing of Wednesday night's visit of Queen of the South. Great confidence was expressed in Manager Jimmy Bonthrone, not least because he was an "East Fife man", and a genuinely nice guy who had played for the club in the past and clearly loved East Fife.

August 9 1989

There can be little doubt that a penalty shoot-out is a lottery.

Some of the best players in the world — Paul McStay, for example, in the Scottish League Cup final against Raith Rovers in 1994 — can miss a penalty, but it is exciting and probably as fair a way of deciding a tie as any other. Seldom can one really complain about being cheated in a penalty shoot-out.

Tonight however came fairly close to it, although the main emotion was sheer bafflement. It was the first game of the season in the League Cup on Wednesday August 9 at Bayview. A good game before 858 spectators against Queen's Park ended 2-2 with Paul Hunter scoring twice for East Fife. East Fife were 2-0 up for a long time but Keith McKenzie and Paul O'Brien equalised for the Glasgow side.

Extra time yielded no winner, and neither did the first five penalties for each side, all well sunk by the players concerned. We went to sudden death and both teams scored. Then Queen's Park missed their seventh.

All East Fife had to do was to score. We did so amidst great cheering and sporting handshakes from the Queen's Park players.

But then we suddenly saw that referee Brian McGinlay was signalling a retake for a reason that baffled everyone. The only possible explanation could be that the ball was kicked twice, or that it hadn't been placed inside the spot.

For whatever reason, the kick was retaken — and everyone could now see the tragic scenario unfolding. Yes, East Fife missed, Queen's Park scored, then East Fife missed again.

This time the sporting handshakes had to come from East Fife, but handshakes with the referee were curt and perfunctory!

Scot Symon on the left with his men, who have won the Scottish League Cup, the Scottish League "B" Division and the "B" Division Supplementary League in season 1947/48

August 10 1957

This was not the way in which one would have chosen to start the season!

In the first place the weather was misty and drizzly, more the weather that one associates with November rather than August.

In addition to that, Jerry Dawson's much changed team of new recruits and youngsters had the misfortune to run into a Hibs team, who, although themselves also much changed, still had Gordon Smith, Eddie Turnbull and Willie Ormond in their ranks.

In spite of the unfavourable conditions, a crowd of about 20,000 appeared at Easter Road and it was pleasing to note a fair representation of black and gold favours among the crowd, enjoying in particular the jousts between the two old warhorses Willie Ormond and Sammy Stewart.

It was Hibs who had the better of the early play and before half time Preston and Ormond had put them 2-0 up. There was a semblance of a fightback in the second half, but then Gordon Smith, arguably Scotland's most talented player of the age, took command. He scored the third and was instrumental in Turnbull adding a fourth as the game ended with the Fifers nowhere in sight.

It was, of course, only the first game of the League Cup section but as the other two teams in the section were Celtic and Airdrie, it was difficult to feel any kind of optimism about the immediate future at least.

Philosophers on the train journey back reckoned that it was all because the small team from Methil had been punching above their weight for many years, and that maybe relegation to the Second Division might not be a bad thing, but others refused to accept that.

August 10 1968

A good view of Bayview at East Fife v Clydebank on August 10 1968

August 10 1968

A good view of the old Bayview stand in that game v Clydebank on August 10 1968. Alan Guild is the East Fife player in the picture

August 11 1962

On a day of sunshine, wind and showers, East Fife opened their season with a trip to Dumfries to take on Queen of the South at Palmerston Park.

It was the first game of Section 7 in the Scottish League Cup. Season 1962/63 like most seasons began with great expectations, for East Fife's supporters were beginning to believe that promotion was long overdue, and the idea that East Fife's natural habitat was the Second Division was one that sat ill with most supporters.

There was a crowd of 5,000 at Palmerston and East Fife were well represented in the ground, but sadly the long trip home was a doleful one after a 3-1 defeat by the Doonhamers. The game was even and hard fought in the first half, and just before half-time both teams scored, Willie McLean for Queen of the South and then George Dewar for East Fife.

In the second half however it became apparent that Queens were the better team, and that East Fife were rather too reliant on their offside trap. A penalty was conceded and converted by John McTurk, and then near the end Derek Frye confirmed the victory of the Doonhamers.

It was just the first game of the season, and no real cause as yet for concern. Montrose had beaten Queen's Park in the same section, and Montrose were due at Bayview on Wednesday night for the first home game.

Elsewhere, the highlight of the opening day was Motherwell's 9-1 defeat of Falkirk, and the Fife derby at Stark's Park between Raith Rovers and Dunfermline ended in a 2-2 draw.

SCOTTISH LEAGUE CUP — First Match

OFFICIAL PROGRAMME
The RANGERS FOOTBALL CLUB LTD
IBROX STADIUM GLASGOW

Directors:—Councillor J. F. Wilson, D.L. (chairman), William Struth, J.P. (vice-chairman), Alan L. Morton, G. C. P. Brown, M.A., John Lawrence, J.P.
Secretary:—J. Rogers Simpson, C.A.   *Manager:*—J. Scotland Symon.

| No. 193 | 11th August, 1956 | Price **Threepence** |

RANGERS 3

		NIVEN 1		
Right				Left
	SHEARER 2		LITTLE 3	
	McCOLL 4	YOUNG 5	RAE 6	
SCOTT 7	SIMPSON 8	MURRAY 9	BAIRD 10	HUBBARD 11

1873   1956

MATTHEW 11	BONTHRONE 10	PLUMB 9	LEISHMAN 8	J. STEWART 7
~~COX~~ *CHRISTIE* 6	~~DAVIS~~ STEWART 5	McLAREN / ADIE 4	~~CHRISTIE~~ *COX*	or ~~WRIGHT~~
Left		WATTERS 1		Right

EAST FIFE 0

Referee—J. LACKIE, Perth   *Linesmen*—L. MILLER, Edinburgh
                                         A. T. WILSON, Edinburgh

FIFERS WILL MAKE STRONG CHALLENGE

WE open the season this afternoon with the first of our League Cup sectional ties, the draw bringing us against resolute rivals in East Fife. We have cause to respect our Methil visitors as worthy opponents, for did they not delay our League Championship success last season by beating us under the Bayview lights on April 9? Yes, and though they have never recorded a win at The Stadium in League or Cup, they have more than once shaken us by their skill and challenge. We have, of course, close ties with our Fife friends, for Manager Scot Symon was with them before going to Preston North End and then returning "home" to The Stadium. And now Jerry Dawson, one of the greatest goalkeepers ever to grace our colours—and those of Scotland, too—is their manager. Everything points to a game justifying the eagerness with which the game's followers have awaited the new season.

August 12 1950

The opening of the season on the "glorious twelfth" of August may have been a good day for grouse shooters, but it was a far from happy occasion for East Fife in their League Cup sectional game, as the League Cup holders went down 0-2 to Celtic in front of a 30,000 crowd at Parkhead.

Indeed it should have been more, for it was one of the better Celtic performances for some time, with Irishman Bertie Peacock outstanding and scoring for his team. John McPhail scored the other goal.

But there was clear trouble for East Fife with Allan Brown and George Aitken refusing to come to terms with the club, and *The Sunday Post* reporting that Aitken in particular, who was working as a plasterer at the Bridge of Earn Hospital, being seen as a spectator at Cowdenbeath v St Johnstone.

To what extent this was simply a plea for more money or perhaps a protest against the somewhat dictatorial methods of Scot Symon (who modelled himself on the legendary strictness of Bill Struth of Rangers) we cannot be sure, but it was certain that it was doing the club no good at all.

The sympathies of the supporters were very much on the side of the club, and there was a general puzzlement as to why any player would not want to keep playing in a team as successful as East Fife had been under Symon. Today at Parkhead, only Charlie Fleming and Willie Finlay emerged with any sort of credit, and East Fife were destined not to qualify from this section.

August 13 1995

Fife fans were given a rare treat this Sunday when Manchester United appeared to play a testimonial match in honour of Jimmy Bonthrone, a man whose achievements at East Fife, both as a player and a Manager were legendary.

Manager Steve Archibald, who had of course played for Aberdeen when Alex Ferguson was the Manager there in the late 1970s and early 1980s, was able to use his connections to persuade his ex-boss to bring a strong side.

The Scottish season had already started but the English one not yet, and Manchester United took the opportunity to play a reasonably strong side in what was, for them, a pre-season friendly.

Unusually for them, they were neither English Cup holders not League Champions in 1995, having been pipped in both tournaments. A crowd of over 5,000 appeared including quite a few bedecked in the famous red of Manchester United. They saw a rather one-sided but good-natured win of 4-0 for United with two good goals from David Beckham, a man who had not yet reached the peak of his fame.

Also playing were Brian McClair, Roy Keane and a man who was frequently joked about as the chinaman of Manchester United — Yung (Young) Li (Lee) Sharpe.

The weather was good, and Alex Ferguson was charming, talking to all the local supporters, while his protégé Steve Archibald made the not unreasonable point that if 5,000 could come along to a pointless friendly, why was it so difficult to attract 1,000 to see a normal League game?

The Bayview

Price 5p.

Printed & Published by Artigraf Printing Company, Buckhaven

"Keeper McDermott secures a loose ball in a recent East Fife v Raith Rovers match"

ALL ABOUT RAITH ROVERS

Formed 1893. Ground: Stark's Park. Manager Andy Matthew. Colours: White with two navy blue hoops, navy blue facings, with shorts and stockings. Record attendance: 30,000 v Hibs, Scottish Cup, first round, 1952, and v Hearts, Scottish Cup second round, 1953.
Scottish League Division 2 Champions 1907-08, 1090-10 (shared), 1937-38, 1948-49; runners-up 1926-27, 1966-67. Scottish Cup finalists 1913. League Cup finalists 1948-49.

SCOTTISH LEAGUE CUP TIE

WEDNESDAY 13th AUGUST, 1975.
BAYVIEW PARK, METHIL.

EAST FIFE
VERSUS
RAITH ROVERS

EAST FIFE FOOTBALL CLUB OFFICIAL PROGRAMME

August 14 1957

The second game of the season, and the first game at home saw a crowd of 12,000 at Bayview to see East Fife take on Celtic in the Scottish League Cup.

It had been a disturbing and ominous summer for East Fife with the decision taken to go part-time instead of full-time. The reason for this was the financial one that East Fife, whose supporters had seen many better days in the recent past, could no longer afford full time wages as the crowds were dropping at an alarming rate, and the days of the big games at Hampden had disappeared.

In addition, there was the bizarre sight of the reserves beating the first team in a pre-season trial, something that was taken with a certain amount of levity but which, nevertheless told a tale.

The first game had been a thumping 0-4 defeat to Hibs at Easter Road, but tonight was a better performance in spite of the 1-4 score line.

The 7.00 kick off time (so that the game could finish in daylight without using floodlights) possibly deterred a few from making the trip from Glasgow, but those who did (and the large local Celtic support) saw their team go 2-1 up at half-time with goals from McPhail and Collins with the only reply being a softish penalty kick converted by Jimmy Bonthrone.

Nevertheless the Fifers stayed in the game throughout the second half (it was a good game with both teams missing chances) and it was only in the last ten minutes that the full-time training told with goals from Mochan and McPhail. But *The Glasgow Herald* was sympathetic saying that "ill luck continued to baulk East Fife".

August 14 2010

Craig Johnstone scores at Recreation Park, Alloa

August 15 1953

Charlie Fleming in action against Aberdeen in 1953

August 15 1903

This was a very significant day in Scottish football, although the weather was awful with very heavy rain.

It was the first day that Celtic wore the horizontal stripes (they had been vertical before), it was the first day that a team called Aberdeen FC (an amalgamation of a team already called Aberdeen and another two called Orion and Victoria) entered the Northern League.

Of course, it was the opening day of East Fife FC who drew 2-2 with Hearts Reserves before a crowd of about 1,000, who paid the large sum of £20 to get in.

The Dundee Courier tells us that the crowd forsook musical performances, flower shows and quoits competitions (a common pastime in mining areas) and was very impressed by some of the players, particularly one John Nangle who scored the first goal.

They are described as "a crack team" and suggests that Fife must keep an eye on this team, which it calls at one point "East of Fife". As yet, the team was not yet a member of any League — the Northern, the Central or the Scottish, but that would clearly be the goal that the team should aspire to.

The team wore green and white hoops, an odd coincidence given what was happening at Celtic Park that same day, but there does not seem to be any connection. It was already clear that the hard work of various people over the past year or so to give Levenmouth a senior team was paying dividends.

August 15 1903

John Nangle, scorer of East Fife's first goal

August 16 1950

This game was generally reckoned to be the best Fife derby of them all. East Fife v Raith Rovers games were often reckoned to be a good pairing, and indeed they were two equally matched sides at this time.

It was a fine sunny Wednesday evening, and the second game of the League Cup section which also contained Celtic and Third Lanark.

East Fife had had a bad day at Parkhead on Saturday, but Raith had done better against Third Lanark. Tonight *The Courier* ran out of clichés, saying that the derby was "rambustious" (sic) (they mean rumbustious, one feels) and that the Fifers are all "bonny fechters", entertaining the 17,000 crowd which packed Bayview.

Within the first 15 minutes, Raith Rovers were two up with goals from Willie Penman and Willie Keith. East Fife however fought back. Henry Morris had what looked like a good goal disallowed for offside, but then Davie Duncan scored from a Charlie Fleming cross before Raith Rovers restored their 3-1 lead with a fine goal scored by Johnny Maule as he ran in to score from a Joe McLaughlin flick.

Before half time Bobby Black rose "like a salmon" according to the writer, who had clearly spent his holidays in the Highlands, to head home a Duncan cross. The second half saw no let-up in the excitement, although there was only one more goal — East Fife equalised when Henry Morris was on hand to score from a Fleming "cannonball" which rebounded off the bar.

3-3 was a fair result in a very good game of football, and all the more creditable because George Aitken was still in dispute with the club and being awkward about signing for the new season.

August 17 1949

12,000 appeared at Bayview on not the most hospitable of nights to see East Fife's first home League Cup game of the season.

Already on a high following their win over Raith Rovers in Kirkcaldy on Saturday, East Fife won again 3-1 over Stirling Albion, but not without a struggle at times.

Stirling Albion, a new team who had risen out of the ashes of the previous Stirling side called King's Park after the Second World War, gave them a very good game with the result in doubt for some considerable time.

It was Allan Brown who scored first, completing a fine move involving Davie Duncan and Dougie Davidson on the left. This was at the key psychological point of just before half-time. Soon after half-time, they went further ahead when Bobby Black sent over a lovely cross for Davidson to head home.

That seemed to be it, but the red-clad Stirling men rallied and fought back putting pressure on a surprisingly shaky East Fife defence and eventually scoring through a man called, funnily enough, Stirling.

Indeed an equaliser looked likely, but in the 75th minute a moment of individual brilliance from Bobby Black eased the pressure as he beat three men to score what proved to be a decisive goal.

Attention now turned to the game against Hearts on Saturday, for, in the four team section, Hearts had beaten Stirling Albion on Saturday and the late night Sports News on the radio told supporters that they had beaten Raith Rovers tonight. Saturday's game, therefore, now became vital.

August 18 2012

No-one really knew very much about it at the time but a dramatic event occurred in the dressing room after the end of this 0-0 draw with Queen of the South. Manager Gordon Durie had collapsed with what looked like a stroke.

It transpired that it was a virus, but the incident was serious enough to compel him to resign his job a few months later on November 4 2012. This was a shame, but it was probably true that Durie, good player though he had been for East Fife, Hibs, Chelsea, Rangers and Scotland, was possibly not cut out for the stresses and strains of managing a small club with limited resources and with supporters who had higher expectations than what was warranted.

He may well also have been suffering slightly from what was going on at Ibrox at the time. He was a Rangers supporter and still had many friends there, including Ally McCoist, and 2012 was the year in which Rangers, after having lived on borrowed time and money for a considerable amount of years, finally went bust thanks to dodgy deals and, in particular, a refusal to pay Income Tax.

While the rest of Scotland tee-heed about all this, Durie must have been badly affected, and indeed his own financial affairs suffered a sharp decline leading to him being declared bankrupt in 2016, a fact gleefully shared by *The Scottish Sun* newspaper.

He is still however held in high regard by East Fife and their supporters, for he is one of the very few players who played for East Fife and then went on to play for Scotland. There are not too many of them nowadays!

August 18 2012

Gordon Durie watches Gareth Wardlaw

August 19 1933

It cannot be often that East Fife find themselves sharing top spot in the Second Division with East Stirlingshire, Stenhousemuir and Forfar Athletic, but that was precisely what the League table of *The Sporting Post* showed tonight. Mind you, they had only played two games!

But today saw a good 2-1 win for East Fife against Leith Athletic, generally one of the better teams in the Second Division. The game was tight, and *The Courier* says that East Fife "just scraped home".

The personality goal scorer of the side, Phil Weir, on whom East Fife had relied so much in the past, was out injured with a badly injured knee. His deputy youngster — listed as Junior, although everyone knew that he was called Craig — played well on the right wing and scored a good goal in the early stages of the game.

Leith's equalising goal was horrific, and although legal and acceptable in 1933 (and for about 30 years after that!), jars on our modern eyes as we read about it. It involved shoulder-charging the goalkeeper, a legalised piece of thuggery. In this case all the worse, as two Leith forwards, Morris and McGillivray, barged poor Kelly in the East Fife goal "rather too violently" (as *The Courier* put it) and Morris was able to force it into the net amidst loud booing, possibly directed at East Fife's own defenders who should have done more to protect their goalkeeper.

However, justice was served: East Fife were awarded a penalty, and Morrison scored what proved to be the winner.

Dom Currie

August 20 1921

4,000 were at Bayview today to see East Fife's first ever game in the Scottish League Second Division.

They were in for a disappointment however; East Fife, in spite of having most of the play went down 2-1 to Bathgate, but "it's goals that count" said *The Sunday Post* with less than stunning originality.

It was a historic day, brought about by the Scottish League successfully making a takeover bid of the Central League, which in some ways had been a better deal for clubs like East Fife.

But the attraction of playing in the "Scottish" League meant a lot to everyone, and as it turned out, most of the opposing clubs were not too far away in West Lothian, Fife, Angus and the central belt. Alloa would turn out to be the first winners of the new Second Division, and East Fife would finish a respectable middle of the table.

Today's game, however, was annoying for the fans. The honour of scoring East Fife's first Scottish League goal goes to Tom Neish, who netted with a penalty, after a previous penalty had been missed.

The general opinion of the Press was that East Fife played a great deal of pretty football, but that they tended to overdo the tricky stiff with Dominic Currie being singled out for this particular fault.

Bathgate's first goal was scored by a gentleman with the unlikely name of Henrietta, and the second by Chalmers. East Fife's team on this historic occasion was J Neish, Stewart and Fleming; Ross, Wightman and Robertson; Kerr, Currie, Cant, Burton and T Neish.

Charlie Fleming

August 21 1954

Following two very good wins in their first two games of the season, East Fife came down with a rather large bump today at Bayview.

A very strong looking Aberdeen team appeared and, frankly, played them off the park. The failure of the East Fife forward line, Charlie Fleming and all, was apparent for all to see.

Even at this early stage, Aberdeen looked a good outside bet for this season's League Championship, and they had considered themselves unlucky to lose last season's Scottish Cup final to Celtic. This was a League Cup sectional game, and there was still time for East Fife to recover, but today was rather discouraging.

East Fife tended to hide behind a rather controversial refereeing decision; Jackie Hather of Aberdeen was in an offside position and the linesman flagged him, but as the ball came to him, the ball struck an East Fife player, Don Emery; thus he was played onside and referee Jackson allowed Hather to go on and score.

Feelings of outrage and righteous indignation however cut little ice, for Aberdeen were already two ahead and well on top with goals from Paddy Buckley and Joe O'Neill. This result actually evened up the section, for although Queen of the South had lost all three games and were now virtually out of it, the other three teams had all won two and lost one.

Meanwhile, in what was perhaps a sign of the times, Aberdeen announced that for their next fixture at Queen of the South, they would fly from Dyce to Prestwick Airport before getting a bus to Palmerston. East Fife however would go entirely by bus to Edinburgh to play Hibs!

August 22 1914

East Fife played their first game in war circumstances in the Central League against Bathgate at Mill Park, Bathgate. They lost 2-1.

This had followed an unsuccessful attempt to get into the Scottish League Division Two in the summer, but in any case, things had changed utterly since the declaration of war on August 4.

The British Expeditionary Force was already in France. There had been reports of "stirring scenes" at various local railway stations as local boys departed for the war, and every football match had a recruiting drive with a member of the Army telling every young man about their "duty" but also stressing what an "opportunity" it was to see some of the world.

Young ladies too apparently found men in uniform irresistible. Indeed there was a great temptation for young men to join up, and excitement was in the air with life in the army looking a lot better than life in the pits or in the docks.

Football itself was under a little pressure, for letters appeared in the newspapers demanding to know why 22 fit young men were "shirking" on a football field and "encouraging loafers in the crowd" to do likewise.

The counter argument was that football gave everyone a chance to keep fit so that they would be better prepared if ever they were required.

The horrors of the war were not yet apparent, and the mood of euphoria would continue for some time, but on a more mundane level, East Fife had started their season badly. The 2-1 defeat could have been a lot worse but for goalkeeper Bernard who was a "gem at saving" according to *The Courier*.

August 23 1939

Spectators would have been forgiven for thinking that the war had already started as they made their way to Methil tonight to see East Fife v Stenhousemuir in the final of the Penman Cup.

Posters were everywhere urging young men and women to join up, and defence works were being built on various sections of the Fife beach, while there was talk of barrage balloons over the Forth.

The BBC Radio News gave the impression that there was no problem, and the game duly kicked off at 6.30 pm, with everybody saying the current cliché of "Cheer Up, It Might Never Happen!"

Attention was turned to the Penman Cup, a relatively minor tournament these days and sometimes not taken very seriously. Tonight for example was the final of last season's competition. It turned out to be a very one-sided 5-1 victory, Stenhousemuir's cause not helped by the early loss of left winger Fenner to injury.

For East Fife, second choice left half Carroll was in goal and had a good game dealing competently with whatever Stenhousemuir threw at him, whereas at the other end, Macartney scored twice.

After half-time, Tommy Adams scored twice and Danny McKerrell added a fifth, while Hill pulled one back for Stenhousemuir. The Cup was duly presented at the end, and the team were given a cheer, with the optimists recalling the great day of a year past April when they picked up another trophy and the pessimists wondering whether this would be the last Cup that East Fife would ever win.

In the meantime talks were going on at a "high diplomatic level" but Hitler was still making these bellicose statements about wanting his corridor to East Prussia and Danzig.

Jimmy Bonthrone

August 24 1963

East Fife continued their fine start to the season with a 3-0 win over Raith Rovers at Bayview in the League Cup sectional stage.

The weather was a great deal better than when the two teams met in the rain at Stark's Park on opening day, and the football was also a lot better, at least as far as East Fife were concerned.

There was little doubt that there was a "buzz about the place" at this time with the feeling that in Jimmy Bonthrone they had appointed the right man as Manager, and people were particularly impressed by young Morris Aitken.

The first game had been a draw but since then, Raith (newly relegated from the First Division) had struggled and East Fife had prospered. Today there was only really the one team in it, in spite of East Fife suffering a bad blow within the first ten minutes as right back Ron Stirrat was carried off with a leg injury.

Substitutes had not yet been introduced (they would be in 1966) and this meant East Fife playing with 10 men. Not that anyone would have noticed it, however, for Ian Stewart scored twice before half time, and then Gray scored in the second half as the disillusioned Raith Rovers supporters began to drift off, not even having the energy to stay and argue, so outplayed were they.

The other game in the section saw a 2-1 win for Arbroath at Dumbarton, a state of affairs which meant that a win at Gayfield on Wednesday night might just be enough for East Fife to qualify. Already League Cup memories of the Scot Symon era a decade ago were beginning to flood back!

August 25 1965

It was the custom in the 1950s and 1960s to play three games of the League Cup section on Saturday, Wednesday, Saturday then the first League game on the next Wednesday before finishing off the League Cup section with venues reversed from the first three games.

It was a good way to start the season, taking advantage of the good weather and the daylight as long as they lasted. This was the Scottish League game on the second Wednesday night of the season, and it was at, of all places, Berwick!

There was a natural feeling of "Why does it have to be us?" but then again it had to be somebody and there was no ground in the 19 team Second Division that was really close to Berwick.

Not a huge support travelled to Shielfield Park, Berwick, although it was a fine night. East Fife had been doing well in the League Cup with defeats of East Stirlingshire and Dumbarton, and only a narrow defeat at Alloa, but tonight they went down 1-2 to the Englishmen with only the goal scored by Morris Aitken to cheer them up.

There was of course a certain body of opinion in Scottish football which felt that Berwick should not be there, not necessarily out of any anti-English feeling, but more because a long trip to the other side of the border was not an economic undertaking.

A few years ago, an attempt spearheaded by Rangers (the Glasgow ones) to get rid of Berwick and four others had been thwarted by court action, and how Berwick would gain their revenge for that one eighteen months from now!

August 26 1953

East Fife this Wednesday night recorded a remarkable victory over Celtic at Parkhead before a 30,000 crowd.

With the news that Airdrie had beaten Aberdeen at Broomfield, East Fife now knew that they were at the top of the Scottish League Cup section with only a visit to Pittodrie on Saturday to come in the final game.

They had seven points and were one ahead of both Aberdeen and Airdrie, whereas Celtic were totally out of it. This was a fine performance, and a dream debut for young Billy Luke, who scored the only goal of the game, after a fine move involving Danny McLennan and Andy Matthew.

There was an element of luck in Luke's shot which was deflected off Jock Stein, but there was no luck involved in this fine victory over a team who would this season go on to win the Scottish League and Cup Double.

Before Luke scored the only goal of the game, both Gardiner and Fleming had hit the woodwork. In the second half, goalkeeper Curran was called upon to make a few good saves, but East Fife's defence were always in control of a disjointed Celtic forward line who earned the wrath of their own fans for their inability to break down the solid defending of Sammy Stewart and Willie Finlay.

History tells that East Fife would go on and win the League Cup this season for the third time. There was no better performance in the competition than this one, and the small band of travelling fans were in raptures at the final whistle.

August 27 1986

A fairly common refrain to Rangers run of success in the late 1980s was "they were lucky".

Never was this truer than tonight as they edged through to the next round of the Scottish League Cup against East Fife on a penalty shoot-out at Bayview before an all-ticket crowd of 10,000.

East Fife's start to the season had been unconvincing, to put it tactfully, but last week they had beaten Partick Thistle at Firhill in the Scottish League Cup (a repeat of the Final of 33 years previously but in totally different circumstances).

Now they drew Rangers, managed by Graeme Souness (but sent off in his first game for them against Hibs!) and grimly determined to restore the old glories to Ibrox.

Tonight, they almost met their match as East Fife held them for the first half, then the second half and might even have edged a winner but for a fine save by the Rangers goalkeeper. Chris Woods had recently in a game against Hibs, when a rammy broke out about the half-way line, charged out of his goal, not to calm everyone down, but to join in!

The game now went to extra time and 120 minutes came and went without any goals, although Ally McCoist had missed a penalty kick!

So it was a penalty shoot-out with East Fife going first. The first eight penalties were all scored, and now with excitement mounting to almost unbearable levels, East Fife's Hugh Hill was the unlucky man to miss, and Rangers, undeservedly, went through to the next round of the Scottish League Cup.

August 28 1948

Jack Harkness, one time Wembley Wizard and goalkeeper for Queen's Park and Hearts, and now a respected journalist of *The Sunday Post* was at Bayview today.

He was extremely impressed with East Fife on his first visit to Bayview since last year's promotion as he saw the Fifers beat St Mirren 3-1. They had now played four games and won two of them, something that was considered to be reasonably satisfactory for the 15,000 spectators who attended this game.

Most of them now were looking forward with relish to the start of the Scottish League Cup fixtures in September. East Fife were of course the holders of that trophy. Today they played football in a "series of terrific, well-thought-out onslaughts, which would have carved to ribbons any team in the League".

The goals were scored by Tommy Adams with his head after Henry Morris had headed the ball across the goalmouth to him, then Davie Duncan scored with a penalty after he himself had been brought down before Charlie Fleming scored a goal which Jack Harkness claimed was the best ever seen at this "compact enclosure" after he swerved to his left, left three men in his wake and crashed home the third goal from well outside the box.

St Mirren had equalised the first goal before half time but were simply swept aside in the early part of the second half, and then when they tried to get back into the game, found themselves unable to do so because of the excellence of the East Fife defence in which Sammy Stewart was outstanding.

August 28 1948

Willie Telfer challenges Davie Duncan on August 28 1948

August 29 1962

George Dewar's goal against Montrose at Links Park tonight which earned a good victory was sadly little more than a consolation prize for East Fife whose League Cup sectional campaign had begun disastrously with three defeats.

It had also included on the first Wednesday night of the season a rather embarrassing 0-5 thrashing from tonight's opponents, Montrose at Bayview. Tonight's result was a little revenge, but it was all too little too late.

On the other hand, it did seem as if a corner had been turned and it was quite clear that Manager Charlie McCaig had made a few necessary changes and had "had a word" with a few other players about attitude and the need to improve.

It was always hard on East Fife and their supporters to go out of the League Cup at the sectional stage, for it was still considered as "their" trophy which they had won three times and they still were the leading trophy winners even though they shared the honour now with Rangers and Hearts.

But times had changed — clearly for the better in the world at large as everyone now talked about "the affluent society" with more or less everyone now owning a television and even a few "working class people" now aspiring to own a motor car, and even contemplating foreign holidays.

But as far as East Fife were concerned, it was clear that the austerity age suited them better, not least because there was a certain equality in all the restrictions. Now teams like Rangers could pay their players astronomical wages. None of this however excused that awful thumping from Montrose two weeks ago, although tonight took the edge off it!

August 30 1930

Since joining the First Division, East Fife had not exactly found their path strewn with roses, and today's 2-6 defeat by Celtic at Bayview represented their fourth defeat out of four.

They did play well against Celtic in patches, and three players at least, goalkeeper John Bernard, Joe Gowdy and Danny Liddle, were able to be considered worthy of the company of the distinguished visitors.

In spite of the general disappointment, it was a great day with long queues to get in, loads of buses disgorging visitors and the atmosphere building up all morning. It was of course good for the local economy, not least the public houses, and in 1930 with unemployment soaring, any boost was a good thing.

Celtic were without Jimmy McGrory, but they did have three Thomsons, two of whom were from Fife. They were inside forward Eckie, whose home was less than a mile away in Buckhaven, and goalkeeper John from Cardenden, although he had been born in Kirkcaldy.

Celtic were 3-0 up at half time with goals from Alec Thomson, Peter Scarff and Cornelius Tierney. In the second half both Scarff and Charlie Napier scored penalties, and then Scarff scored again.

In the meantime, East Fife had fought back with a penalty from Arthur McGachie and a tap-in from Jock McCurley to make it 3-2 and it looked like a close game until a defender foolishly gave away a penalty, which effectively won the game for Celtic.

The lesson for East Fife was that when you are up against a good team, you must play well all the time, and not be foolish enough to give away penalties!

August 31 2013

East Fife supporters at Ibrox in 2013

August 31 1964

In what was generally regarded as being one of the best games ever played between these two grand old clubs, Forfar defeated East Fife 4-3 at Station Park.

Funnily enough, though, this result was not looked upon as a disaster this Monday night by fans of East Fife because it was only the first leg of the Supplementary Round of the League Cup.

Both teams had (convincingly) won their sections but as there were nine sections, there had to be a play-off. With little time for manoeuvre, the first leg was at Forfar on Monday and the second leg at Methil on the Wednesday.

In front of one of Forfar's biggest crowds for many years, Forfar scored first through Hamish Watt, before good work from Andy Waddell levelled the scores. Forfar regained the lead but then Ian Stewart scored twice to put East Fife 3-2 up.

In a tense finale, Kenny Dick scored for Forfar to equalise and then in the final minute Jake Young had the mortification to divert a ball past Andrew Kruzycki to give Forfar victory on the night.

The man of the match was undeniably Andy Waddell and the sizeable East Fife contingent were convinced that this narrow defeat could be overturned in two nights' time — it was now known that Celtic awaited the winners — and so it turned out. But tonight at Station Park both teams were given a deserved ovation at the end for a wonderful game of football and the following day's newspapers agreed with their assessment.

East Fife with the Second Division trophy and the Fife Cup in 2016. Photographer Jim Corstorphine is in the photo, yet he took the photo! How did he manage that? Is he a magician as well?

September

East Fife in 1927. They were the first team from the Second Division to reach the Scottish Cup final

September 1 1956

It was the final day of the League Cup Qualifying Section, and Celtic were at Bayview.

Earlier reverses meant that East Fife themselves could not qualify, and this was a shame because East Fife had done so well in previous years of this competition. But the key players had been sold on, and the good times had, to a large extent, gone. Nevertheless a crowd of 16,535 appeared at Bayview including a very large contingent from the west.

Celtic had drawn with Rangers on Wednesday night, and another draw here would be enough to see them qualify. But the traditions of Celtic, even without the injured Charlie Tully, would not allow them to sit back and defend, and a hard game ensued, occasionally a bit too hard with the referee, W D Liston of Larbert, compelled now and again to "have words" with several players on both sides.

Yet the atmosphere between both sets of supporters was good with everyone behaving (although one or two Celtic supporters dented their haloes a little outside the ground and found themselves staying in Fife for the weekend before visiting the magistrate on Monday!) and East Fife supporters were not slow to tell Celtic supporters that they had already won this Cup three times, whereas Celtic had yet to grace Hampden on League Cup final day.

The only goal of the game came through that superb practitioner of the game, Fifer Willie Fernie from Kinglassie, who weaved his way through several East Fife defenders before laying it off for Billy McPhail to score. Celtic would then go and break their duck in the competition this year.

September 2 1939

East Fife had an off day today going down 1-2 to a late goal scored by Airdrie's Steven at Broomfield, Airdrie.

It was a fine goal and was naturally greeted with a loud cheer from the Airdrie supporters, but there was a great deal of sadness and anxiety as well, both of which emotions were shared by the travelling supporters from Methil.

It was as if they knew that there would be no more football for a while. Germany had invaded Poland the day before, and this Saturday afternoon, the House of Commons met in emergency session to discuss sending an ultimatum to Germany.

Everyone now knew that war was inevitable — indeed it had been inevitable for some time — and, unlike 1914 when there was a certain amount of enthusiasm and euphoria in the air, the atmosphere was one of grim determination.

The game was started with a spirited rendering of "God Save The King", and there was a genuine hand-shaking at the end. It was noticeable too that the Disabled Enclosure (for men who had been badly injured in the 1914 - 1918 war) was full of men who were weeping, for their sacrifice twenty years ago had now been all in vain.

East Fife hurried away to get their train home. Rumours spread to the effect that London had already been bombed, and that the Methil docks would be next, although once they got home and were able to listen to the BBC Radio News, a more sober mood prevailed.

It was one of the most bizarre games that East Fife have ever played, and no-one really talked much about Airdrie's winning goal.

September 3 1949

Referee G MacDonald of Stirling is singled out for praise in *The Courier* for his control of this League Cup qualifying tie which might well have got out of hand and descended into a "rough house".

Basically East Fife were two points ahead of Hearts, but if Hearts won by more than one goal, they could qualify on the complicated system of goal average.

This was long before the days of calculators, so those who were good at mental arithmetic at Buckhaven High School were at a premium in the large crowd of 20,000 at Bayview today.

At one point Hearts were ahead, winning 2-1 in the first half, but Henry Morris equalised and then Allan Brown put the Fifers ahead. Jimmy Wardhaugh then equalised for Hearts and things were very tight indeed with the tension on the field mirrored by the tension on the terracings, but then Bobby Parker of Hearts handled in the box and Davie Duncan settled matters from the penalty spot.

Then East Fife's defence which had not been all that great, the normally reliable Sammy Stewart in particular, asserted control of the situation and the game finished a very creditable East Fife 4 Hearts 3.

In fact they won the section by four clear points. Indeed it was a good day for Fife because Dunfermline and Cowdenbeath qualified as well, leaving Raith Rovers (who had been in the same section as East Fife) the only team from the Kingdom not to qualify.

East Fife would of course go and win the Scottish League Cup that year, but never did they have a tougher day than this afternoon in Methil.

September 4 1948

15,000 were at Bayview today to see East Fife continue their impressive start to their First Division campaign with a 2-0 win over Partick Thistle. The crowd is astonishing, but a potent reminder of the support that East Fife and other clubs had in those post-war days.

Industry in Methil was booming, everyone was in work and the mines in particular offered loads of overtime, such was the need for coal to keep the post-war recovery going. In addition, football never at this stage made the mistake of pricing itself out of the market, and going to the football on Saturday afternoon and then the pictures on Saturday night was well within the capability of almost everyone.

Today the East Fife supporters saw a good game and a fine performance from the coming star, young Charlie Fleming, although *The Sunday Post* reporter was of the opinion that his enthusiasm for shooting was just a trifle misplaced when he tried it from too far out.

However he scored the first goal with his head following a cross from Allan Brown. That was in 20 minutes, and then the second came just before half time when Tommy Adams managed to slip home a rebound off the post.

Thistle fought back in the second half but their shooting was wayward, and they failed to reduce the leeway. The final whistle brought great scenes of joy, for it meant that East Fife were fourth in the First Division, only two points behind joint leaders Hibs and St Mirren.

September 5 1931

On a day well known for a sombre event involving a Fife goalkeeper, East Fife were on the wrong end of a heavy 4-1 defeat at Bayview in the derby game against Raith Rovers.

Both teams were now back in the Second Division, and may have lost a little credibility in the eyes of some supporters as a result, but this was a local derby and 4,500, including a lot of Rovers supporters on special trains made their way along to see the game on a hot, sultry kind of day with the threat of thunderstorms.

The 4-1 win, however, was a little flattering on Raith Rovers, and Rovers were indebted to the three B's — Andy Bell, Tommy Batchelor and Jock Beath — for their solid defending. For Rovers, Joe Cowan scored twice and the other goals were scored by Jacky Archibald and Jacky McLaren.

It was a fine win for the Rovers whose form this season had been inconsistent so far, but whose supporters, naturally on a high following a derby win, now felt that this might be the year for promotion again. East Fife on the other hand must have wondered why they only had one Danny Liddle goal to show for their efforts.

When the evening papers came out, the report of the Rangers v Celtic game stated that John Thomson of Celtic had been carried off with a head injury. This was a shame, for several players knew "Jock" Thomson, and indeed some had played with him at Wellesley Juniors.

Worse news followed when the Sunday papers appeared the following morning after a night of speculation and anxiety. John had died at 9.30 pm the previous evening.

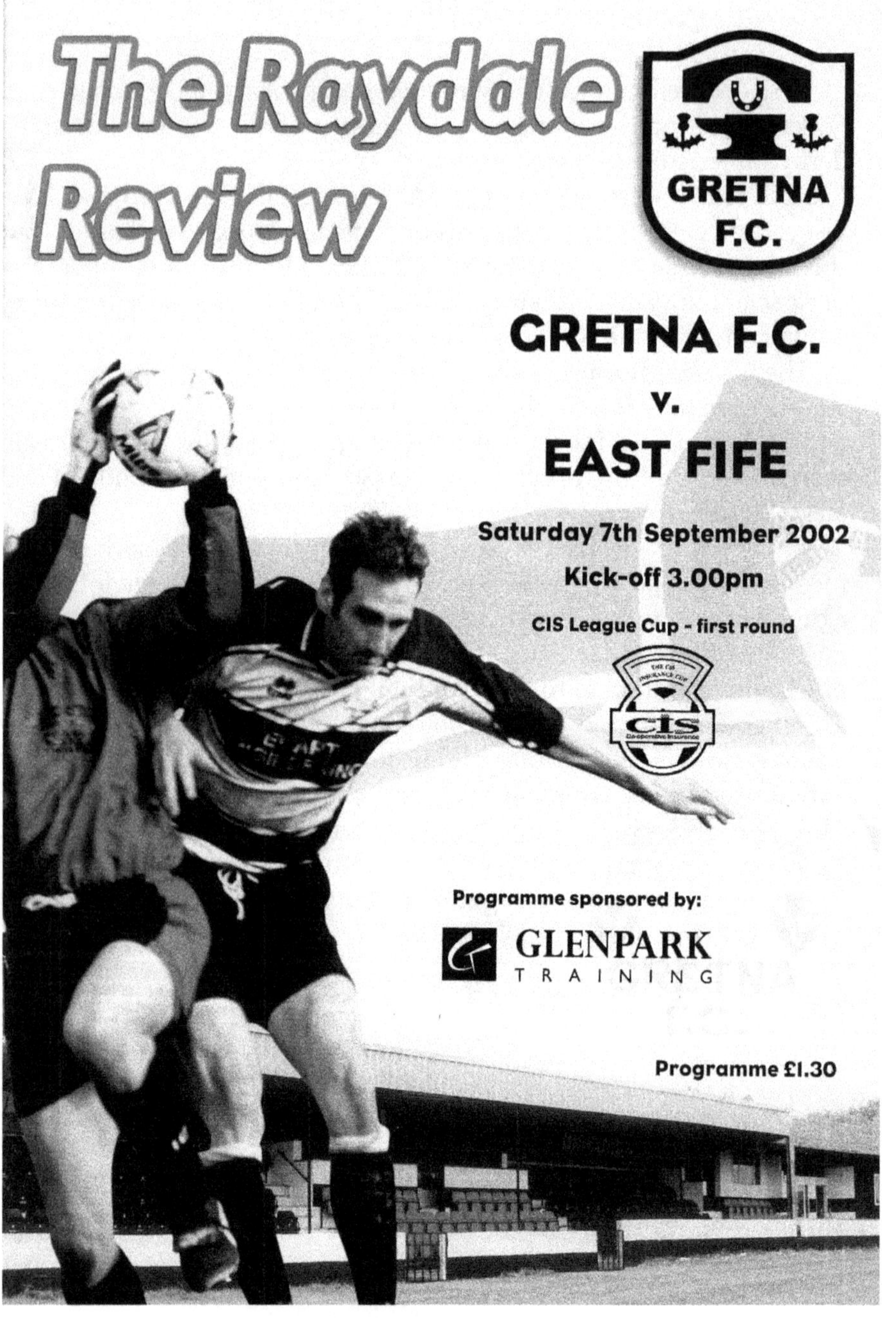

The Raydale Review

GRETNA F.C.
v.
EAST FIFE

Saturday 7th September 2002

Kick-off 3.00pm

CIS League Cup - first round

Programme sponsored by:

GLENPARK TRAINING

Programme £1.30

September 6 1924

East Fife sustained their first reverse of the League season with an unlucky 1-2 defeat at Volunteer Park, Armadale.

They had defeated King's Park and Dunfermline and drawn with Broxburn so far this season. On a pleasant day, Armadale scored first through Chisholm, but it looked suspiciously as if another Armadale player, Cheetham, was offside.

The significance of the man's surname was not lost on the East Fife supporters who immediately told each other about the famous London firm of solicitors called "Cheetham and Bolt".

In spite of this early reverse East Fife stuck manfully to their task, and had the bulk of the pressure in the second half, being profligate with their shooting until Peter Edgar got an equaliser with a fine shot. Scarcely however had the cheering from the small band of East Fife supporters died down when Armadale took the lead again when Porteous managed to get past two defenders to score.

Fairly soon after that Patrick Cahill, while defending a corner sustained a bad blow to his knee and had to be taken off, compelling East Fife to play with 10 men for the last 15 minutes. Chances then fell to both teams, and the general feeling was that East Fife deserved a draw.

They certainly had little to reproach themselves for, because they had played well enough. Meanwhile, the first Labour Government of Ramsay MacDonald, a hero among the East Fife supporters, was still hanging on in spite of being a minority one, and had just concluded a deal with France about disarmament, as well as recognising the Soviet Union.

September 7 1974

Derek O'Connor scores for East Fife against Raith Rovers in September 1974. Observe the long hair, and the hideous enclosure in front of the railway

September 7 1963

It was derby day at Stark's Park, Kirkcaldy but the persistent rain kept the crowd down to a good deal less than 10,000, when about ten years ago, this fixture would have attracted about 20,000.

Both teams had declined somewhat since their heyday and Raith Rovers had now joined East Fife in the Second Division. This was not, of course the first time that they had met this season, for East Fife had already beaten them and drawn with them in the League Cup sectional stage.

East Fife had won the section, and now awaited the arrival of Rangers next midweek. 1963 saw the net slowly tightening around the Government of Harold McMillan after scandal. His Minister of War was having an affair with a lady called Christine Keeler who was simultaneously having an affair with an attache from the Soviet Embassy.

Jokes naturally abounded about the sexual nature of all this, but no-one was telling jokes after this entertaining affair in which both teams claimed that they had done enough to win, but a 1-1 draw was the final result. Jimmy Bonthrone, who had had problems with injuries, was happier than Raith Rovers Manager Doug Cowie.

Both goals came in the middle of the first half. First Jimmy Gilpin scored for the home side, and then Morris Aitken hammered home the equaliser from the edge of the penalty box after goalkeeper Bobby Reid had punched the ball out.

In the second half, it was a typical derby tussle with heavy tackles, close things and penalty claims but neither side was able to achieve the breakthrough.

September 8 2018

Unlike the Scottish League Cup and indeed the Scottish Cup (to a lesser extent), East Fife have no great pedigree in the League Challenge Cup (the competition for all Scottish clubs other than the Premier League clubs and in recent years for the occasional club for Wales, England and Ireland), so it was all the more satisfying to record a victory over Partick Thistle, a team who, until recently were in the Premier League.

This game was played on an "International weekend" (on the night before, Scotland had gone down to a shocking 0-4 defeat from Belgium) and even though the weather was good, they attracted a disappointing crowd of only 932 to New Bayview.

However the small crowd saw a stirring performance for the Fifers who were 0-1 down at half-time to a goal scored by Andrea Mbuyi-Mutombo, but fought back well in the second half to score two great goals from Scott Agnew and Rory Currie, the second one a particularly spectacular one.

The news that in the same competition Raith Rovers had gone down 0-5 to Ross County at Dingwall put East Fife's triumph into some kind of perspective and the hope was expressed that East Fife could now go on and have some kind of a run in this often despised tournament — despised usually by those whose team met an early and little noticed exit, a fate that sadly had often come East Fife's way in the past!

Most supporters agreed however that the bread and butter Scottish League fixtures against the likes of Forfar and Stenhousemuir were the important things.

Mark Lamont evades a challenge from Alloa's Iain Flannigan at Recreation Park last Saturday

SPFL Ladbrokes League 1
East Fife FC v Stranraer FC
Saturday 10th September 2016   Kick off 3.00pm
Match Sponsor:
First Mortgage, Edinburgh

Issue No. 6   £2.00

September 9 1964

East Fife pulled off one of their best results for many years this Wednesday night at Bayview.

In their favourite trophy, the Scottish League Cup, they beat Celtic 2-0, a result all the more creditable because Celtic came into this game on the back of a 3-1 victory over Rangers.

The only problem as far as East Fife were concerned was that it was only the first leg of the two-legged quarter final and everyone knew that Celtic at Parkhead in a week's time would be a totally different proposition indeed.

On tonight's showing there was little doubt who the better team was. Having survived an early shock when John Hughes hit the post in the fourth minute, East Fife were one up at half-time when George Christie deflected in a Donnelly shot with his head, and in the 65th minute, they began to fancy their chances when Stewart passed to Andy Waddell to put them 2-0 ahead. East Fife then defended well with Jake Young outstanding and only John Hughes looking as if he could get through the defence. Late in the game, it could have been even better when a Donnelly shot hit the bar with Fallon beaten. The crowd was a healthy one of about 10,000 — one of the best crowds at Bayview for a long time — and it included a fair amount of disappointed green and white bedecked supporters.

The field was invaded at full-time as everyone ran to congratulate their heroes and plans were now being laid to attend the second leg at Celtic Park next week.

September 10 1967

All of the East of Fife and indeed all of Scotland awoke this Sunday morning sadly aware of the disaster at the Michael Colliery, East Wemyss yesterday.

It was now known that nine men had lost their lives in the cataclysmic fire which broke out underground. Three bodies have never been recovered.

There was a certain criticism of the football authorities for allowing the Cowdenbeath v East Fife game to go ahead yesterday, but to be fair, at the time that the football match kicked off, it was not yet apparent just how bad the tragedy was.

The score was 2-1 for East Fife, all the goals being scored in the first half. Andy Rolland had scored for Cowdenbeath, and Andy Waddell and George Dewar for East Fife.

In normal circumstances, this game would have been much talked about and dissected by the East Fife supporters, for a derby win is always very welcome, but as it was, people talked about nothing other than Philip Thomson, Andrew Taylor, James Tait, Harry Morrison, Andrew Thomson, Johnson Smith, Alex Henderson, Hugh Gallacher and James MacKay.

Quite a few of these men were East Fife supporters and were personally known to some of the players and other supporters. Prayers were said in Churches for the families of those who had died. The Michael Colliery, the biggest in Scotland at the time of the disaster has never re-opened, and the whole business remains a poignant reminder of the dangers to those who mined our coal, in 1967 still the major source of energy.

SEASON 1968-69 377

Official Programme 6d.

EAST FIFE v. HIBERNIAN

KEEP THIS PROGRAMME — IT MAY BE WORTH £1

September 11 1963

It was one of these nights that make old-timers nostalgic for the Old Bayview.

A packed crowd, great atmosphere, the players close to the pitch and everyone able to say that they were only three feet away (at times) from Jim Baxter.

Rangers were the guests at Bayview for the First Leg of the quarter Final of the Scottish League Cup and were held to a 1-1 draw. The ground was full, and Rangers brought a large crowd with them including a special train all the way direct from Glasgow to Leven.

It was hardly a level playing field, for Rangers were replete with Internationalists, whereas a few injury problems meant that the 11 players who ran out for East Fife were more or less all that they had!

The Rangers supporters must have been totally taken aback by the way that the Fifers played, for it would have been difficult to say which team was the First Division outfit until the last quarter of an hour when the part-timers tired, yet the full-timers were themselves too exhausted to apply the finishing touch.

Rangers had possibly had it too easy this season for their League Cup qualifying section had included two 3-0 wins over a poor Celtic team whom they had managed to "psych" into some sort of paralysis.

Not so East Fife. Although Rangers scored first when a Davie Wilson corner was deflected in by Harold Smith, East Fife fought back and George Dewar scored with a cracker. Towards the end, the home crowd barracked Jim Baxter, who of course had played for Raith Rovers, but Rangers would, sadly, have the last laugh in the second leg.

September 11 2010

Lloyd Young in action at Station Park, Forfar in 2010

September 12 1903

The first ever photograph, taken on September 12 1903 about a month after their first game. The team are wearing green and white, Celtic type, jerseys.

September 12 1953

An astonishing game at Methil in the Scottish League Cup quarter final first leg against Dunfermline Athletic saw Charlie Fleming score five goals!

"Charlie is the Methil darling" trumpeted the Glasgow *Evening Times* as East Fife won 6-2 before a very large and enthusiastic crowd on a lovely warm day at Bayview.

This result over their Fife rivals seemed to put East Fife well on the way to the semi-final and possibly even another trip to Hampden for the final, but there were at least two down sides to this day.

One was that although Fleming scored five goals and had a hand in Jimmy Bonthrone scoring the other, the rest of the game was pretty even and there were times when the Pars were clearly the better side, so that if Dunfermline could find a way to neutralise Fleming, the second leg might well be a different story.

The second down side, concomitant on that one, was the question of how long East Fife could hope to hold on to Charlie, given the interest shown in him by wealthy English clubs, not least Sunderland, whose Director, Mr Hall, was at Bayview and "in raptures" according to *The Courier* about Charlie's performance.

Sunderland had already spent £160,000 over the summer in buying new players, and had never hidden their admiration for Charlie. A bid was expected, and it remained to be seen whether the East Fife directors would be financially strong enough (and mentally strong enough) to be able to turn down a very large sum of money.

September 13 1924

A good win for East Fife today at Bayview when the local side beat Dumbarton 2-1.

The Sons of the Rock, as they were called, were a famous old Scottish team, but even in the 1920s, not everyone would believe you when you said that they were the winners of the Scottish League for the first two years of it in 1891 and 1892, and had won the Scottish Cup in 1883.

Although Dumbarton and Dunbartonshire are in many ways looked upon as the cradle of Scottish football, they were a small town team and had no real answer to the introduction of professionalism and the rise of the big city clubs in the 1890s.

Nevertheless for many years they were a force to be reckoned with in Scottish football, their ground being called "fatal Boghead" because of the number of times that teams like Celtic and Rangers came a cropper there.

Now, sadly, the Sons of the Rock had fallen on bad times and were in the Second Division. The Sons were off to a good start, however, in season 1924/25 and today was their first defeat in a game that "pulsated from start to finish" according to the writer of *The Sunday Post*.

Weir and Duncan scored for East Fife and Kennedy for Dumbarton, but it was thrill-a-minute stuff with even a mini-crowd invasion when a man ran on to remonstrate with the referee Mr Innes of Glasgow for being biased in favour of the West coast clubs and failing to award East Fife a penalty. He was "hustled off", and the game continued with *The Sunday Post* saying at the end that "the result rather flattered Dumbarton".

September 13 2008

Dene Shields and Andrew Cook capture the essence of the Fife derby here in September 2008

September 14 1935

This would have to be described as a poor game today at Forthbank in Stirling where East Fife lost 1-2 to a now defunct team called King's Park.

One of the reasons why King's Park went defunct after the Second World War and were replaced by Stirling Albion was because their ground was damaged by enemy bombs; today, even in 1935 there were already signs of troubling brewing in Europe.

In Germany, for example, Hitler had forbidden "mixed race" marriages of Jews and Aryans on the grounds that the German people were under threat, but at least that nonsense at the moment was confined solely to Germany itself.

More worrying was Mussolini's designs on Abyssinia, which could only really be described as bullying — for Italian tanks and aircraft were always likely to get the better of Abyssinian spears! Those who admired what Mussolini had done in Italy — and he had many admirers — found it difficult to defend what he was trying to do in Africa.

By no means oblivious to all this, East Fife went to Stirling and lost 2-1. It was a feisty game, and referee Mr Grant at one point had to talk to the police about the threatening behaviour of some spectators after a player was injured.

The Courier insists that East Fife were worth a share of the points, but simply did not get the breaks. George Scott scored East Fife's goal, but the star men for East Fife was the wee trickster who had made such an impact since joining the club at the start of the season — Tommy Adams. Sadly, his play was not matched by other members of his team.

September 15 1923

East Fife had a good win against Alloa Athletic today at Bayview on a crisp autumn day before 3,600 spectators.

Alloa were an interesting team. They had won the Second Division of the Scottish League in its revamped format in season 1921/22, but had come straight back down again, clearly finding the gap between the two divisions something that was difficult to bridge.

At the moment that were hamstrung by a dispute involving Arthur McInally, a talented but wayward individual and brother of the equally quixotic Tommy, who had fallen out with Celtic and was now playing for Third Lanark.

East Fife's form so far this season was disappointing but today they won 1-0, a little more comfortably than the score line would have suggested, with Phil Weir scoring the only goal of the game.

This season had seen a further expansion of the Scottish League with a Third Division now in place, and automatic relegation from the Second Division for the two lowest placed clubs. This was an effort to bring more competitiveness into the Scottish League fixtures, but it was doomed to failure simply because too many Third Division clubs could not sustain the financial costs of travel in a national League and preferred a regional one.

In the meantime trouble was brewing in the mining industry. It had been brewing since the end of the War, because demand for coal had slumped and owners were threatening to close down pits and to lay miners off. The obvious wealth of the Wemyss family made it hard for anyone in the Levenmouth area to believe they had any kind of a problem, however.

September 16 1964

East Fife's hopes of defeating Celtic over two legs crashed at Celtic Park tonight.

Winning 2-0 from the first leg and with hopes of possibly adding another (Billy McNeill was still out injured) to make life difficult for the green and whites, they travelled with optimism.

Sadly the predictable happened on the wet pitch, and Celtic won 6-0 with Steve Chalmers scoring five and Jim Kennedy getting the other one.

What a tragedy tonight was for goalkeeper Andrew Kruzycki who palmed the ball into the net for Celtic's first goal, and never really recovered. All the goals were in fact good ones, usually from a distance, but one wonders what might have happened if it had not been for Kruzycki's early unfortunate error.

It was clear that Celtic had worried about this game for they had drawn 1-1 with Clyde on the intervening Saturday, but they were up for the game, as indeed were their supporters.

East Fife got a good share of the 25,000 gate, and even on occasion got a round of applause from the chivalrous Celtic Park crowd with Donnelly and Waddell in particular attracting welcome attention. It was noticeable too that Celtic's goalkeeper John Fallon went out of his way to commiserate with Kruzycki at the full time whistle — every goalkeeper could sympathise with his error, and his confidence may well have been shattered after an encounter with a lout at Station Park, Forfar a few games ago.

It was an unhappy party that returned home that night, but they had the satisfaction of knowing that they had at least put the wind up Celtic after their first leg.

September 17 1949

A crowd of 5,962, Forfar's biggest crowd since well before the Second World War, packed Station Park to see East Fife, whose supporters arrived on several trains and quite a few buses to see a great game.

Forfar, without being disgraced, managed to hold the First Division East Fife to 1-3 in the first leg of the Scottish League Cup quarter final.

The most popular man on the park was Tommy Adams, now with Forfar, but a man who had made his name with East Fife. He was one of the many unfortunate football players of that era whose career was badly disrupted by the war.

Forfar started brightly and Sunter might have scored an early goal which would have made all the difference to them, but it was East Fife who opened the scoring through Bobby Black in a goalmouth scramble.

Forfar also suffered a bad blow when their inside forward Perrie broke his arm and had to leave the field.

The writer of *The Forfar Dispatch* is clearly nostalgic about the recent passing of the cricket season for he talks about the "tea interval" when it is more normally referred to as "half-time".

In either case, the crowd were well entertained by the Kirriemuir Pipe Band. But after the resumption, Henry Morris scored twice, one being a great header, and the other when he squeezed between two defenders to score.

This effectively knocked the stuffing out of the gallant Forfar side, but there was still time for a consolation goal scored by the diminutive Tommy Adams when he glided a Rodger cross beyond John Niven, and earned a cheer from his former admirers in the East Fife support.

September 18 1965

Heavy rain overnight and on the morning of this game restricted the crowd to a lot less than what one would have expected for a Fife derby, with the Raith home fans in particular reluctant to turn up following their 8-1 hammering from Celtic in the League Cup quarter final first leg on Wednesday night.

But East Fife were not exactly away to the best of starts this season either, having been bundled out of the League Cup at the sectional stage and having lost 1-2 to Albion Rovers the previous weekend.

Manager Jimmy Bonthrone therefore rang a few changes and brought in some new faces. One of them, Alan Guild, who had recently joined the club from Forfar West End, crossed for George Christie to score in a goalmouth scrimmage.

Before half time Christie had put East Fife further ahead with a neat header following a good move down the right. This was clearly not to the liking of the Raith Rovers faithful. The slow hand-clap was heard and their team left the field to boos ringing in their ears.

But East Fife's fans were a great deal happier and became absolutely ecstatic when George Dewar picked up a Morris Aitken pass and scored off the post. At this, the Rovers fans decided than enough was enough and went home, missing their consolation goal near the end. It is always sweet to win a derby game, and this one was particularly so, although the good form was not always maintained this season.

September 19 1953

In a hard fought game at Stark's Park before a large crowd on derby day, things ended up all square and the 2-2 score was no disgrace to anyone.

With East Fife now in the Scottish League Cup semi-final and Charlie Fleming the man of the moment, it was no great surprise to the 17,000 crowd when "Legs" put East Fife ahead in the 15th minute. But, although they remained on top for most of the rest of the first half, they could not add to the score and in a five minute spell in the second, Raith Rovers equalised and then went ahead.

The Courier is in little doubt that the catalyst was Raith Rovers' Andy Young who first slipped the ball through to Ernie Copeland to equalise, then started a move which led to the second goal.

It was a funny one too, for Eddie Kelly was brought down in the penalty box for what was a clear penalty but referee Bobby Davidson from Airdrie saw that the ball was heading for the goal line, and allowed the ball to cross the line before awarding not a penalty for Raith Rovers, but a goal!

East Fife's players and supporters argued furiously about this, but Mr Davidson was correct in his rather unusual allowing of the "advantage" rule. The game was now an exciting one as Raith Rovers worked hard to go further ahead and East Fife fought to level it, and it was East Fife who did level it with a good strike from Jimmy Bonthrone. Sometimes, "derby" fixtures can be one-sided and boring. This one wasn't.

September 20 1972

East Fife hinted tonight that the great days of the Scottish League Cup could be on their way back with a fine performance in the first leg of the Second Round of the tournament as they beat Partick Thistle 1-0 at Bayview.

Partick Thistle were of course the holders of the tournament which they had won last year by beating Celtic 4-1 in what was generally regarded as being the biggest upset in the history of the League Cup.

In addition, East Fife v Partick Thistle had been the final of the 1953/54 competition, and no-one in Methil needed reminding about that!

The set-up in the League Cup was now of course all different, for two teams qualified from each section and there was now an extra round, and this was it. Tonight however it was a bright performance from East Fife before a slightly disappointing crowd of about 5,000, and Partick Thistle had goalkeeper Alan Rough to thank for keeping the score down to 1-0, the goal coming eight minutes from full time from a header by Doug Dailey, one of Manager Pat Quinn's signings.

Glasgow's *Evening Times* the following night criticised Thistle for being far too fond of the "frills and fancy stuff" and warned them that the second leg in two weeks' time at Firhill would not be plain sailing. They did not seem to heed this warning and the second leg was a 0-0 draw meaning that East Fife were now in the quarter finals of the League Cup.

September 21 1949

East Fife duly qualified for the semi-final of the Scottish League Cup this Wednesday evening at Bayview with a fine 5-1 win over Forfar Athletic, whom they had already beaten 3-1 the previous Saturday at Station Park in the first leg.

The 7,000 crowd saw some good football and even felt magnanimous enough to cheer on Tommy Adams, East Fife's great right winger now playing out the last days of his career with Forfar.

The star of the game was undeniably Henry Morris, who was celebrating his selection for the Scottish team. He scored twice in the first half, one a tap-in and one a more difficult goal where he calmly chose his spot as three defenders converged on him. He had also laid on other goals for Jack Davidson and Allan Brown.

But for John Smith in the Forfar goal having an inspired game, the score line would have been a lot more, but Forfar kept plugging away and eventually scored a goal through Menzies before Bobby Black finished off the scoring.

Forfar's right back was Sam Smith, a crusty character who would become Forfar's Chairman in the 1970s and lead them to unbelievable heights. Forfar's current Chairman in 1949, the legendary James Black, who had been involved in Scottish football since the 1880s, was heard to say that East Fife were as good a team as any he had seen.

Indeed, East Fife did look a good bet to repeat their success in the Scottish League Cup of two years ago, but their semi-final opponents would be either Rangers, Hibs or Dunfermline Athletic.

September 22 2012

Paul McManus and Kevin Twaddle of Ayr United

September 22 2012

Considering that neither team had won a League game this season, it was rather surprising that 575 turned up at New Bayview to see East Fife v Ayr United.

In fact they saw a very good game with both sides playing better football than their lowly League positions would have suggested, even though the end result was another heartbreak, agonisingly late in the game for East Fife.

Jamie Pollock got East Fife off in the right direction with a fine low drive early on, but then defensive frailties let them down again after a fine combination from Michael Moffat and Davie Sinclair.

In the second half Sinclair scored again for the Honest Men of Ayr, and heads went down as East Fife seemed to be heading for defeat. So they were, but the action wasn't all over yet and Robert Barr equalised with a cracker from well outside the box.

Only a couple of minutes remained and a goal looked a possibility for either side, but sadly for East Fife it was scored by Kyle McAusland of Ayr United, Sinclair was involved again for it was he who sent the ball across for McAusland to score.

Sadly it was too late for Gordon Chisholm's men to fight back and East Fife were now rock bottom of the Second Division with only two points and four defeats in a row. Life was not destined to be a bundle of laughs or an awful lot of fun for East Fife supporters the rest of this season!

September 23 1950

This derby win over Raith Rovers at Bayview came as a welcome and much needed boost for East Fife, for the start to the 1950/51 season had not been a good one.

They had failed to qualify from their section in the League Cup and they had already sustained two heavy defeats in the League. The cause was easily discerned.

George Aitken and Allan Brown were both in dispute with the club, both wanting transfers to larger clubs, and basically refusing to play for East Fife.

East Fife, for their part, were equally bloody minded, and the result was an impasse. The fans' opinion was split on this one. While some sympathised with the players, more thought that they were acting like spoilt brats and everyone agreed that it was doing the club no good at all, for everyone else was unsettled.

Today, East Fife showed that they were still the best team in Fife with a good performance including two excellent goals, and both involved Charlie Fleming, who scored one himself and made another for Jimmy Bonthrone. The other Bonthrone goal was less spectacular, but enough to win the game with a degree of comfort.

Doug Stockdale scored Raith Rovers' only goal in a game that lacked nothing of the passion that one should associate with "derby" fixtures with a few hefty tackles from two sides who were not prepared to give an inch to each other.

Meanwhile, the Korean War which had broken out in the summer was showing no signs of abating, and already reports of casualties were causing concern.

September 24 1966

East Fife won again today to stay at the top of the Scottish League Division Two with a hard fought but worthy win over Berwick Rangers.

Berwick Rangers were always difficult opposition. They were the only English team to play in the Second Division of Scottish football and it was often felt that their future was quite precarious.

A few years ago for example, Glasgow Rangers had produced a "blueprint for the survival of Scottish football" which had involved the axing of five clubs — and Berwick Rangers had been one of them.

Berwick Rangers would very soon wreak their spectacular revenge over the other Rangers, but no-one could have predicted that. There was often a Scotland v England aspect to games involving Berwick, and this year of course there was an added edge to all that, for it was less than two months since England had won the World Cup!

Six League games had been played by East Fife before this game started and there was only one defeat, admittedly a painful one against Raith Rovers.

The good start to the League was enough to make supporters forget about their early League Cup exit to Greenock Morton. East Fife had beaten Brechin City 4-0 on Wednesday night, and although today's victory over a stuffy Berwick Rangers side was less spectacular, it was no less welcome.

It was a bright autumn day at Bayview and before a slightly disappointing crowd of 1,500, goals from George Christie and Jimmy Walker saw them through. It was of course, as discerning supporters could see, the way in which League titles could be won and promotions gained — by the steady grinding down of one's opponents and challengers.

September 25 1954

For the second year in a row, East Fife qualified for the semi-final of the Scottish League Cup.

Having drawn the first leg 2-2 on Wednesday night at Cappielow, they today beat Morton 2-0 at Bayview to join Motherwell, Airdrie and Hearts in the semi-final, and they were now hoping to repeat last year's success and win the trophy for the fourth time.

But it was not as easy as it seemed, for Morton, a "B" Division team, fought well and for a long time in the second half, they were certainly the better team. But Jimmy Bonthrone scored in the 23rd minute of the first half, and everything looked fine for a spell, but the Fifers then took the foot off the pedal.

After a few lucky escapes on the East Fife goal with Morton's Alec Linwood giving the East Fife defence no end of bother, Charlie Fleming with one of his trademark goals (hence, of course, his nickname the "Cannonball") eased the pressure in the 72nd minutes, and sent the 15,000 crowd home with a smile on their face.

East Fife's record in the Scottish League Cup was little short of phenomenal, for they had won it three times out of eight starts, more than Rangers' and Dundee's two.

In spite of some indifferent form in the League, they were now the favourites, even though they had been lucky to qualify from a difficult section which included Hibs and Aberdeen. But manager Jerry Dawson was very confident about his team's ability to repeat last season's success.

September 26 1931

East Fife supporters were reeling from two blows in autumn 1931.

One was the collapse of the Labour Government in August and the other was the tragic death of John Thomson on September 5, a man known personally to many of the East Fife players and supporters.

Very soon the new National Government would go to the country to ask for a "Doctor's Mandate" to increase unemployment and cut unemployment benefit.

Times had been better for East Fife supporters, and today produced very little balm for them with a hefty 0-3 defeat to St Johnstone at Muirton Park, Perth.

The game was to a very large extent spoilt by over-zealous refereeing on the part of the referee, Mr Kilbride of Polmont, who seemed to enjoy blowing his whistle on every conceivable occasion and refused to let the play flow, to the obvious annoyance of the players and the 5,000 crowd.

This could not however be said to be the cause of East Fife's defeat because St Johnstone, a slick side who would earn promotion this season, won the game well.

East Fife were the better team in the first half but suffered two bad blows on either side of half-time — one was a bad goalkeeping error from Robertson, and another was an inadvertent own goal deflected past his own goalkeeper by defender McKee.

St Johnstone then took charge of the game, and there was no obvious way back for East Fife, especially when Cameron scored with a brilliant overhead scissors kick after a corner kick. All in all, an unfortunate time for East Fife.

September 27 1947

In one of the best Cup ties ever played at Tynecastle, East Fife beat Hearts 4-3 after extra time before 23,000 spectators to reach the semi-final of the Scottish League Cup.

Unlike the previous year, the quarter finals of the League Cup were only one game this year because of the reluctance of the government to allow midweek football and encourage absenteeism in industry when everything was required for the post-war recovery. (Ludicrously, Winston Churchill, now leader of the Opposition, was encouraging everyone to emigrate!).

The game almost did not happen for left half George Aitken, because about half an hour before the start, he was not going to be playing because of a niggling injury. However after a chat with manager Scot Symon, he found himself in the team, and played brilliantly.

East Fife opened the scoring through Dougie Davidson, but then Ken Currie equalised, Davie Duncan put East Fife ahead again, Currie equalised yet again and the game went to extra time.

Hearts then went ahead through a remarkable goal when Archie Kelly managed to get to a ball before John Niven did and to hook it into the net from the edge of the box.

Naturally Tynecastle erupted at such brilliance, but their joy was short-lived as Tommy Adams, not for the first nor last time, won the day for East Fife.

First he scored direct from a corner kick, and then with time running out, Adams scored again, slipping round goalkeeper George Paton to prod home, and put East Fife into the semi-finals along with Rangers, Falkirk and Aberdeen.

September 28 1946

East Fife finished a phenomenal League Cup qualifying section by beating Alloa Athletic 6-0 in their final game.

Because midweek football was discouraged in 1946 (lest it interfere with the post-war recovery) all the sectional games in the first League Cup tournament were played on successive Saturdays.

East Fife had simply demolished the opposition of St Johnstone, Dunfermline Athletic and Alloa with an aggregate score of 22-0, and curiously they won all their away games 2-0!

Today Alloa were simply swept aside and newly demobbed David Paris, who was still in the forces in midweek, scored to-day, leading *The Courier* to chortle that it was three Dundonians who had scored for East Fife — David Paris, Dougie Davidson and Henry Morris.

It was the only member of the forward line not to score who had made it all happen — this was the mercurial, quixotic, will o' the wisp Tommy Adams whom many East Fife supporters claimed was the best there had ever been.

The Scottish League Cup would now be put into cold storage over the winter — a very hard winter, as it turned out — until March when there would be a two-legged quarter final with East Fife drawn against Hearts.

The crowd of over 10,000 still contained a fair sprinkling of military uniforms, for demobilisation was a slow process, although most men were home by now, many of them wearing their broad brimmed "demob hat" given to them by a grateful nation. Manpower was particularly required in the local Fife area, for coal was in great demand. It was in total contrast to the days of the 1920s when mines would stand idle. Every single miner was now required.

September 29 2007

Paul McManus has just scored

September 29 2007

It is difficult to dislike Stenhousemuir, clearly one of the great survivors of Scottish football (and one of the three clubs who have two u's in their name, the other two being Dundee United and Queen of the South!)

Their crowds are usually very poor, and one has to give credit to the men who have kept the show on the road at Ochilview. A few hundred yards down the road, however, at the Tryst is their cricket team, a team who have done consistently well in Scottish cricket circles.

The football team have had their moments, putting Aberdeen out of the Scottish Cup in 1995, for example, but today was certainly not one of them, for they went down 7-0 to a rampant East Fife team at New Bayview, and had two men red-carded into the bargain!

They were simply outplayed, and yet at half-time the score was 0-0 and Stenny would have had cause to congratulate themselves on holding the League leaders. But then the roof fell in and Paul McManus scored 4, Jonathan Smart scored 2 (both excellent headers) and Paul Walker 1.

Steven Ferguson and Ross Hamilton managed to get red cards in that Stenny horror story of a second half, and in truth such was the play of East Fife that double figures would not have been entirely out of the question.

Those East Fife supporters who sympathised with Stenhousemuir would find that their compassion would be much diluted by the time that the teams met again a few days before Christmas, for they beat us 2-1 at Ochilview!

September 30 1939

The country had been at war for a month now, and it was still not 100% clear what was going to happen to Scottish football.

In a knee-jerk reaction, all football had been stopped the day after war was declared, but now some games were being allowed — friendlies and in Fife, the Penman Cup, a trophy which had had its moments but was hardly looked upon as the highlight of anyone's season.

East Fife defeated Raith Rovers 3-0 in this Penman Cup game, all the goals coming in a six minute spell at the start of the second half, the goal scorers being Wilkie, Wilson and Fleming.

The crowd was smallish — 2,000 — and the Raith Rovers part of them in particular departed very unhappy, cheerfully ignoring however the appeals to people not to travel lest they disrupt troop movements.

There was indeed a great deal of "troop movement" with sad, emotional farewells often to the accompaniment of pipe bands, as young men, sometimes reluctant conscriptees, left to join their units, but at the moment there was no great action, certainly not in Europe.

The "phoney war" had begun, but there were still a few hopes being expressed that peace could yet be negotiated. That view was not however shared in Poland, which had been virtually obliterated by the German Army, in alliance with their equally evil henchmen the Russians.

In the meantime, the argument was expressed very strongly that football must be allowed to continue for reasons of morale. In any case, it was an excellent way for 22 young men to keep themselves fit for what was to come.

October

East Fife in 1927. The photographer seems to have made a mistake in making the players look into the sun!

October 1 1949

Henry Morris in his Scotland colours for his one and only International

October 1 1949

Scotland, October 1 1949 with two East Fife players – George Aitken and Henry Morris. Aitken is third from right in the back row, and Morris is third from right in the front row. Observe the referee and the two linesmen in the photo as well!

October 1 1949

This was an excellent day for East Fife.

Not only did they beat Queen of the South 4-1 at Bayview before an appreciative crowd of 10,000 supporters, but they did it with a weakened team, and the team was weakened for the very good reason that two players, George Aitken and Henry Morris were playing for Scotland!

The International was played against Northern Ireland in Belfast, and Scotland won 8-2, a score-line which brought as much joy to Methil as did East Fife's own result.

For Scotland, the hero was Henry Morris who scored a hat-trick — Scotland's first with a header which goalkeeper Kelly misjudged, Scotland's sixth with a shot after he had been left unmarked, and the eighth with a miskick which *The Sunday Post* described as "the softest ever".

The Courier is similarly damning with faint praise about Henry's hat-trick and says that he was "one speed" throughout. All this does not really explain however how it came about that Henry Morris was never again chosen to play for Scotland.

Allegations of discrimination in favour of bigger clubs may be valid, although they do not always stack up in the face of evidence, and Morris's subsequent rejections can only really be put down to the general strange and quixotic behaviour of Scotland's selectors.

George "Dod" Aitken was generally held to have had a good game, but the consensus of opinion was that Willie Waddell was the man of the match.

Scotland's team was Jimmy Cowan (Morton), George Young (Rangers) and Sam Cox (Rangers); Bobby Evans (Celtic), Willie Woodburn (Rangers) and George Aitken (East Fife); Willie Waddell (Rangers), Jimmy Mason (Third Lanark), Henry Morris (East Fife), Billy Steel (Derby County) and Lawrie Reilly (Hibs).

Photograph Opposite: Back Row: Evans (Celtic), Woodburn (Rangers), Cowan (Morton), Cox (Rangers), Aitken (East Fife):
Front Row: Waddell (Rangers), Mason (Third Lanark) ,Young (Rangers), Morris (East Fife), Steel (Derby County), Reilly (Hibs).

George "Dod" Aitken

October 2 1999

Changes were afoot at the turn of the century.

Two more teams were to be added to the Leagues and therefore three teams were to be promoted to Division Two for the following season.

It was rather complicated to work out but it meant that East Fife had more chance this year of moving upwards than they would normally have.

They had already advanced twice in the League Cup by dint of a penalty shoot-out and they were due to play Hearts in the next round at "home", although safety concerns about the new Bayview would mean that "home" would have to be Stark's Park, Kirkcaldy.

Today, however, on a bright and breezy autumn day, a trip to Glebe Park, Brechin was the order of the day.

Glebe Park is a very unusual and indeed charming ground with its small match box stand, and the hedge running down one side of the park. They have the smallest "catchment area" of any club in Great Britain, and today's crowd of 365 (one for each day of the year!) was slightly above the average for Glebe Park.

East Fife's League form was inconsistent and they had stumbled of late, but today they had a good game, winning 3-1 with a couple of goals from Barrie Moffat and another from Stuart McKay.

In the meantime as the millennium approached, rumours spread that there was to be a millennium bug which would paralyse everyone's computer because no computer could cope with the change in the date — but if you believed that, you would believe anything!

October 3 1953

When Charlie Fleming left Bayview on the Thursday night to join the Scottish party to go to Ireland, his team mate Henry Morris might have said to him "Mind what happened to me! I scored a hat-trick for them four years ago, and they never gave me another game!"

The "Cannonball" might have laughed at that, but more or less the same thing happened to him. He scored twice... and never played again for Scotland!

His first was a fine goal from a distance, one of those which earned him the nickname "Cannonball". The second goal was a less aesthetically pleasing goal — a rebound off the goalkeeper's leg — but it was a goal nevertheless, and Scotland silenced the 55,000 crowd at Windsor Park, Belfast by winning 3-1.

So what was the problem? In fact Charlie, according to some newspapers did not have a good game, *The Courier* being particularly hard on him saying that he was in "one of his can't do anything right moods" and then the Special Correspondent goes on to say "I can't recall him ever taking the ball in his stride and getting on with the job".

Indeed it appeared that Northern Ireland were the better team with the Scottish based pair of Billy Simpson of Rangers and Charlie Tully of Celtic being singled out for special praise.

But Scotland won 3-1! Maybe all of this goes a little way to explain why "Legs" didn't get another Scotland cap, but it did seem hard on him at the time. His club form was consistently good. East Fife clearly missed him, for they went down 1-3 to Clyde at Shawfield that day!

October 4 1924

It is very easy to dismiss Albion Rovers as an irrelevance to Scottish football.

Those who enjoy sneering at poverty have a great deal to go on there, but it was not always so for the Cliftonhill men.

Not many people know that they contested the first Scottish Cup final after World War I in 1920, losing narrowly to Kilmarnock before a crowd given as 90,000!

Until 1923 they had been in the First Division, and today at Cliftonhill they shocked East Fife by going four goals up before half-time, then scoring another before East Fife pulled two back through two goals scored by Duncan and Hunter.

Indeed *The Courier*, always keen to say something to cheer up the local support, says that East Fife could have scored more but for "poor shooting" and says that of the five goals lost, goalkeeper Neish was very unlucky, particularly as one of them was a penalty.

Frankly, this seems like "clutching at straws" and the truth was that East Fife were well beaten 5-2.

Meanwhile, the fate of the first Labour Government lay in the balance. It had been a minority Government, dependent on Liberal support, but the enlightened and progressive signing of a trade deal with the Soviet Union had alienated Liberal support and encouraged bogus ideas among the establishment that Ramsay MacDonald was little other than a front for Bolshevism.

Among East Fife miners however, and working people generally his popularity remained high... but his Government had only a few weeks to live, and the smear campaigns were in full flow.

October 5 1957

Everyone agreed that Hearts were very impressive this season (they would indeed win the Scottish League) but not a lot of people saw this one coming.

East Fife, although now a few years past their glory days but still well supported, travelled to Tynecastle and received their heaviest ever hammering to the tune of 9-0.

Frankly, they were simply outclassed as the talented Hearts team ran through a panic-stricken defence with ease, with only Sammy Stewart showing any sign of being able to stop them.

Fortunately, there was an International on that day (Scotland drew 1-1 against Northern Ireland in Belfast) and East Fife were able to "hide" behind that one as far as the newspapers were concerned, but no-one could pretend other than that they were in a great deal of trouble, and indeed they would be relegated at the end of the season.

Willie Bauld scored two, Jimmy Wardhaugh scored a hat-trick, Dave MacKay, Alec Young, John Cumming and Jimmy Murray scored one each.

East Fife never looked remotely like scoring, or getting back into the game at all and W M Syme's final whistle brought great relief that double figures had not been reached.

Hearts would go on and win the League that year. East Fife's form was now two wins, two defeats and one draw, but this game signalled the beginning of the end of East Fife's great side.

A joke ran round Levenmouth to the effect that an East Fife supporter had asked his Hearts-supporting girlfriend to marry him. She was learning German at the time at Buckhaven High School and said "Nein! Nein! Nein!"

October 6 1951

It was a sign of the times that East Fife were actually disappointed not to have anyone in today's International match against Northern Ireland in Belfast.

They consoled themselves with a 2-0 win over Greenock Morton at Cappielow while Scotland went one better and defeated Northern Ireland 3-0.

Morton were always a quixotic team in Scottish football, and today they were two men short, for goalkeeper Jimmy Cowan and attacker Tommy Orr were with the Scottish team. Today's game had a crowd of 10,000 and most of the Morton supporters were prepared to admit at the end that their side been well beaten by the team from the opposite coast of the country.

Ian Gardiner scored the first goal for East Fife, and it was due to a wise piece of refereeing by Jack Mowat of Rutherglen, generally regarded as the best referee in the country at the time. Gardiner was fouled but Mowat wisely played advantage and allowed him to run on and score.

In the second half, Jimmy Bonthrone scored a second, a softish goal from a throw-in which was then headed on to the unmarked Bonthrone to put the ball past Hamilton, Morton's deputy goalkeeper.

Once again, it was the play of Charlie Fleming which attracted attention. He did not score that day, but he was hardly ever off the ball in the second half, spraying passes to the other forwards. This result moved East Fife up to joint top of the table alongside Hibs with 4 games won out of 5 played, and only one defeat, against Hearts at Tynecastle.

October 7 1972

Kevin Heggarty, himself an ex-Bairn, was the man mainly responsible for East Fife's ultimately rather narrow 4-3 victory at Brockville today.

East Fife, now in the their second year back in the First Division, had been very lucky to escape relegation last year, but this year they had made a far better start and had now won four games out of six.

Today's victory at Falkirk was particularly rewarding, for Falkirk were old rivals and a team with a lot in common with East Fife in terms of their support, local area and a tendency to yo-yo between the Divisions.

Falkirk were likely to be relegation candidates by the end of the season as well, so it was all the more necessary for East Fife to beat them, particularly as the Bairns had delighted their fans with a win over Aberdeen in midweek.

This was a curious game with East Fife being 4-1 up at half-time and apparently cruising thanks to Heggarty's two goals, and one each from Honeyman and Dailey. Heggarty's two goals were both remarkable in their own way with the first coming in 37 seconds, and the other when the Falkirk defence stood still foolishly claiming offside and allowed Heggarty to run on and score.

The Bairns did not give up and their two second half goals ensured a lively finish for the 5,000 crowd, but East Fife's impressive defence of Gorman, Duncan and Printy; McIvor, Martis and Clarke were more than up to the task, and ensured that East Fife were in a position of mid-table respectability.

October 8 1949

October 8 1949

It was a bitter-sweet day for East Fife as they reached the final of the Scottish League Cup for the second time in four years. They did this by beating Rangers 2-1 before 76,000 at Hampden Park, and will now face Dunfermline in what will be an all-Fife final.

But the triumph came at the cost of the death of East Fife's Chairman, John McArthur, who collapsed as he stood up to cheer the winning goal. He died a few minutes later in the dressing room. He had had a serious heart attack some time ago and was attending the game today against medical advice.

The game itself was a thriller with East Fife taking the lead through an Allan Brown header in the first half, then finding themselves pegged back while Rangers mounted assault after assault until they equalised following what many people thought was a foul on goalkeeper John McGarrity. Referee Mr McDonald of Stirling, however, thought otherwise.

This happened heartbreakingly late in the game, which now went to extra-time. There was nothing to separate the teams until Charlie "Legs" Fleming took over. He picked up the ball just inside his own half and started to beat one man, then another, then yet another, but the East Fife supporters feared that he might throw it all away. Not a bit of it!

He hammered the ball past Bobby Brown in the Rangers goal for a spectacular winner which was generally believed to be one of the best ever seen at Hampden. But the glory must be shared with full back Sammy Stewart for his part in the taming of the ever-dangerous Willie Waddell.

October 8 1949

John McArthur, Chairman

October 9 1948

Hearts v East Fife at Tynecastle in 1948. The result was a rather severe 6-1 defeat

October 9 1954

In retrospect, this was really the end of the great Scottish League Cup adventures of East Fife.

Today at a sadly deserted Hampden in the drizzle, East Fife lost 1-2 to Motherwell in the semi-final, and East Fife would never again reach such dizzy heights as a League Cup semi-final.

And all this was in spite of scoring first through Ian Gardiner in the early stages of the game and for a long time after that, they remained on top.

This fine Motherwell side had a strange existence in the early 1950s winning the Scottish League Cup in 1950/51, the Scottish Cup in 1952, getting relegated in 1953 and then promoted in 1954.

They gradually took control, until, as the papers put it, "Kilmarnock scored for Motherwell", a reference to a free kick taken by Willie Kilmarnock, the right back of Motherwell.

This happened just before half-time, and from then on, Motherwell never looked back and scored a winning goal through Alex Bain at about the hour mark.

East Fife had a few half chances squandered by Andy Matthew, and at one point made the strange decision to play Charlie Fleming on the right wing, but they simply could not get the ball past the red sweater of Hastie Weir in the Motherwell goal.

All in all, it was a somewhat depressing experience for East Fife, but the small crowd of less than 20,000 in the huge Hampden bowl perhaps told its own story of a small town team which had reached its limit. Maybe an Edinburgh ground might have been a better venue.

October 10 1953

Without necessarily convincing anyone that they were indisputably the better side, East Fife eased themselves into their third Scottish League Cup final as they beat Hibs 3-2 before a crowd of 38,000 at Tynecastle.

Partick Thistle beat Rangers in the other semi-final at Hampden on the same day.

At Tynecastle, Jimmy Bonthrone headed the first goal of the game from a Willie Finlay free-kick but then Hibs hit back through Lawrie Reilly who scored with a shoulder charge (still legal in 1953, but this law was coming under increasing pressure) and then a fine header.

As the game entered its last quarter of an hour, Hibs looked the more likely winners but then their centre half Hugh Howie handled needlessly in the box, and referee Jack Mowat pointed to the spot.

The onus was now on full back Don Emery, a burly Welshman who had been a renowned penalty kick taker when he played for Swindon Town. To counteract his nerves, he had an agreement with Charlie Fleming, who would place the ball on the spot for him, so that all he had to do was run up and score. This he duly did, and East Fife were level.

But then Howie conceded another penalty when he fouled Andy Matthew. This time Emery had to wait while Matthew received attention, and admitted after that his stomach was churning, but he took the kick, Younger saved, but Emery scored at the second attempt.

Only five minutes now remained, but the East Fife defence were good enough to hold out against the last frantic attempts of Hibs to equalise.

October 11 1947

33,000 turned up at Dens Park, Dundee to see the League Cup semi-final between East Fife and Aberdeen.

It was a thrilling game won 1-0 by East Fife, while in the other semi-final Falkirk beat Rangers 0-1, so instead of a repeat of last year's final between Aberdeen and Rangers, the second League Cup final would be East Fife v Falkirk.

The Tay Road Bridge was still twenty years away in the future, so if you travelled by road, you had to queue for the "Fifie" as the Tay Ferries were known, and long delays were reported with some supporters not getting across on the homeward journey until about 7.30 pm.

Rail would have been a better option, one feels, although that might have involved changing at Kirkcaldy. However the East Fife supporters were all in a good mood, for Henry Morris scored the only goal of the game, although Aberdeen had their chances as well and just couldn't take them.

The Courier was very impressed by the *esprit de corps* of East Fife under Scot Symon, for all the wives and girlfriends were there as well to see the game, and they all went out for tea to the Café Val D'Or.

Goal scorer Henry Morris was, of course, himself a Dundonian (as were several others of the East Fife team) and he had played for Dundee Violet before he signed for East Fife. Other players to be singled out for praise were the two Davidsons, Davie Duncan and Sammy Stewart, and full credit was paid to referee Willie Webb from Glasgow for his control.

October 12 1946

Today East Fife put up a tremendous performance to defeat Fife rivals Dunfermline Athletic 7-0 in the sectional stages of the inaugural Scottish League Cup.

The trophy had been competed for in the unofficial war years and had been called the Southern League Cup, although the concept "southern" seemed a little misplaced when it was won by Aberdeen in 1946!

1946/47 was the first official season after hostilities, and East Fife showed an early love of the trophy that they were fated to win three times in the near future, by winning their section of six games without losing a goal!

Today this 7-0 hammering of the Pars was as emphatic as it sounded, although *The Sunday Post* states that in the first half at least, Dunfermline had as much of the ball as East Fife did, but were thwarted by "over-eagerness in finishing". On the other hand East Fife were more clinical and were 2-0 up.

In the second half Dunfermline "crumbled badly" and their goalkeeper with the unfortunate name (for a goalkeeper) of Still was badly at fault for several of the goals. Duncan and Canavan scored two each and the others came from Davidson, Morris and Adams.

The referee was the famous veteran Peter Craigmyle of Aberdeen, a man who enjoyed the dramatic. After a goal was scored, he stood still for a second or two so that everyone could see him, then pointing histrionically up the field, having planted the seed of suspicion that he might not give it. He did that seven times today to the delight of the East Fife crowd.

October 13 1923

This was a historic day in the city of Dundee, when East Fife had the honour of being the last team to play against Dundee Hibernian.

In the following midweek, the Tannadice team agreed to change their name to Dundee United. This was an attempt to widen the base of the club to more than the Dundee Irish, and it was felt that, in view of the ongoing troubles in Ireland in the early 1920s, it was better to change the name.

They wanted to be called Dundee City, but Dundee FC objected, and perhaps surprisingly, the Tannadice team gave way to their objections and called themselves Dundee United. Old habits died hard, however, and even as late as 30 years down the line, old Dundonians could be heard cheering on the "Hibs".

It was a shame that the last game of Dundee Hibs' existence was such a dull one, but even *The Courier* says it was poor stuff and neither team really did well enough to score a goal, so the game ended 0-0. Such highlights as there were centred on a penalty for Dundee Hibs which Swan drove straight at Neish, and then the same goalkeeper saved a free kick just at the very end.

The pitch was wet after several days' heavy rain, and the crowd was a disappointing one at a dismal ground with no shelter apart from a small stand. It was difficult for Hibs supporters not to look across the ground at the First Division club called Dundee FC and feel jealous of them, but for East Fife it was not a bad result, confirming their mid table respectability of 10 points from 10 games.

October 14 1995

East Fife were off to a good start in their Division Two campaign, and this fine breezy autumn day attracted to Bayview a crowd of 1,128 to see the visit of the "Bully Wee" Clyde.

Clyde, a team with a great tradition, had an attraction in their ranks today in the shape of the now ageing but still talented Charlie Nicholas who had joined them at the start of the season. He was of course up against an equally famous man in Steve Archibald who was now player-manager of East Fife.

Nicholas's talents had often outshone his achievements, it was felt, and it was not only Celtic supporters who felt that he had made a mistake in leaving them in 1983 to Arsenal where he achieved very little other than a League Cup medal.

He returned to Scotland to Aberdeen, won a Scottish League Cup medal and Scottish Cup medal in 1989/90, and then returned to his first love Celtic, unfortunately at the time that the Parkhead club were at the nadir of their fortunes. He had played for them in last season's League Cup final against Raith Rovers.

Now in the twilight of his career (before becoming a TV pundit) and instantly recognisable with his hair in a pony tail (something that earned him a few homophobic jeers from the East Fife fans) the old touches of magic were still there, but neither Clyde nor East Fife were able to enforce a victory or even to score a goal. Both teams had chances, and both felt ill-treated by the referee, but the game finished 0-0. East Fife had now played 9 games, won 7, lost 1 and drawn 1.

October 15 1966

It was announced that Charlie "Legs" Fleming, probably East Fife's best ever player was to try his luck in American football. From time to time, attempts had been made throughout the 1950s and 1960s to start a major League in the USA, but they were never really successful in spite of the apparently limitless supply of money in that country.

This time there seemed to be more likelihood of it happening, and "Legs", with his experience of playing for East Fife and Sunderland and managing Bath City, announced from his home in Blairhall his intention to give it a go.

Meanwhile East Fife had a poor game this Saturday losing 0-1 to Arbroath at Bayview. It had been a reasonable game but it was Arbroath's Jimmy Cant who scored the only goal of the game to the disappointment of the 2,000 crowd.

Both teams had started the season well, but the top two in the Second Division Table were Morton and Raith Rovers, and Raith Rovers had shown their desire for promotion by yesterday buying Gordon Wallace from Montrose.

The Second Division in Scotland had contained 19 teams up to this season, some of them not very good (to put it mildly!). This season, the League had been increased to 20 with the introduction of Clydebank who last season had (incredibly!) been amalgamated with East Stirlingshire, but had now been severed from them by court actions etc.

20 teams at least put an end to the absurdity of having one team idle every Saturday. Meanwhile the "swinging sixties" continued. Although they weren't necessarily all that "swinging" in Methil, nevertheless it was still an era of full employment and peace, although more and more concern was beginning to be expressed throughout the world about America's continuing and unsuccessful involvement in the war in Vietnam.

Alan Guild

October 16 1965

Away form had not been too good recently, so today's 2-0 win at Recreation Park, Alloa came as a pleasant and welcome surprise, and East Fife were now in a respectable place in the Scottish League Division Two.

The goals came from Jimmy Walker with a penalty and Willie Rutherford. The crowd was possibly slightly less than 1,000, and that was a reflection of the gradual dropping of attendances since about 1960.

However the crowd did contain a bus load from Methil and they returned happy, particularly with the performances of wing halves Alan Guild and Henry McLeish.

But happiness was in short supply this day as far as Scottish football was concerned, for Scotland on Wednesday night had broken the hearts of a nation by going down 1-2 to Poland at Hampden in a World Cup qualifying match.

They had been 1-0 up with a goal from Billy McNeill, but had failed to add to their lead and paid the penalty when they conceded two late goals to lose the game and thus to seriously imperil their chances of World Cup qualification.

The crucial thing this year was that the World Cup was to be played in England, and a World Cup without Scotland would be unthinkable. Such thoughts dominated the conversation of the East Fife supporters as they travelled to and from Alloa, but they were at least cheered up by the performance of their own team.

It would be nice to think that East Fife could return to the First Division someday, but we had not been there now since 1958, and that was now seven years ago — the seven years of famine, as someone with a Biblical inclination might have said.

The Bayview

EAST FIFE FOOTBALL CLUB OFFICIAL PROGRAMME

5 np

DON'T CRY BERTIE — YOUR A BIG BOY NOW   Photo: Ricky Jannetta

EAST FIFE
v
CLYDEBANK

October 17 1903

Considering that the club had only been in existence for a couple of months, a 0-1 reverse at East End Park, Dunfermline in the Fifeshire League should not really be considered to be a disaster.

But *The Courier*'s reporter is far from sympathetic to the new club, and in addition shows clear signs of bias in favour of Dunfermline Athletic.

He opens by saying that it was "far below the standard witnessed in the Northern League fixtures, which was owing to the poor opposition served up by East Fife".

Dunfermline, apparently, "bombarded" the East Fife goal, but instead of praising the East Fife defence for a gallant rear guard action, he bemoans the luck of Dunfermline until Wood of Dunfermline headed the ball into the net after a corner kick with "a nice piece of judgement".

Yet the score stayed at 1-0. It is important to realise however that in 1903 the standard of reporting was not always good, and it was highly unlikely that *The Courier* would have sent a professional reporter to this game.

They were far more likely to have simply asked the opinion of someone at the club, and he might have been somewhat biased! In fact the new club East Fife was doing reasonably well.

It did have the support of its local area, and its current ambitions were little more than to do well enough to be admitted into the Northern League sometime in the future. Most of the existing members of the Northern League were sympathetic, but reports like that one in *The Courier* were distinctly unhelpful.

October 18 1913

Profligate shooting was East Fife's problem today at Forthbank Stadium, Stirling, the home of King's Park in this Central League game.

The game should have been well and truly won before half time but the shooting of the East Fife forwards was totally reckless, and a goalless draw resulted.

East Fife had now played 7 games in the Central League, won 4, lost 2 and drawn 1. King's Park were further down the table and probably counted this draw to be a good result.

There was a strong wind blowing, and East Fife, taking advantage of it in the first half were well on top but "time after time the ball went sailing over the bar, and in no previous match at Stirling had so many substitute spheres to be at hand" according to *The Courier*.

The issue of "substitute spheres" was a potent factor in the finances of clubs, for footballs were quite expensive. However, King's Park seemed to have enough of them.

In the second half, it was their turn to press, although their pressure was never as constant as East Fife's had been in the first half, and in any case, East Fife's defence was magnificent with centre half Lowther particularly good, although well supported by Simon and Brown.

The Central League consisted of 14 clubs — East Fife, Kirkcaldy United, Lochgelly, Forfar Athletic, Arbroath, Stenhousemuir, Armadale, Bo'ness, Broxburn, Bathgate, King's Park, Alloa Athletic and the reserve teams of Dundee and Falkirk.

It was quite competitive, but the ultimate aim, of course, was to be invited to join the Scottish League, something that would not happen for East Fife until after the War.

October 19 1957

After a reasonable start to their Scottish League season (the Scottish League Cup had been an unmitigated disaster) East Fife's progress came to a shuddering halt today at Brockville in Falkirk as they went down 1-4.

Even as early as 1957, Brockville was a stadium that was showing its age, and had a few dangerous spots as far as crushing was concerned.

Falkirk were, of course, the Scottish Cup holders, having won the trophy last April against Kilmarnock in a replay (they had also won it in 1913 beating Raith Rovers) but they were still reckoned as one of the weaker teams in the Scottish League Division One. They were a team that East Fife would have been expected to beat, if they were to avoid relegation (to which they had come mighty close last year).

Wins over Queen's Park and Raith Rovers however encouraged their supporters to be optimistic, but today was a rather severe beating from "the Bairns" with the 4-1 score line a fair reflection on the balance of play, and only Jimmy Bonthrone's second half consolation provided any sort of comfort for the Fifers.

It was therefore a sad bunch who travelled back to Methil, but they were at least in good company, for they saw on the road a few Rangers buses full of similarly depressed people who had seen their team go down 7-1 in the League Cup final that day to Celtic, something that the form of Celtic in their two League Cup encounters with East Fife in August had hinted at.

October 20 1951

East Fife were now second in the Scottish First Division, equal on points with Hibs (who beat Partick Thistle 5-0 today) but having played one game more.

This followed a rather remarkable game at Bayview against St Mirren which ended in a 3-3 draw but in which all six goals were scored in the first half. The defending and the goalkeeping of both sides was absolutely woeful in the first 45 minutes, although things tightened up in the second half.

It was a pity however that East Fife had not managed to score in the second half — both Fleming and Gardiner had reasonable chances — for that would have meant that they would have topped the table. But Johnny Lynch in the St Mirren goal was in inspired form and took everything that East Fife threw at him.

The first half was quite amazing with Ian Gardiner scoring first after both Duncan and Fleming had grazed the bar all within the first 10 minutes! But then goalkeeper Johnny Curran fumbled a shot and St Mirren's Stewart in ran to score.

This turn of events seemed to floor East Fife and they very soon conceded another two goals to Gemmell and Rice. By the 30 minute mark they were 1-3 down, but no game was ever lost when Charlie Fleming was around!

"The Cannonball" lived up to his name with a fine drive from a distance, and then just on half-time a free kick from just outside the penalty box yielded another.

The crowd needed their half-time interval to recover from all that, but there was no slackening of the pace in the second half. The only difference was that there were no more goals!

OFFICIAL PROGRAMME 20p

FORFAR ATHLETIC FOOTBALL CLUB

SCOTTISH LEAGUE DIVISION TWO

Forfar Athletic v East Fife

STATION PARK, FORFAR :: SATURDAY, 23rd OCTOBER 1982

October 21 1972

East Fife had enjoyed a few good results of late, but harboured no realistic hope of getting anything out of this game against Celtic at Parkhead.

They set out to defend, and actually had a reasonable degree of success in this respect, for it was half-time before Harry Hood broke the deadlock with Celtic's third attempt after the East Fife defence had blocked the first two attempts.

Then more heroic defending by Pat Quinn's team in the second half until the 80th minute when Deans scored, although to the small band of East Fife supporters, it looked as if he had fouled goalkeeper Gorman first.

But then Lennox scored another to put the issue beyond doubt. Gorman had had a heroic game in the goal and Kevin Heggarty showed up well for East Fife in the forward line, but to no effect.

In the context, it was hardly a total disaster for East Fife who would end up in the middle of the table that year. But the very few supporters who turned up at Bayview today (less than a hundred) to see the reserve game had a real and unexpected treat when Jimmy Johnstone ran out with the Celtic reserve team.

Jimmy, temporarily out of favour with Big Jock Stein (not the first nor last time!), had been shipped off to Methil to play for the reserves. He didn't play all that well, it was believed, but he earned the respect of the young East Fife reserves by shaking their hands and saying "Thanks for the game, big man!" Everyone was a "big man" for wee Jimmy, though!

October 22 1955

East Fife were well beaten 3-1 at Tynecastle by a Hearts team that were now beginning to emerge into the strong team that they would be by the end of the decade.

East Fife, now shorn of some of their great players like Charlie Fleming, who was now impressing everyone at Sunderland, were beginning to struggle (last week they had drawn with 1-1 with Clyde, and the week before they had gone down 6-3 to Falkirk).

Angus Plumb today returned after a long absence, but that made little difference against very accomplished opposition for whom Alfie Conn scored twice and Alec Young once.

But the man of the match was Kirkcaldy's own Johnny Urquhart who had a hand in all three goals. Kirkwood scored a late consolation goal for East Fife.

The weather was poor and the attendance was a good bit short of 10,000, it seemed.

Aberdeen were winning the Scottish League Cup for the first time by beating St Mirren 2-1 at Hampden in front of a disappointing crowd.

The big talking point on the news was the romance between Princess Margaret and Group Captain Peter Townsend. The snag was that Townsend was divorced, and today Princess Margaret is reported as being in discussions with the top brass of the Church of England about the possibility of marriage.

Sadly, the Church would say no. This was a shame, and in some ways her subsequent behaviour can be explained by this decision. Had she been allowed to marry Townsend, she might not have become "Mad Meg" after all!

October 23 1937

Bob McCartney scored four goals for East Fife today at Station Park, Forfar where the team beat the home side 5-3 in what all newspapers describe as a great, entertaining game of football. Larry Millar scored the other one.

Yet the game could easily have turned out differently if both defences had not been so careless. Forfar scored two early goals, and then in the ten minutes immediately preceding half time, four goals were scored, three for East Fife and one for Forfar, so that the teams went in at half-time with the score at 3-3.

It was only in the second half that East Fife took command and even then they were helped by a few errors from Forfar's goalkeeper. The last ten minutes saw the game turn rather feisty with some players lucky not to get booked by referee Mr MacKay from Glasgow.

Matches between East Fife and Forfar in those days tended to have a good reputation for being entertaining and this one was no exception. After a September that could be described as "indifferent", East Fife had now recovered and had won their last three games, having beaten Dumbarton and Airdrie before their trip to Forfar.

The world situation was now beginning to cause grave concern with no let-up in the slaughter in Spain, and Hitler keeping making warlike noises about wanting to take over central Europe.

Quite a lot of East Fife supporters enjoyed their trip to Forfar, for the bridies, of course and not least because of the banter with their local counterparts. The Forfar loons roared with laughter when someone from Methil said that East Fife might win the Scottish Cup this season. What nonsense!

October 24 1953

East Fife have just won the League Cup by beating Partick Thistle on October 24 1953

October 24 1953

East Fife with the League Cup won in 1953. Charlie Fleming is sitting second from the left with a bandage on one of

October 24 1953

38,529 turned up on a fine, dry October day at Hampden on October 24 to see what was, in playing terms, one of the better League Cup finals with a good fightback and a twist at the end.

East Fife wore white shirts with gold collars and black pants, while Partick Thistle were in a most unusual blue with white sleeves. There was not much of a wind, and four of the five goals were scored at the Mount Florida end of the ground.

The teams were:

East Fife:Johnny Curran, Don Emery and Sammy Stewart; Frank Christie, Willie Finlay and Danny McLennan; Jackie Stewart, Charlie Fleming, Jimmy Bonthrone, Ian Gardiner and Andy Matthew.

Partick Thistle: Tom Ledgerwood, Jimmy McGowan and Bobby Gibb; Willie Crawford, Jimmy Davidson and Andy Kerr; Johnny McKenzie, Bobby Howitt, Willie Sharp, Alex Wright and Jimmy Walker.

Referee; Mr J S Cox, Rutherglen.

East Fife were 2-0 up at half-time — an early freak goal from Jimmy Gardiner which looked more like a cross, and then a better one from Charlie "Legs" Fleming, even though he got the benefit of a deflection.

These were early goals, but that was the score at half-time. But Partick them mounted a great fightback with goals from Jimmy Walker and then from the excellent Johnny McKenzie.

From then on, Thistle looked the better team, but Frank Christie (a man who had spent some time with Liverpool) lashed home from the edge of the box after Thistle had failed to deal with a cross ball. This was just three minutes from the end, and not enough time for Thistle to mount another fightback.

It was a great triumph for Manager Jerry Dawson, who had played in the goal for Rangers and Falkirk, and had actually played in the goal for Falkirk in the 1947/48 Scottish League Cup when they had lost to East Fife.

Scot Symon, Manager of the last two League Cup winning sides and now with Preston North End, sent a telegram with his congratulations.

October 25 1947

35 buses left Methil and Kirkcaldy today (and countless more supporters travelled by train) for Hampden Park to see the second Scottish League Cup final.

Today it was East Fife v Falkirk. East Fife's team contained two men who played in the Scottish Cup final of 1938 — Willie Finlay and captain Tommy Adams, and the side also had Doug Davidson, a man who had now recuperated well after being badly wounded in September 1944 when it was believed that he would never play again.

The teams were generally agreed to be evenly matched and *The Courier* cannot resist a joke that the Falkirk defence is "Jerry built", for their goalkeeper is Jerry Dawson, one time of Rangers.

The crowd was 53,000 but they were disappointed at what they saw — a nervous Cup final ending up 0-0 after extra time.

Quite a few players were clearly overawed by the occasion, and defences were on top throughout, with goalkeepers Jerry Dawson and John Niven singled out for special praise. East Fife probably had the balance of pressure — they certainly forced more corner kicks — but Falkirk had a few chances as well.

Stan Cullis, the manager of Wolves was there to run the eye over George Aitken, East Fife's half back, and he must have been quite impressed. But no goals, and a replay next Saturday at Hampden, although Mr McArthur, the Chairman of East Fife, made a strong bid for the game to be played at Tynecastle. That, however, would have involved an all-ticket game, and there was not enough time to get tickets printed and sold.

October 26 2013

Liam Buchanan v Rangers. Observe the temporary accommodation behind the goal.

October 26 2013

"Quantum mutatus" is a phrase often used to describe a mighty change.

It was used originally to describe the Trojan hero Hector when he was visited in the Underworld by Aeneas after this death. Robert Burns talks about "A devilish change indeed" when projecting his own death.

Rangers had, of course, died in February 2012 as a result of gross incompetence and corruption, allied to an arrogant refusal to pay Income Tax.

This was a new Rangers, their supporters perhaps a tad more humble and less arrogant, but even so it was difficult not to feel a little sadness for the old club especially for supporters old enough to recall the titanic battles of the 1950s.

There were enough supporters of the new Rangers to establish a ground record for New Bayview with temporary accommodation installed to allow for a 4,700 crowd.

This was in truth a very poor East Fife side — they too had undergone their fair share of trauma — and the 0-4 defeat left than anchored at the bottom of the Scottish League Division One (the third tier of Scottish football — and the fourth one was now beckoning!)

East Fife held them until half time, but then Gary Thom conceded an own goal, and the roof fell in (metaphorically speaking!) when Jon Daly scored a hat-trick. Daly was a Roman Catholic from Dublin.

One wonders what he made of all the tribal nonsense in the hymns of hate which still permeated the Rangers support. But for East Fife, it was a grim day, and the pain would not go away all season.

October 27 1956

A couple of small wars were brewing in the world, either of them capable of starting something a great deal bigger.

One was the Hungarian rebellion against the Soviet Union, and its savage repression. The other was the vainglorious attempt of the British to bully Egypt over the Suez Canal.

In Glasgow the Scottish League Cup final was being played between Partick Thistle and Celtic (it would end in a dull 0-0 draw) but at Bayview there was a thrilling Fife derby for the fans to savour between East Fife and Dunfermline Athletic.

Tom "Tiny" Wharton was the referee, and his huge bulk in itself usually prevented things from getting out of hand. No problems here in any case, for it was a fine sporting contest with Dunfermline just edging home.

Dunfermline had now been in Division "A" for just over a year and there were those who felt they had been lucky to escape relegation last season, whereas East Fife after prolonged success and three Scottish League Cups were showing signs that they had reached their peak and were now heading downwards.

Felix Reilly scored twice for Dunfermline before half time, but that was not enough to give the Pars the lead, for East Fife had scored three times. Two of them it would have to be said were flukes — one was an own goal from Harry Colville and another went in off the back of Angus Plumb, but the other was a good strike by the same player.

3-2 at half-time, but in the second half, without necessarily convincing anyone that they were the better side, Dunfermline nevertheless got the two goals — one from the industrious right winger George Peebles, and the other from Felix Reilly again. 4-3 for Dunfermline was the final result.

It was a breath-taking game, and East Fife had every reason to feel that they deserved at least a draw.

October 28 1967

East Fife's good start to the season encountered a slight blip today with a 3-6 reverse at Gayfield, Arbroath.

Both teams were going hard for promotion along with St Mirren, and a reasonable crowd turned up to Arbroath's ground a matter of yards from the North Sea.

It is of course a very old ground and the venue for the world record 36-0 score line for Arbroath against Aberdeen Bon Accord in September 1885.

Arbroath won well today, but East Fife contributed hugely to the occasion with two goals from Walter Borthwick and one from Jimmy Kinsella. Arbroath's top man however was centre forward Jimmy Cant, who scored a hat-trick.

It was not the first time that these two teams had crossed swords this season, for each had a victory over the other in the Scottish League Cup section.

East Fife, however, had won the section before losing to Dundee, and today Dundee were playing in the final of the Scottish League Cup at Hampden. That also turned out to be a high scoring game but the Dens Park men lost 5-3 to Celtic, who immediately after the game flew to Argentina to play in the World Club Cup final.

For East Fife it was back to League action, and although they fought hard all this season (and there was of course a particular incentive to gain promotion this year because Raith Rovers were now in the First Division), they were just a little short at the end, and the promotion spots went to St Mirren and Arbroath.

October 29 1949

Davie Duncan scores for East Fife in the Scottish League Cup final against Dunfermline in 1949

October 29 1949

East Fife recorded their second success in the Scottish League Cup when they beat Dunfermline Athletic 3-0 at Hampden Park before a somewhat disappointing crowd of 39,744.

Dunfermline Athletic were still in Division "B" at this time, and a certain amount of support had been expressed by the neutrals for them, but today saw East Fife take control at an early stage, score three goals in the first quarter of the game and then await the final whistle well on top. The Pars were never really in the game apart from the time when Clarkson hit the post.

The goals were scored by Charlie Fleming pushing home a Davie Duncan cross, Davie Duncan himself hammering home another cross from right winger Bobby Black, and then with the game less than a quarter over, Henry Morris scoring a third after a good through ball from the same Bobby Black.

East Fife were wearing a new strip of old gold and black collars and cuffs (looking not unlike Wolverhampton Wanderers), and Dunfermline wore black and white hoops.

The teams were

East Fife: McGarrity, Laird and Stewart; Philp, Finlay and Aitken; Black, Fleming, Morris, Brown and Duncan.

Dunfermline Athletic: Johnstone, Kirk and McLean; McCall, Clarkson and Whyte; Mays, Cannon, Henderson, McGairy and Smith.

Referee: W Webb, Glasgow.

The Courier reports rather improbably that "hosts" of representatives from English clubs like Manchester City, Newcastle United and Burnley were there, virtually cheque book in hand to persuade Scot Symon to part with his men.

This was unlikely, but it was certainly true that East Fife contained quite a few players who would fit in rather well at a richer team than East Fife.

October 30 1926

It was generally agreed that the miners in late October 1926, both in Fife and elsewhere, were on their knees.

They had been on strike since early May, and when the General Strike collapsed a fortnight later, they were left to fight on alone with no support from fellow workers and increasingly losing out to the coal owners. Wiser leadership might have negotiated some sort of deal at any earlier stage, but as it was, starvation beckoned and more and more of them were forced back.

East Fife however provided some sort of relief to their beleaguered community by today beating Clydebank 4-2 at Clydeholm in Yoker in the Scottish League Division Two. (This "Clydebank" had no direct connection with the later one which played at Kilbowie Park).

East Fife's hero was once again two-goal Jock Wood, the other two coming from MacKay and Barrett, but Clydebank did not really help their cause by missing two penalties.

It was a shame that there were so few spectators there (the crowd was described as "in the hundreds"), but Clydebank were never a well-supported team, being just too close to Rangers who tended to attract men who worked in the shipyards.

East Fife had, at this time, very few supporters who could make afford to travel with them.

In addition there was an International at Ibrox that day in which Scotland defeated Wales 3-0, and quite a few "waverers" might have gone to Ibrox instead of Clydeholm. Clydebank struggled on for a few years after this, but eventually financial problems compelled them to resign from the Scottish League in 1931.

October 31 1998

Old Bayview's last match v Livingston on Hallowe'en 1998

October 31 1931

Just as this game was kicking off at East End Park today, vague rumours (as often happens) were reaching the crowd of some explosion at the Number 1 Pit at Bowhill, Cardenden this Saturday morning and that a number of men were trapped underground.

News like this naturally affected a mining community, but as the details were scant, the game went ahead and provided astonishingly good entertainment for the crowd.

Unfortunately for East Fife, the game finished 4-3 for the Pars, but most newspapers agreed that a draw would have been a far fairer result for the men from Methil.

East Fife were 3-1 ahead at half-time, but everything seemed to hinge on two penalties, one for each side. Dunfermline netted theirs, but East Fife missed, and the Pars never looked back after that.

The Dunfermline penalty saw a strange incident with Dunfermline's manager Mr Knight actually on the park to encourage Archie Young to take it.

He was immediately sent packing by the referee, and in any case it was George Paterson who took the penalty — and scored! For East Fife, Phil Weir and Arthur McGachie are given honourable mentions.

Scotland also beat Wales at Wrexham that day but all football talk was soon submerged with the news that 10 men had lost their lives in the Cardenden disaster. This was confirmed that night at about 10.00 pm after an anxious afternoon and evening spent waiting at the pithead.

It was yet another blow, coming only seven weeks after the death of John Thomson. 1931 was far from a happy year for Fife.

November

East Fife in 1971. Back Row: Clarke, Cairns, Borthwick, Gorman, Martis, McQuade, Finlayson: Front Row: Miller, Quinn, Hughes, Honeyman, McPhee

November 1 1947

Before a disappointing crowd of 31,000, East Fife beat Falkirk 4-1 at Hampden in the replay of the Scottish League Cup final to win the trophy for the first time.

The teams were:

East Fife: John Niven, Willie Laird and Sammy Stewart; Jimmy Philp, Willie Finlay and George Aitken; Tommy Adams, Doug Davidson, Henry Morris, Jack Davidson and Davie Duncan.

Falkirk: Jerry Dawson, Jock Whyte and Jim McPhie; Bobby Bolt, Bob Henderson and Jimmy Gallacher; Jim Fiddes, Jimmy Alison, Archie Aikman, Jackie Henderson and Ken Dawson.

Falkirk lost an early goal thanks to a bad goalkeeping error by Jerry Dawson, a man, who had excelled for Rangers in the past but whose best days were clearly behind him.

He was also partly to blame for at least one of the others, as Tommy Adams scored one and Davie Duncan three with only one goal in reply from Archie Aikman. It was a well taken goal by the Falkirk centre forward but there was little else for the "Bairns" to cheer about.

The Courier tells a story which says a great deal about the professionalism of Scot Symon, even at the greatest moment of his career so far. The players had been presented with the now famous three-handled trophy on the field of play. They then disappeared into the dressing room along with manager Scot Symon. Symon then locked the door, even excluding a couple of East Fife Directors who had a bottle of champagne to commemorate the occasion!

Then, after the players had had their shower and were dressed, they were allowed out to celebrate. The adoring public was well out in strength at Bayview that evening even in spite of the heavy rain as the Cup was shown to all who assembled, some of whom were unashamedly in tears.

November 1 1947

Davie Duncan scores his third and East Fife's fourth in the Scottish League Cup final of 1947

November 2 1946

It is often said by Celtic historians that one of the weaknesses of Jock Stein as a Manager was that he was not very good at dealing with goalkeepers, a breed whom he generally distrusted.

His dislike of the science of goalkeeping may well have stemmed from this game when he was playing for Albion Rovers against East Fife at Cliftonhill.

An injury to goalkeeper McGregor compelled centre half Stein to don the yellow jersey to take over in goal for about 40 minutes of the game during which East Fife already two up, added another two. Jock hated that experience!

The final result was 4-1, and most newspapers agree that, although the loss of the goalkeeper was a blow to Albion Rovers, East Fife would have won comfortably anyway.

The Sunday Post praises the hat-trick of Henry Morris and the goal of Davie Duncan. Morris, it claims, is in the "Rolls Royce" mould, a reference to the very posh make of motor car which people in "austerity" Britain of 1946 could only dream about.

But the player that *The Sunday Post* goes into ecstasies about is left half "Dod" Aitken, and it wishes that the Scotland Selectors had been there to see him that day on the desolate, dreich terracings of Cliftonhill.

One East Fife player not happy that day however would have been goalkeeper John Niven who after a series of clean sheets, conceded a goal and it was a fumble which allowed Doonan to score a consolation goal for the Rovers.

The promotion race promised to be an exciting one that year, with Dundee and Airdrie both heavily involved as well as East Fife and Albion Rovers.

Celtic Football & Athletic Co. Ltd.
FOUNDED 1888

DIRECTORS
Desmond White, C.A. *(Chairman)*
Thomas L. Devlin
James M. Farrell, M.A., Ll.B.
Kevin Kelly

MANAGER
John Stein, C.B.E.

OFFICIAL ADDRESS
Celtic Park, 95 Kerrydale Street,
Glasgow, S.E. *Telephone:* 041-554 2710

Celtic v. East Fife
CELTIC PARK

LEAGUE CHAMPIONSHIP
Saturday, 3rd November 1973 Kick-off 3.00 p.m.

Price 5p

November 3 1917

The war continued its weary course, but this Saturday, East Fife were able to put out a team at Bayview and to earn a 0-0 draw against Armadale in the Eastern League.

Raising a team was not easy in 1917 and often teams like East Fife were heavily reliant on soldiers who happened to be stationed nearby, those who were home on leave or enthusiastic youngsters.

Even so, the Bayview men were still at the bottom of a League which was stronger than it had been in the past, for it now contained Dundee and Raith Rovers who had been compelled to resign from the Scottish League last summer because of the difficulties involved in fulfilling fixtures in the west of Scotland. Other teams in this League were Armadale, Dunfermline, Cowdenbeath and Dundee Hibs.

The small crowd at Bayview enjoyed this game, even though defences were well on top, and *The Dundee Courier* gives plaudits to Dom Currie and Wattie Robertson.

There was a resigned acceptance of the war, but the good thing was that with coal required in great quantity there was no unemployment and in a funny sort of a way, there was a general prosperity, although certain foods and goods were in small supply.

This however did not mask in any way the horrific casualties on a daily basis in the front line. The Americans were now in the war but had not yet arrived in sufficient strength to make any difference, and in any case, it was feared that Russia would soon collapse as it was engulfed in its own domestic agony.

It was of course a "revolution" but the newspapers dared not use that term lest it put any ideas into the heads of people in Great Britain!

November 4 1961

East Fife had started this season reasonably well, and the games against Rangers in the quarter finals of the Scottish League Cup, although the results were disappointing, had seemed to ease financial problems, at least temporarily.

But since then, things had not gone quite so well and today saw a trip to Douglas Park, Hamilton and a 1-2 defeat. The weather was cold, although crisp and pleasant, but the Fifers lost out to a competent (but no more than that!) Hamilton Academical side.

Although George Dewar had headed home an equaliser before half time, the home team scored again in the second half. This result left East Fife third from the bottom of the Second Division, a position which supporters of a team who had been third from the top of the First Division not all that long ago and several times in the last decade, found hard to accept.

The financial problems were ongoing, and like everyone else, East Fife were finding it difficult to persuade their supporters to turn up when TV (and TV ownership was now more or less universal) was offering alternative entertainment on a Saturday afternoon and then gave the football scores as well!

Admittedly, the "entertainment" was often things like Wrestling (and fairly obviously "faked" Wrestling at that!) but it did deter the gullible from coming to watch the football. Today's attendance at Hamilton for example was little more than 1,500. Five years previously, it would have been a lot more than that.

November 5 1921

This day in the years immediately after the Great War was always a difficult one.

The Armistice itself on November 11 was not easy for the war veterans either, but November 5 with all the explosions associated with Guy Fawkes could trigger off all sorts of unhappy and traumatic memories for the shell shocked.

Today however saw the first time in history that East Fife faced a team called Dundee Hibs in the Scottish League. They had met before, of course, in other competitions but this was the first year of the Scottish League and Dundee Hibs would finish second bottom this season and therefore lost their place for the 1922/23 season.

The Hibs, apart from their Irish connections, were also looked upon as the poor man's team of Dundee with newspapers like *The Courier* and *The Evening Telegraph* making that quite clear in the amount of space allocated to them in comparison with the markedly more successful Dundee FC.

Today however at Bayview a small but enthusiastic band of ill-clad and bedraggled "ragamuffins" arrived with the team. The green shirts of Dundee Hibs were lucky to get off with a 0-0 draw. They finished the game with only nine fit men after two serious injuries and were heavily indebted to their goalkeeper Henderson for keeping them in the game.

East Fife felt that they should have won, claiming that refereeing decisions went against them, but it was a poor game and *The Courier* condemns it unequivocally by saying that "it was as chilling as the weather".

November 6 1976

Bottom team East Fife played one of their better games of the season so far as they held League leaders St Mirren to a 3-3 draw at Bayview today.

This was a First Division game, but "First Division" now meant the second tier of three! This was the second year of the new structure and last year the 14 team First and Second Divisions of the League finished in February, and fixtures were supplemented by a Spring Cup which disappeared almost as soon as it appeared.

This season, therefore, all teams played each other three times — something that was grossly unfair because East Fife, for example, played St Mirren once at Bayview, but twice at Love Street! Incredible, but true.

Yet today was a good game. The defending of both teams was deplorable, but the 1,300 crowd (a large proportion of whom seemed to have come from Paisley) were well entertained.

The St Mirren team containing men like Tony Fitzpatrick, Frank McGarvey and Billy Stark were shocked by Drew Rutherford's two early goals for East Fife. In between the two of them, Donnie McDowell had scored for St Mirren, and then the Saints equalised with a strange goal when a mishit shot from Alex Bennett hit a defender and was deflected into the net.

When Billy Stark scored a third, East Fife feared the worst, but in the second half, Harry Kinnear equalised and then in the last few minutes, both teams could have scored in a rousing finish.

St Mirren's Manager wondered why East Fife were bottom of the First Division. He was a fellow called Alex Ferguson.

November 7 1953

It was quite a surprise that East Fife went down 2-3 to Stirling Albion at Annfield today.

Having won the Scottish League Cup a fortnight ago, and then having beaten St Mirren 2-0 last week, Stirling Albion did not seem to be too much of a problem today.

Only in existence since 1945 — when they replaced another Stirling team called King's Park, whose ground had been bombed during the war — Stirling Albion were already called the "yoyo" team because they kept getting relegated and promoted, and they would enjoy that role for many years in the future. Today they were certainly on the up, with a man called Archie Kelly netting a hat-trick, as against one from Jimmy Bonthrone and one from Charlie Fleming for East Fife.

The general feeling was that East Fife looked tired and listless. Maybe this was a natural reaction from their success two weeks ago, but more likely it was because they had just returned from England where they had played two friendly games under floodlights.

East Fife and Hibs in particular were very keen to see the development of floodlights and their extension into Scotland to allow games to be played in the evenings on weekdays, but there was still a genuine conservatism and indeed suspicion of such things particularly high up in the SFA.

There was even some wild talk of games being played against European opposition in midweek in some sort of European Cup, but quite a lot of people remained convinced that floodlight football was dangerous, expensive and simply a gimmick that would quickly pass.

November 8 1930

It is a well-known fact that all Scottish days in November are dreich, not desperately cold necessarily, but damp and the sun disappears far earlier than it used to.

It is also a well-known fact that teams at the bottom of the Division do not get the breaks that teams higher up the League get.

East Fife today welcomed Greenock Morton, a team that they might just have defeated with a bit of luck. They started the game with only one win, and that was six weeks ago against Ayr United, and one draw.

Morton on the other hand, Scottish Cup winners only eight years ago, and comfortably placed about the middle of the Division got all the breaks that they could reasonably expect.

The Courier however says, tellingly, that there were no stars in the East Fife team, although "they played a whole-hearted and eager game". They went in at half-time two goals ahead thanks to Phil Weir, and the 6,000 crowd were confidently expecting more goals. But it was a tale of two goalkeepers. Wilson in the Morton goal was impeccable, but Bernard made a crazy mistake for the Morton winner when he went up for a ball and simply misjudged it so that it went through his hands.

This happened late in the game after McCurley of East Fife had conceded a foolish penalty with a piece of unnecessary handling. Thus Morton's two goals were mistakes, but already in November, some supporters were wondering out loud how long East Fife could stay in the First Division.

Poppies had been sold at half-time, for Armistice Day, always a poignant time, was approaching.

The Gable Ender

THE OFFICIAL MATCHDAY PROGRAMME OF
MONTROSE FOOTBALL CLUB

SEASON 2002/03

Programme Monthly — PROGRAMME of the YEAR THIRD DIVISION 2001/2002

SHIRT SPONSOR
RGIT MONTROSE

BELLS LEAGUE DIVISION THREE

v EAST FIFE

SATURDAY, 9th NOVEMBER 2002
KICK OFF 3.00pm

£1.00

November 9 1907

In spite of incessant heavy rain both before and during the game, a large crowd (no-one knows how large, but they paid £30) saw East Fife beat Kirkcaldy United in the semi-final of the Fife Cup at Bayview.

The crowd included a large contingent who had travelled along from Kirkcaldy "by car". This does not mean the private motor car as we know it, (for they were very few and owned only by people like doctors in 1907), but rather the tram car, which were the pride and joy of Kirkcaldy since they had opened in 1903 and could now travel out of town.

Several of them made the journey along to Methil in appalling weather, but must have wished that they hadn't, for East Fife won 2-0. Kirkcaldy United, drawing their support from the Overton and Pathhead area of town and now losing out to Raith Rovers who had been in the Scottish League for several years, were nevertheless the holders of the Fife Cup.

Today East Fife won 2-0 with two second half goals from Jimmy Peggie. Peggie's performance was impressive enough to earn him a move to Hibs in a few weeks' time, and *The Fife Free Press* describes him and Scott as "the sprightliest" forwards on view.

Because of the wretched weather and the imminent gloom, referee Mr Walker of Kilmarnock shortened the half-time "interlude" and blew his whistle early, but as the game became rather one-sided in the second half, many of the crowd had gone home in any case.

November 10 1956

For the second week in a row, East Fife lost heavily in Glasgow.

Last week they suffered a 3-0 defeat at Hampden from Queen's Park, and today a visit to Celtic Park saw a 0-4 beating. It was in fact difficult to avoid the conclusion that East Fife were past their best, and were possibly even candidates for relegation.

The great players had now all gone, and although there quite a few decent players around like Andy Matthew and Jimmy Bonthrone, men like the mighty Charlie Fleming and George Aitken were now elsewhere.

Yet there was a certain feeling that today could have a produced a shock, for Celtic had a good few injuries, and had Jackie Stewart and Angus Plumb taken advantage of a few early opportunities, it might have been a different matter.

Celtic had Neil Mochan and Charlie Tully and very soon took command, and goals by Mochan, Ryan, Haughney (with a penalty) and Higgins finished the game for Celtic. The clincher was the penalty just on half-time which made it 3-0, and it was one of these penalties which might not have been given to a team with a smaller support.

There could be no disputing the result on what was a rather depressing day for East Fife. They did however meet an old friend in the Celtic Boardroom. It was called the Scottish League Cup, won by Celtic 10 days ago but which had East Fife's name on it three times.

Meanwhile the Suez crisis was now settling down, but Britain's humiliation and duplicity were all the more apparent.

November 11 1922

This was the first time since 1918 that Armistice Day had fallen on a Saturday, and as usually happened in those days, everything stopped at 11.00 am — even cars, buses and trains.

When East Fife travelled to East End Park, Dunfermline there was more commemoration, for everyone knew someone who had failed to return, and there were an awful lot of blinded and otherwise disabled supporters in the crowd, the blinded all being ushered into a special enclosure in front of Dunfermline's somewhat primitive stand to hear a commentary from a volunteer.

They "saw" or rather heard a very good game, won 1-0 by East Fife with a goal scored by Phil Weir in the first half, and that was immediately after the same player had hit the crossbar with a header.

With ex-Ranger Jimmy Gordon now back, after a lengthy spell with injury, dominating the midfield, Dunfermline Athletic pressed hard in the second half but East Fife's defence held firm.

It was a day however with a lot more than football to animate the population for on Wednesday a General Election was to be held. The Great War Coalition had now split up, and the Conservatives and Liberals were now on separate tickets with the added complication of the new party, the Labour Party, which was threatening to make huge gains to the terror of the Establishment!

East Fife supporters who lived in Methil voted in the Kirkcaldy Burghs (who already had a Labour MP as a result of a by-election), whereas those outwith Methil would vote in the constituency called "East Fife".

In both cases the Liberals won on the following Wednesday, but the Conservatives of Andrew Bonar Law formed the new Government.

November 12 1904

The organisation of East Fife FC was not of the best in the early days!

One of the problems was persuading young men (not always very literate and certainly rather unfamiliar with the world outside their immediate circles) to understand the workings of the railway system.

It was indeed rather complicated in 1904 with the rival railway companies doing little to make life easier for customers who travelled some of the way on a different line.

Methil to Bo'ness was not necessarily very easy and no attempt seems to have been made to travel together, but the general plan was that everyone should meet at Polmont on the Edinburgh to Glasgow line at about 1.30 pm then travel to Bo'ness for the Eastern League game.

Sadly, four East Fife players got lost, apparently getting on a train at Edinburgh which went to Glasgow, but without stopping at Polmont. Mobile phones were about a century away, and indeed telegrams were the only way of communicating, so what could one do?

While the four lost boys had a Saturday afternoon in Glasgow, going to see Third Lanark v Kilmarnock, the remaining players and a reserve turned up at Newton Park, Bo'ness where the local side, very considerately, allowed them one of their reserves, then asked members of the crowd if anyone wanted a game.

Two enthusiastic youngsters thus made their East Fife debut, but in the circumstances, it was hardly surprising that East Fife went down 1-2. Football at minor levels in Edwardian times sometimes was a hit or a miss business.

November 13 1948

There is a first time for everything, and today East Fife, in their first season in Division "A" recorded their first ever win at Celtic Park as they beat Celtic 1-0.

The goal came from a Davie Duncan rebound as Celtic full back McGuire tried to clear. But the real heroes were the East Fife half back line of Philp, Finlay and Aitken who knew how to take the sting out of the Celtic attack, even with their talismanic Irishmen Charlie Tully on board.

Celtic had a huge crowd (55,000!) but a poor team at this point in history, and it was a particularly rewarding day for East Fife because their last visit to Parkhead had resulted in a 9-1 thumping.

Celtic actually scored but it was correctly ruled out by Mr Benzie of Irvine. Paton took a corner kick, the ball hit the post and rebounded back to Paton who immediately kicked it again to Leslie Johnstone who "scored". This was of course illegal.

Very few of the 55,000 crowd knew this rule, but Mr Benzie did, and an indirect free-kick was awarded to East Fife from the place where Paton kicked the ball the second time.

A great day for East Fife, and it remains the only time that East Fife have beaten Celtic at Parkhead in the Scottish League.

But this event, great though it was, was not the main news of the day, for crowds were already gathering at Buckingham Palace for news of Princess Elizabeth who was imminently expecting her first child. The baby duly arrived on Sunday night, a boy to be called Charles.

November 14 1998

History was made today as East Fife played their first ever game at New Bayview.

1,462 (a great deal more than the average) were there to see East Fife take on their old adversaries Forfar Athletic, and East Fife won 1-0 with a goal scored by Barrie Moffat.

The ground had been worked on since the summer and consisted of only one grandstand and an uninterrupted view of the sea and Largo Law and other places on the other three sides.

The proximity to the sea could be alarming on a blustery, windy day, but then again Arbroath's Gayfield had had the North Sea as its neighbour for well over a century.

The new stand was comfortable but as it faced the east, it tended to be a little cold on occasion. It was however difficult to imagine the sun ever getting in anyone's eyes!

The emphasis was on sociability with a bar and lounge open, something that was not without a touch of controversy for since 1981, alcohol and football did not really mix in the eyes of the Scottish public.

But this was, of course, alcohol after the game, and it was still strictly forbidden to drink alcohol while the game was in progress.

This was a great day for East Fife and the win (the second in a row) was welcome but it was ironic that the two teams playing today, East Fife and Forfar Athletic, were the two teams who would be relegated to the lowest tier at the end of the season!

Partick Thistle Football Club

SCOTTISH LEAGUE

FIRST DIVISION

v. EAST FIFE. SATURDAY, 15th NOVEMBER, 1975 — 10p

THE BALL FOR TODAY'S GAME WAS DONATED BY—

"Mr. Glasgow" himself
Glen Daly

November 15 1998

On the day after New Bayview was opened, Old Bayview was closed down.

This happened after an Under-18 youth game, and supporters were generally allowed to cannibalise and take away bits of the stadium as souvenirs.

It was probably true that the ground could not continue as it stood, but many supporters felt that the New Bayview could have been built on the original site, but the club received an offer they could not refuse and the money they received was used to finance the development of the new ground.

Yet one could not help feel sad at the loss of another old Scottish ground — Muirton Park, Perth had gone the same way some 10 years earlier — for the ground absolutely bristled and teemed with the traditions of Scottish football. Those supporters lucky enough to have been alive some 50 years earlier during the great days found it difficult to hold back the tears.

Rangers and Celtic teams of long ago had often been happy and relieved to leave Bayview with a point, and a lot of this was due to the atmosphere of the ground with the crowd almost on top of the players and everyone feeling part of the game.

Memories of the ghosts of the past — "Dod" Aitken, Jimmy Philp, Henry Morris, Davie Duncan — mingled with the excited noise of the souvenir hunters as they dug up bits of the turf to take home or helped themselves to chunks of the old stand! It was a very sad day, but then again one has to move on, it is said.

The stand at new Bayview filled to capacity in November 2008

November 16 1946

East Fife continued their good form today with a fine 3-1 win over Alloa at Bayview.

This victory was all the more creditable because they played virtually the whole game with 10 men. Left winger Mudie had to withdraw with a muscle injury and as substitutes were still 20 years away in the future this meant 10 men v 11 men.

Not that anyone would have noticed it though, for the ten men of Methil turned on an absolutely splendid performance with wing halves Jimmy Philp and George Aitken signalled out for praise in *The Sunday Post*.

In the forward line, East Fife's method of combating the fact that they were a man short seemed to consist of Tommy Adams playing in both wings, for he kept turning up all over the place leading an Alloa supporter to wonder if there was "more than one of him"!

Dougie Davidson scored first and then Danny McLennan managed to score at each end — an own goal which he could not get out of the way of, and then a happier occasion at the other end — before Henry Morris finished off the scoring.

Incredibly, Morris had already scored 30 goals in all games this season, and this was considered to be a quiet day for him, well policed as he was by Alloa's Skivington.

Considering that this was a Second Division match on a not particularly hospitable November afternoon, the crowd of 6,000 spoke volumes about how much the local community was watching and supporting their team. More or less all supporters were now back from the war, and a feature of the crowd was not so much the previously almost universal cloth cap as the "demob hat" which was given to ex-soldiers on their return.

Jim Philp

November 17 1928

A fair amount of Arbroath supporters had made their way to Bayview today. Several ladies were well dressed in the club's maroon colours, and engaging in some gentle, good-natured, even a little flirtatious, banter with the East Fife supporters in the stand.

There was also an old man who when Gibb scored Arbroath's second goal, encouraged them to make it 10. "And when did Arbroath ever scored 10?" asked some East Fife fans. "10, I've seen them score 36!" said the old man in a reference to the 36-0 world record score against Aberdeen Bon Accord in 1885.

This remark provoked a certain amount of ridicule, until the old timer said "In fact, I scored some of them!" Cue more laughter, until one of the Arbroath ladies introduced the East Fife supporters to the old guy, one Jim Buick who had indeed played in the 36-0 game! Mr Buick and the Arbroath ladies enjoyed this game, for the Red Lichties, now second in the League and going for promotion, won 3-2.

East Fife did have some hard luck though, for the last ten minutes saw frantic saves by the Arbroath goalkeeper and more than one the ball was kicked desperately off the line. Arbroath were 2-0 up at half-time, but then McGachie pulled one back, Arbroath scored again (Gibb scoring a hat-trick) before McBeth again reduced the leeway.

It was clear from the demeanour of the Arbroath fans that they considered this 3-2 score line to be a great victory and that they considered East Fife to be one of the more difficult teams in the League.

November 18 2017

Following two rather depressing defeats to Raith Rovers and Forfar Athletic in the Scottish League First Division, East Fife today travelled to Second Division Clyde on Scottish Cup business.

Their small support in the 522 crowd were delighted with a 2-0 win on the artificial pitch at Broadwood, a strange ground with what looks like offices behind each goal!

It was a creditable result for the team with injuries and some loan players not being made available to play by their parent clubs. It was also a very cold day, but the team did well and Manager Darren Young had cause to feel happy with what they had achieved.

Kevin Smith scored in the first half after a rather dull first half hour, and that seemed to settle the Fifers, so that they added to their score in the second half when Jonathan Page scored with a header in the 67th minute after some fine play on the left.

From then on, things were rosy for East Fife, and Clyde's cause was not helped when Martin McNiff received a red card for a rash (although not necessarily evil) challenge on an East Fife player.

It was good progress in the Scottish Cup (both Raith Rovers and Forfar Athletic fell today at the first time of asking) but only a real footballing anorak or geek could have told you that this game was played between the last two winners of the Scottish Cup before the outbreak of war in 1939! Things had changed somewhat since then!

November 18 2017

Jonny Page has just scored against Clyde at Broadwood. The Clyde defenders don't look as if they can believe it!

November 19 1955

A large crowd turned up to Bayview to see the Fife derby between East Fife and Dunfermline Athletic.

Dunfermline were new to the First Division having been promoted last year, and although their form had been none too impressive, they brought a large crowd with them.

It was a dull, foggy sort of day and Dunfermline surprised both sets of fans by appearing in red jerseys with white sleeves and looking for all the world like Arsenal.

They had had a struggle to get a team together because of injuries, and East Fife took full advantage of their weakened defence, leading 3-0 at half-time with two goals from Tommy Wright and one from Frank Christie.

It seemed all too easy for East Fife, but then, as sometimes happens, things changed. In the 70 minutes, East Fife conceded a foolish penalty and Mailer converted. It was as if someone had pressed a switch and Dunfermline suddenly realised that they could get something out of this game against a tiring and hitherto complacent defence.

Spurred on by Felix Reilly and George O'Brien, they pressurised the East Fife defence and goalkeeper John Curran, who had hitherto been little other than a spectator was suddenly called into action, and very quickly became a hero.

In the last 20 minutes, the Pars could easily have won the game, let alone earned a point, but a combination of brilliant goalkeeping, a few goal line clearances and belated realisation on the part of East Fife that they had to buck up their ideas saw East Fife home to a victory that should have been a foregone conclusion.

November 20 2010

Early days for the 2011 Scottish Cup, but the competition had been recently re-vamped to include some Junior teams, and the whole thing started earlier.

The Scottish Cup, the second oldest competition in the world and around since 1873 had seen a few changes in its time, but it still retained its mystique and its aura.

It was still, however, hard to imagine what it would be like at Hampden in the summer sunshine in May as one looked at New Bayview this November day which seemed to be a very good dictionary definition of the word "dreich" with the mist, the drizzle and the waves crashing on to the rocks.

In the circumstances a reasonable crowd of 695 turned up, and they were well rewarded with a good game in which East Fife emerged 3-1 winners over a gallant Forfar team which might well have earned a draw on another day.

East Fife with the experienced Bobby Linn and Steve Crawford on board were the better team today. The first goal was scored by Robert Sloan with a well-placed penalty kick, but the key thing for the Fifers were the two goals scored on either side of half-time, always key psychological times.

Thus East Fife were 3-0 ahead and remained that way until Forfar pulled one back late in the day through Andy Tod, another man who had been around a great deal.

The referee's whistle came as a relief to everyone and East Fife could now look forward to the next round. League form had been far from encouraging so far, and it was nice to have something to smile about.

November 20 2010

Steve Hislop scores against Forfar

November 21 1903

East Fife's first season continued today with a Fife League game against Dunfermline at Bayview.

They lost 1-2, but the reporter of *The Courier* pulls no punches when he apportions blame. "But for the lack of judgement displayed by the East Fife custodian, Dunfermline would have returned home defeated".

The East Fife goalkeeper was a man called Moffat, and twice he left his goal to narrow the angle as a Dunfermline player charged in on him "with fatal results to his charge".

Yet the reporter is far more critical of the Dunfermline team than he was of the East Fife players, whose supporters would have been very disappointed to lose after dominating the play in the second half.

But the East Fife forwards "lacked sting in their shooting". But he also says "Football there was none. Let us just say that the elements were to blame for that". By this he presumably means that it was difficult to pass a ball with any degree of accuracy on a heavy pitch.

But it was difficult in every sense for the founding fathers of East Fife in the first season of their existence, and it says a great deal for their perseverance that they kept going. The first season is always likely to be difficult, and there is never any guarantee that the club will not fold at any given time. Evidence too was beginning to appear of strife and dissension among those who had formed the first committee.

Senior football in Levenmouth was precarious in 1903.

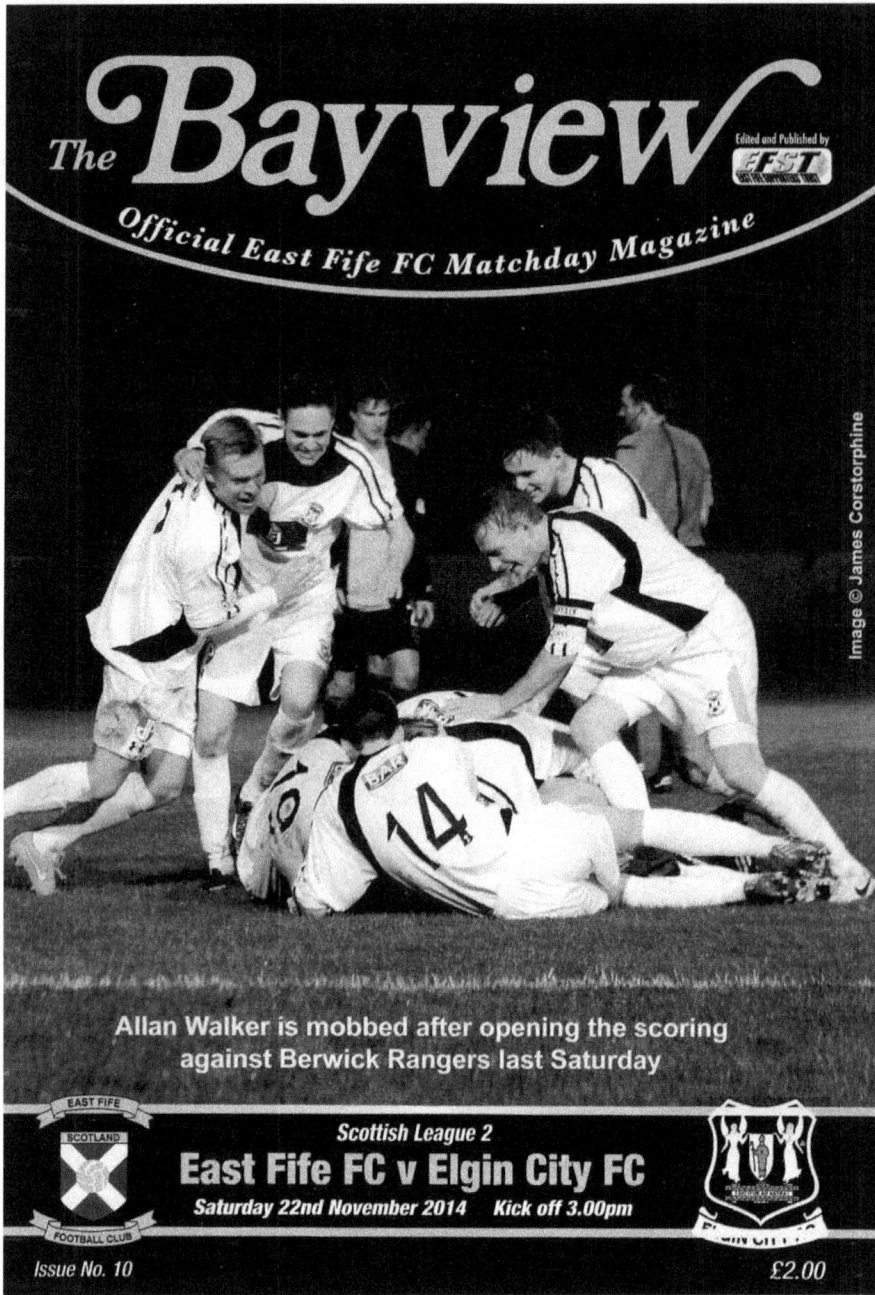

November 22 1930

The impression that East Fife were misfits in the First Division was slowly gaining ground even in Methil itself and to-day's events at Douglas Park, Hamilton did East Fife no favours.

It was the first time, apparently, that East Fife had ever played on this ground, and it was a truly awful experience in every way. As the team travelled to the west, they went through heavy rain, and once they reached the "Ducal Toon" (as Hamilton was called), the temperature dropped and the rain turned to snow but not deep enough for referee Mr Quinn of Bellshill to consider calling it off.

The game was played in steady sleet, and apparently the attendance was as low as Douglas Park had seen with large swathes of the uncovered terracing containing not a single soul.

The pitch began to cut up as well and a "passing game" over the wet and uneven surface was virtually out of the question. *The Courier* and *The Leven Mail* try manfully to gloss over East Fife's manifest problems, but the truth was that the Fifers were never in it, apart from the one consolation goal from "Dangerous Dan" Liddle.

Hamilton scored four times and only a good performance from goalkeeper Steele kept the score down to respectability. It was a day that East Fife would try to forget, and it was a mercy that the awful weather meant that very few East Fife supporters travelled through to Hamilton. If there is any truth in the maxim that Scottish football is not for softies, then this was a prime example!

November 23 1963

Normally one minute's silence is held before a game if an ex-player has died, or possibly a Director and sometimes even a well-known and revered supporter.

What was unusual about this one, held impeccably before the start of the East Fife v Berwick Rangers game was that this one was for a man who had probably never seen a football match (certainly not a Scottish football match) in his life! It was for President John F Kennedy shot the previous night in Dallas, Texas for reasons that no-one yet has satisfactorily explained.

It was a shock to the world that this young President, apparently so idealistic and peace-loving, had met his death so suddenly, and the pessimists predicted a nuclear war! In tune with this — as all the religious Jeremiahs began to enjoy themselves and to tell us that the end of world was not far away — the weather was dull and wet, and another excellent example of the Scottish word "dreich".

It did not seem to affect East Fife all that much though, for after the 1,500 Bayview crowd had stood in reverential silence in the rain, the team thumped a very poor Berwick Rangers side 6-0.

The team had been going well under Jimmy Bonthrone and very now sixth in the League with two goals from Jimmy Walker, and one each from Andy Waddell, Morris Aitken, George Dewar and an as yet unnamed youngster who rejoiced in the unlikely name of Newman.

The Second Division this year, however, was dominated by Greenock Morton who had yet to lose a game.

November 24 2012

Mercy me, East Fife have won two games in a row!

Following last week's success at Albion Rovers, Billy Brown's men today beat Arbroath 2-1. Is this the start of something, one may ask?

Well no, actually, but it did at least give the supporters something to cheer about. The crowd was 570, and that owed a little to Arbroath who, as always, brought a reasonable crowd of spectators with them.

It was only the fourth win of the League season in Division Two (the third tier of four in season 2012/13), but it was welcome nevertheless.

An ill-mannered laugh was heard when the Arbroath team was read out and they had a man called "Banjo" playing for them, but any sympathies for the unfortunately named gentleman evaporated when he was yellow carded by referee Barry Cook for a bad foul.

It was East Fife who opened the scoring with the first goal of the season for Sean Jamieson as he picked up a pass from Robert Barr. East Fife now looked comfortable for a spell but then everything happened on either side of half-time.

First, the Red Lichties equalised when Paul Currie seemed to get in the way of a colleague's effort and the ball entered the net to allow Arbroath to go in at halftime on level terms. But the best goal of the game came immediately after the restart when Scott McBride thundered home a great shot from well outside the box.

The game then became quite entertaining as Arbroath came close on several occasions, but East Fife held out to register a win and three much-needed points.

November 24 2012

Craig Johnstone in action against Arbroath, one of whose players has the unlikely name of Banjo!

November 25 1961

This was one of the less pleasant days of watching East Fife.

They lost 1-4 to Clyde at Shawfield in Glasgow, but it should have been a great deal more, for the Fifers were frankly outclassed by a team who would go on and deservedly win the Second Division Championship this season.

The weather was atrocious with heavy rain and hail reducing the crowd to the low hundreds. Clyde were not a very well supported team at the best of times — they were geographically far too close to Celtic. In addition, a side effect of the ongoing work to demolish Glasgow's slums was that more and more people were being decanted to new towns like East Kilbride and Cumbernauld. Furthermore, today, in spite of a new player called Divers having joined them from Hamilton Academical, the weather was a massive deterrent.

Tommy Ring was no longer with Clyde, trying his luck unsuccessfully in England, but the other great Clyde man of the 1950s, Harry Haddock was still with them and although his Scotland days were now behind him, he was still an outstanding full back.

For Clyde, in the gloom, Currie scored twice and Divers and Steele once each, while Yardley scored for East Fife in a rare breakaway. For East Fife, this was a profoundly depressing experience, and it was maybe just as well that very few supporters had ventured out of Methil to Glasgow that day.

It was probably true that the financial crises of the past few years were now being solved, but there seemed to be no solution to the problem of getting quality players back to wear the colours.

November 26 1949

East Fife and Partick Thistle played out a 1-1 draw at Bayview today — something that kept both teams towards the top of Division "A".

There was a 10,000 crowd and they were well entertained with both goals a delight. Henry Morris put East Fife ahead with a lovely header, and Alex Stott, one time of Dundee, who had scored a hat-trick last week, earned a point for Partick Thistle with a late equaliser.

Indeed, he might well have scored a winner but for a good save by goalkeeper John Niven. Both Managers Scot Symon and Davie Meiklejohn were Ibrox legends in their time and both agreed that a draw was a fair result.

East Fife supporters were a little perturbed to hear that George Aitken had submitted a transfer request. This was in addition to the one submitted by Henry Morris a few days earlier. It was, one supposes, the price that East Fife had to pay for their success.

Appearances in Hampden Cup finals did attract attention from English club who, although we lived in an age of a theoretical maximum wage, did have more money to splash about than did provincial East Fife.

There were also rumours that some players did not always get on very well with Manager Scot Symon who had inherited from Mr Struth of Rangers high expectations of standards of dress and strict discipline, including Church attendance. Fortunately for East Fife, they managed to hold on to both players for at least a little longer, and East Fife would remain a power in the land for some time yet.

November 27 1994

East Fife fans are not, in general terms, small-minded, parochial or bigoted.

Good heavens, no! Where else could one find such a bunch of tolerant, welcoming, generous and magnanimous people?

Nevertheless, they were put to a severe test this Sunday. In the first place they had to read the Sunday papers about the appalling display yesterday when Steve Archibald's side went down 0-3 to Morton at Cappielow. Those who had been there came back with phrases like "never in it" and "totally useless" peppering their conversation.

Today however was worse with close rivals Raith Rovers in the League Cup final against Celtic at Ibrox, and the game was on terrestrial TV, so there was no escape.

You had to say, unconvincingly, things like "it would be good for Scottish football, if..." or you could develop a sudden and unusual love for the green and whites. Sadly those who did just that found themselves supporting a Celtic team barely worthy of the name.

Raith Rovers went ahead, but Celtic came back and looked likely winners until Gordon Dalziel scored to take the game to extra time and penalties, and it was Raith Rovers who won through in the lottery of the shoot-out.

So what could an East Fife lover do? You could say "nothing to do with me", you could try to avoid any trip to Kirkcaldy for the next six months, or you could say through gritted teeth "good for football in Fife".

Or, of course, you could get your grandad to tell you all about Henry Morris and Charlie Fleming. Now, that was the way to win the League Cup — THREE times — and no penalty shoot-out nonsense then!

November 28 1964

An unusual and rather dramatic game took place today at Somerset Park, Ayr today in the wind and the pitiless west coast rain which Robert Burns possibly had in mind when he wrote his Tam O'Shanter.

Ayr United were rock bottom of Division Two (an unusual place for Ayr who had been known to flirt with the First Division in the past) and this no doubt contributed to the poor crowd which the *Evening Times* describes as "practically non-existent" at the 2.15 pm start.

East Fife had not been doing all that well either but were comfortably placed in the middle of the table. Ayr won the toss and chose to play with the wind and the rain at their backs in the first half, and in 20 minutes they were 3-0 up before a crowd which had swollen to 800. Goals had been scored by Paterson, Gilshan and Paterson again — and it should have been more!

The second half saw no let-up in the conditions at the exposed Somerset Park, but this time East Fife had the benefit of the wind and when George Dewar scored within a minute of the restart, things looked better. But Ayr held out in the gathering gloom until the 80th minute when Jimmy Walker added a second, then more or less at the very end, East Fife won a free-kick which Walker took and scored from.

No player seemed at all unhappy when referee Mr Wilson of Glasgow pointed to the pavilion, but East Fife had the reward of knowing that all their efforts had paid off and that they had earned a 3-3 draw on a dreadful day for football.

November 29 1930

East Fife played a good 4-4 draw with Falkirk at Methil today.

The Courier says "East Fife may be the bottom dogs in the Scottish League, but in the vicinity of their own kennel, they can bite".

Continuing (and straining) the metaphor, he continues to say that "the only thing is that they do not seem to put enough snap into their bite".

East Fife in their only season in Division One so far, had managed to amass only three points at the start of this game, but they did at least entertain their fans today, even though a lot of them had deserted their posts in the last 10 minutes when Falkirk were 2-4 up.

Certainly Arthur McGachie did not seem to have heard the word "relegation", for he scored a hat-trick — and three good goals they were as well. He tackled with "vigour and unrelenting tenacity" and this was needed for East Fife who had two defenders out injured (often, in football as in life, when one is down, one does not get the breaks) and a better team than Falkirk might have given East Fife a real doing.

As it was, while Falkirk were the better side, East Fife nevertheless fought well and, although most of the supporters were already, at the end of November, reconciled to relegation, nevertheless, the draw with its two late goals put a smile back on some of their faces and the name "McGachie" did at least cheer everyone up.

And cheering up was necessary for the depression was now beginning to have its effect, and unemployment showing signs of getting out of control.

November 30 1957

East Fife came very close to beating Rangers at Ibrox today, but a 3-3 draw was still a creditable performance from East Fife.

Sadly however the Glasgow-based *Evening Times* makes a prophecy that did not come true. It states that "East Fife ought not to worry about their future status."

Sadly they would be relegated at the end of the season, but today at least they played a good game to impress the large Glasgow crowd.

Both teams came into this game suffering from recent painful hammerings. On October 5 1957, East Fife had gone down 0-9 to Hearts, and two weeks later Rangers had endured an even more painful experience as they lost 1-7 in the Scottish League Cup final to their old rivals Celtic.

Rangers, now managed by ex-East Fife Manager Scot Symon had recently bought centre half Willie Telfer from St Mirren in an attempt to stop the flood of goals but it did not look to be all that successful at half time when East Fife were 3-1 up with goals from Andy Matthew, Dennis Mochan (singled out for booing by the Ibrox supporters because his brother was Neil Mochan of Celtic!) and Jimmy Ingram as against one from Maxie Murray.

Booing, early departures and the slow handclap were the order of the day as the second half progressed but eventually Rangers got back into the game when Sammy Baird managed to edge the ball over the line after a goalmouth scramble, and then Harry Davis scored with a long range hopeful shot which evaded everyone.

All this was hard luck on East Fife, and the Sunday papers were in unanimous agreement that Jerry Dawson's side were the better of the two.

December

East Fife with the huge Scottish Qualifying Cup which they won in season 1920/21. They were not allowed to field thirteen men, though. Two were reserves! Back Row: Robertson (Trainer), Ross, McGlashan, Wightman, Neish, Main, McBride, Stewart; Front Row: Neil, Currie, Moffat, Burton, Wilson and Brown

December 1 1951

Little doubt about it — the team of the moment was East Fife!

Today they entered December at the top of the table with Hibs hot on their heels. Both East Fife and Hibs won to-day, but Hearts dropped a point. Neither Celtic nor Rangers were anywhere in sight.

East Fife consolidated their position at the top today with a fine 3-1 victory over Airdrieonians at Bayview. The weather was dull for the 2.15 kick off and the crowd was given as about 10,000 which was not bad, considering that Airdrie did not bring a large support.

With their distinctive strip and the small number inside the V at the top of their neck, Airdrie were always a tough team, and they did not make it easy for the Fifers.

East Fife showed the visiting journalists from the west of Scotland (some of them there for the first time and clearly impressed by the team, if not the facilities!) just why they are top of the League.

Both Gardiner and Fleming came close before Jimmy Bonthrone opened the scoring with a snap shot in the 34th minute, a lead that was consolidated soon after half time before Charlie Fleming added another.

Airdrie scored a consolation goal, but they were well defeated. The only worry was an injury to Davie Duncan, and the talk in the pubs of Methil that night was whether East Fife could really make a challenge for the Scottish League.

The Scottish Cup and the Scottish League Cup had been won in the not too distant past. But Scottish Champions?

December 2 1905

The weather was mild enough for December, but there was a strong wind blowing at Bayview and this would have a great effect on the course of the game between East Fife and Arbroath in this Northern League game.

East Fife won 2-1. Arbroath were the League leaders and stayed League leaders in spite of this reverse, but East Fife now moved into third place.

Arbroath had the advantage of the breeze in the first half and led 1-0, but East Fife scored twice late in the second half to first equalise through Andrew Horne and then win the game when "they rushed the leading goal". *The Courier* says that play was "of a regular Cup tie sort" and there was never "a dull moment".

The Courier has an odd reference to "the Bees" meaning East Fife. One might think that this meant that East Fife were now wearing black and gold, but the *Arbroath Herald* clearly calls them "the Green and White".

This is clearly the first time that the writer of the *Arbroath Herald* has been to Bayview for he says that "Methil is about the most out-of-the-way place that can be imagined" (a little harsh, one feels, but then again the railway was everything in 1905 and most other football grounds were reasonably close to a rail link) and Arbroath arrived "after a journey that was not all by train".

However, he then goes on say "The pitch is the best in Fifeshire, is set on the top of a hill, and must be pretty on a calm day".

December 3 1921

It was the first visit of Stenhousemuir to East Fife on Scottish League business.

One of the few times that the clubs had ever met, today they served up a good game of football for the 3,000 spectators who came to Bayview this dark but comparatively mild December day.

Stenhousemuir were a remarkable team who were generally reckoned to be the poorest supported in Scotland, and there were indeed very few people shouting for Stenny that day.

The 4-0 score line for the Fifers was rather flattering, for three of the last four goals came in the last quarter of an hour, but this perhaps says something about the superiority of East Fife's training methods.

Indeed up to the interval, Stenhousemuir were the better side with Jock Neish in East Fife's goal looking a little shaky from time to time, but gradually East Fife took control. It was Burton who scored the first goal, Warrender the second and then Cant finishing things off against a Stenhousemuir team, now dispirited, who would have cause to rue their poor finishing in the first half.

East Fife were now fourth in the table, although no-one looked like catching the impressive Alloa team. Meanwhile in the Scottish Qualifying Cup final at Ibrox, Nithsdale Wanderers and Montrose drew 3-3.

On the broader front, things looked optimistic for a settlement of the Irish question. The problem however was that the British Government were offering a Free State, not a Republic, and that the six counties of the north would not be part of it. Sinn Fein turned the proposals down.

OFFICIAL PROGRAMME

MEET YOUR FRIENDS at
"THE ARGYLL"
47 MURRAY PL., STIRLING

THE POPULAR RENDEZVOUS
For Choice Quality
WINES and SPIRITS

Proprietor,
HAMILTON A. WATTERS.

READ
DONALD CAMERON'S
SPORTS REVIEW
The Brightest and Snappiest
Sports Page in Scotland
in the
STIRLING JOURNAL
EVERY THURSDAY
Order from Your Newsagent NOW
Telephone Nos. 5444/5

STIRLING ALBION
Football Club Ltd.

versus

Nº 103

EAST FIFE

Saturday, 3rd December, 1960   Kick-off 2.10 p.m.

football fans read

NEWS OF THE WORLD

expert reports

December 4 1982

The weather was wet, the day was dark — but East Fife today delighted their supporters in the paltry crowd by defeating League leaders Meadowbank Thistle 5-0 at Bayview.

Originally known as Ferranti Thistle, they had been admitted to play in the Scottish League in 1974 as Meadowbank Thistle, using the stadium which had been used for the Commonwealth Games when they were staged in Edinburgh in 1970.

Their first few years had been a struggle, but season 1982/3 was their first good season, and indeed they would be promoted at the end of this season, second to Brechin City. In 1995 they would move to Almondvale in Livingston and adopt the name of that town.

Today was a curious blip for them, but East Fife supporters were tearing their hair out at the inconsistency and unpredictability of their side. Today was one of the better days for East Fife this season with a hat-trick from Paul Burt. George Scott and Robin Thomson (with a penalty) got the other two.

East Fife had not a bad run about this time (they beat Queen of the South 2-1 the following week, for example) but sadly never raised their game to such an extent that they challenged for promotion from the 14 team Second Division.

It was an odd arrangement, one often felt, for there being 14 teams, it meant that each team played each other three times twice home and once away or vice versa. It was undeniably unfair, but of course a good team will triumph over everything.

December 5 1951

This Wednesday afternoon at Ninian Park Cardiff against Wales a special match was arranged to celebrate 75 years of the Welsh FA since 1876. Charlie Fleming was given the singular honour of being chosen to play for the Rest of the United Kingdom.

Five Scotsmen were chosen to play in the UK side — George Young of Rangers, Tommy Docherty of Preston North End, Jimmy Cowan of Morton, Gordon Smith of Hibs and Charlie Fleming of East Fife. Of the five, Charlie was the only one who had not yet played for Scotland, but his selection for this game clearly showed that he was in the frame for a Scotland cap.

Indeed many thought that he should have had one already. Before a crowd of about 35,000 Welshmen, the UK side, playing in white satin shirts, failed to make any impact — something that was hardly surprising, for some of them had not even met before the game — and were 3-0 down well into the second half and it was only when Fleming scored one of his trademark goals from a distance that the UK made any impact on proceedings.

The Rest of the UK then scored another and the game finished 3-2, and the Welsh were well worth their victory. It was a great experience for Charlie, still just a young lad from Blairhall, and a banquet was held at the end of the game before they returned home the following day.

It was no secret — in fact it was a big bore in many sections of the Press — that many English teams were keeping an eye on Fleming, already famous for his speed, his shot and his ability to produce quality balls for other members of the forward line.

December 6 1930

For an East Fife team down on their luck and needing every break to escape relegation, Queen's Park were one of the teams that they might reasonably expect to beat, even at Hampden, but East Fife today went down 1-5 to the Amateurs.

With New Year now approaching, this left East Fife with still only one victory in Division One — against Ayr United on September 27. Today, there seemed to be little that anyone could say to comfort supporters — *The Courier*, for example, in a brilliant euphemism says that they "did not create a very favourable impression on the spectators who turned up to see their match".

It then says more overtly that "it is difficult to visualise them escaping the Second Division". And of course, bitter experience of life teaches one that when one is down on one's luck and needs a break, that is exactly the time when one is not forthcoming.

The first goal was a total fluke — a bizarre deflection. Just as East Fife were beginning to come on to a game, they lost another two, and thenceforth never really made much impact other than a consolation goal by Wilson.

Queen's Park were not a great eleven by any manner of means, but they were far too good for East Fife who had the "pallor of death" written all over them. Indeed it was openly discussed in the pubs, mines and schools of Levenmouth that it had been a great mistake to join the First Division. Refusing promotion might have been a better idea.

December 7 1929

East Fife's good form continued with an excellent 4-1 win over Forfar Athletic at Station Park, Forfar.

Forfar had been going well of late as well, and a good game was expected. It was a strange game with a cold wind blowing but it attracted a crowd of about 1,000, including quite a few who had travelled by train and arrived at Forfar Station (about 100 yards from the ground) just before kick-off.

East Fife won the toss and rather surprisingly chose to play against the wind. Arthur McGachie scored early on, although Forfar claimed that he was offside, but then Davie Kilgour equalised for Forfar.

Forfar then failed to capitalise on the benefit of the wind, whereas East Fife played more sensibly with their short passing game, crucially keeping the ball on the ground, and James Rarity took advantage of two defensive errors to put East Fife 3-1 up at half time.

In the second half, Forfar, playing against the wind now, simply could not get back into the game, and when they did try their strategy of shooting from a distance, they found an unstoppable barrier in goalkeeper John Bernard.

Phil Weir scored a fourth goal for East Fife. This game consolidated East Fife's second position in the Second Division, behind Leith Athletic.

An unfortunate incident occurred when a spectator tried to assault East Fife's Jimmy Gabriel. The embarrassed Forfar officials apologised profusely for this and said it was "some tinkie led" (i.e a representative of the travelling community) who was responsible.

December 8 1923

The country of Great Britain was in a crisis.

The General Election held on Thursday December 6 had produced a "hung" parliament.

The whole business had been unnecessary because the Conservatives had had a majority, but the new Prime Minister Mr Baldwin had felt he needed another mandate.

This he did not get, and now if he were to continue as Prime Minister he would need the support of the Liberals. Otherwise there would be the unpalatable (to the establishment) prospect of a Labour Government!

The trouble was that the Liberals under Asquith disagreed fundamentally with Baldwin on Free Trade, and were in any case better disposed towards the Labour party.

While such weighty considerations were going on, (and they would continue well into the New Year) East Fife sustained a defeat at Newton Park, Bo'ness today and what was unacceptable about it was that it was all so sudden.

East Fife had scored first through a Phil Weir miskick which the goalkeeper had allowed to trundle past him. They had then looked comfortable until two goals within a minute both from a distance and with which goalkeeper Jock Neish had no chance, sealed the fate of the Fifers.

The double whammy seemed to knock the stuffing out of the visitors and there was no fight back, something that caused a certain amount of distress to the small band of travelling supporters. East Fife had now lost nine games in the League as distinct from winning six.

The supporters looked upon their form with a certain degree of disquiet.

December 9 1916

In what was described as a "stubborn" game of football, East Fife today beat Lochgelly United 2-0 at Recreation Park.

This was a Wemyss Cup tie, and it was almost considered a luxury for fans to be able to see any kind of football, such was the increasing shortage of manpower; indeed some clubs were having to go into abeyance for the duration of the war.

East Fife played in the Eastern League normally, a somewhat makeshift organisation with only ten clubs, most of whom were struggling to put out eleven men.

All this is not to say that football had in any way lost its popularity, and today a crowd of over 1,000 enjoyed this game. An obscure character called A Allan according to *The Courier* scored first for East Fife, and then the second goal was scored "in a scrimmage".

The second half saw some strong Lochgelly pressure but they could not breach the East Fife goal, and there was no further scoring.

In the meantime, another "East Fife" man had fallen from power. This was Herbert Asquith, MP for East Fife, who had been removed from his position as Prime Minister after a coup organised by the treacherous Lloyd George.

Asquith had been a good Prime Minister in peace time but was clearly not suited to the demands of wartime leadership of the country. He was a benign politician, sometimes rather too fond of a drink and often criticised for being too cautious, his catchphrase often being "wait and see".

Lloyd George on the other hand was not always well liked but was generally seen as far more dynamic than Asquith. There seemed to be no end in sight to the war, and the casualties continued to horrify.

Phil Weir

December 10 1949

The weather was cold and the pitch was icy, but this being 1949, a huge crowd of well over 20,000 appeared at Dens Park to-day to see a local derby between two teams who were going well.

The economic climate was usually described as "austerity". In fact it was a time of gradual prosperity with everyone in work, and the National Health Service still in its infancy but determined to defeat the pre-war horrors of diseases like tuberculosis.

Dundee were still suffering the horrors of hell at the recollection of the way in which they had comprehensively blown their chances of winning the Scottish League in April, whereas East Fife were on the crest of a wave after their recent win in the Scottish League Cup final.

But today rather to the disappointment of the large contingent who had followed them from Methil, it was Dundee who triumphed 1-0, their secret according the Press being their rubber boots which gave them a far better grip on the hard ground.

Yet East Fife had started well enough, and were a little unlucky in not getting an early goal, something for which they had a certain reputation in 1949. But although Bobby Black in particular and Charlie Fleming tried hard, Henry Morris (himself a Dundonian, of course) was well policed by the Dundee defence, and full time came with only one goal registered and that was by Gerrie of Dundee.

Today's result was a bit of a setback for East Fife who were flushed with their League Cup success and were even beginning to nourish hopes of a serious challenge for the Scottish League itself.

December 11 1937

This was a remarkable day at Methil as East Fife recorded their highest ever score to beat Edinburgh City 13-2!

It is important to stress that this was *not* the Edinburgh City as we now know them. Edinburgh City were an amateur team who played at Powderhall, Marine Gardens and City Park and went out of existence in 1955, having become a junior side soon after the Second World War. Even as early as 1937 they were struggling, never more so than on this day at Bayview.

On a day when many other games were off because of the weather, this game passed a pitch inspection but twice in the first half while East Fife were playing against the wind, they had to face a fierce hailstorm, as the 1,500 crowd huddled together for warmth. In spite of that, East Fife were 3-2 up at half-time.

In the second half, the wind settled down and East Fife scored another ten with the supporters having to ask themselves what the score was. Both the Edinburgh goals were scored by a man called Carruthers (by coincidence, the referee was also called Carruthers — no relation, presumably, but rare to find two men of that name on the same Scottish football field!)

For the record, Eddie McLeod and Tommy Adams both scored hat-tricks, John Sneddon scored two penalty kicks, Bob McCartney scored two, there was an own goal, and Joe Cowan and Jimmy Henderson had one each. Latterly the game became rather boring and some of the crowd were seen to go home.

The Courier, never given to kicking anyone when they are down, says that "the amateurs had the spirit but little else".

December 12 1964

This dull December day saw a bit of history created when East Fife paid their first and only trip to Kilbowie Park, Clydebank to play a team called East Stirlingshire Clydebank.

The name of the team leads a little explanation, for at first glance it appears absurd. Indeed it was, for a glance at a map of Scotland will indicate that East Stirlingshire and Clydebank are many miles away from each other. What had happened was that in the summer East Stirlingshire, in financial problems not for the first or last time, had been rather forcibly taken over by a team called Clydebank who thus gained their place in the Scottish League.

This action was much disputed by East Stirlingshire's supporters, but it had the backing of those in high places, notably at Ibrox. Some called the Steedman brothers of Clydebank "entrepreneurs"; others used words like "gangsters".

Legal action followed, and this hybrid team were separated like a pair of Siamese twins for the following season. They were actually doing rather well in the Second Division in December.

Today they attracted a fair crowd of 2,000 on a rather unpropitious day. East Fife's victory, therefore, was a good one. Quite a few supporters travelled from Methil to see this new ground and team, and they were rewarded with a narrow and hard-fought 2-1 triumph.

Kemp scored for ESC (as they were often referred to) but then George Christie with two goals in two minutes turned the tables and earned the Fifers a deserved victory.

December 13 1930

More gloom for East Fife came at Ibrox. It was a miserable day, although all games were played in Scotland.

Only a little over 6,000 appeared at Ibrox today to see the current League champions take on the little rated men from Methil. Even Mr Struth, Rangers legendary Manager seemed to lack interest in this game for Bob McPhail was given a rest, and reserves McDonald, McGowan and Conlin were given a game.

East Fife approached the game in exactly the wrong spirit — coming out like men going to the dentists, expecting a hammering and of course getting one. Phil Weir did a lot of running and was clearly looking for the ball, but the ball seldom reached him, and in any case he was up against Davie Meiklejohn.

Some other players were given pass marks — goalkeeper John Bernard, for example, but then again, if your defence is overwhelmed to the extent that East Fife's was, the goalkeeper is bound to have at least some good saves!

Rangers' best player was "the wee blue de'il" Alan Morton but he was poorly supported today by a lacklustre Rangers side. Even so, Rangers still won 4-0 with two goals from James "Doc" Marshall and another two from Bob McGowan.

So one-sided was the game that even some of the meagre crowd had departed long before the final whistle. When some of the home supporters tried to cheer themselves up by singing their current anthem "The Wells O' Wearie", others were heard to remark that "weary" was indeed the appropriate term for this game of football.

December 14 1974

For all sorts of reasons, December 1974 was a depressing time, but today East Fife lightened some of the gloom by travelling to Annfield, the home of Stirling Albion (their new home at Forthbank was some way in the distance) to win 3-1 and put themselves back on top of Division Two.

One of the goals coame from Gillies and the other two from a "Newman" who turned out to be called Sammy Frickleton. The crowd was meagre, the atmosphere was non-existent on that bleak day, but at least it was a victory.

It was a strange season, for every team was playing for its place in next year's Leagues. The League was changing from two Divisions to a Premier Division of 10, a First Division of 14 and a Second Division also of 14.

As things stood, East Fife looked likely to be in the middle Division, but it would be nice to be the winners of the last ever old Second Division. 1974 had been a depressing year with two General Elections in the United Kingdom and the resignation of President Nixon in the USA.

Rampant inflation causing even such normally docile people like dustmen and teachers to go on strike, as the second Labour Government of Harold Wilson tried manfully to cope with the problem.

Football still had not got its act together either as attendances dropped with people less than totally happy to go to grounds which were frankly dangerous, unhospitable and in some cases insanitary (Bayview not excepted!) so it was good to see some good news in the dark, depressing month of December.

December 15 1928

This was a remarkable game of football won 6-3 by East Fife against Dumbarton at Bayview.

Normally one is very suspicious of statements which imply that because there were a great deal of goals, this must have meant that the standard of football was uniformly high. Not always, for it usually means also that the standard of defending was shockingly poor.

In any case, anyone who has been to a basketball game where "goals" are scored all the time will testify to the fact that it can be boring watching scores and goals all the time.

Not today however. This was a fine game with even Kirkcaldy's *Fife Free Press* lapsing into ecstatic utterances about the quality of football played and giving this game more prominence than Raith Rovers!

The weather was cold with the pitch having a light covering of snow but referee Willie Webb of Glasgow had no hesitation in declaring the game on.

East Fife scored within a minute through Arthur McGachie and in quarter of an hour they were 4-0 up, Weir, Nairn and Brown scoring the others.

But Dumbarton were not out of it. With a young right winger called John Jackson (who earned a special cheer from the East Fife fans for he was the nephew of Alec Jackson, who had scored a hat-trick for the Wembley Wizards in March this year) supplying loads of crosses, they came back and by half way through the second half, the score was 4-3.

But then East Fife took control again as Dumbarton tired and Nairn and Kyle scored before the end. Nine goals was enough to warm anyone up on a cold day!

December 16 1903

Clear signs are reported in *The Courier* today of some sort of major problem at the new football club called East Fife.

Rumours of strife had been circulating in the town for some time, and it was clear that many men had agreed to serve on the Committee without really having any idea of the sheer amount of hard work, determination and no little expertise required to run a football team.

"It is a lot more than simply turning up on a Saturday" was the common wisdom, especially the absolute necessity for everyone to work together.

Today *The Courier* reports that it is the President himself, Mr John Adamson from Leven, who had resigned, stating that he was not prepared to risk a repetition of the "gutter oratory" of the last meeting.

This remark was seen as comment on the behaviour of Councillor Birnie, who had taken Mr Adamson to task for looking upon the Presidency as a sort of a figurehead, rather than a job which demanded a great deal of time and attention.

Clearly there was some "previous" between Adamson and Birnie, but the Committee now moved on, electing James Campbell as President and James Brunton as Vice President. The hope was expressed that the new club would now, in every sense of the word, prosper.

There was, for example, a game against the Black Watch on Saturday. There had been a certain feeling of disappointment in the attendance at some of the matches, but a wise man said that "Rome Wasn't Built In A Day".

In any case, the best way to attract people to see the team was to be successful and win some games.

December 17 1949

Had this been a Celtic team worthy of the name, this game might have gone down in history as one of East Fife's best ever performances. They crushed Celtic 5-1 at Bayview today.

The weather was mild enough but very windy. The 14,000 crowd were a bit frustrated at half time when the score was 1-1 with goals from Davie Duncan for East Fife and Jackie Gallacher for Celtic.

The Sunday Post was at a loss to know what Manager Scot Symon said to his players at half-time but certainly East Fife came out to face the strong wind coming from the west, and within quarter of an hour, they were 4-1 up. Goals from Bobby Black, Charlie Fleming and Henry Morris silenced the large Celtic crowd, who had until then dominated proceedings with their songs and backing for their team.

By the time that Morris scored the fifth with only a few minutes to go, they had all more or less departed for their trains and buses. Celtic's only real star was the irrepressible Charlie Tully. His trickery and artistry delighted even the East Fife crowd who were forced to give him a reluctant round of applause from time to time.

But this was a fine East Fife team who possibly lacked any great individual player like Charlie Tully but knitted together far better as a team. This result meant that East Fife were still behind Celtic in the League race but thanks to their League Cup campaign, they still had games in hand.

Celtic's woes continued, however. Top of the table were Hibs.

December 18 1920

East Fife recorded their first ever major success in any national competition when they won the Scottish Qualifying Cup.

They beat Bo'ness 3-1 in the final at Central Park, Cowdenbeath before a crowd given as around 20,000. If this figure seems a trifle high for midwinter, one must remember that this was the heyday of Scottish football with attendances very high indeed.

Everyone was concentrating on football to help them forget the horrors of the War which had just ended and the continuing labour and other social problems of the age. The Qualifying Cup was a huge trophy (huge in both size and prestige), and apart from the trophy, it guaranteed admission to the Scottish Cup itself and the possibility of a large gate.

It would also lay down a marker for any ambitious team like East Fife who had ambitions about joining the Scottish League. The weather was surprisingly mild for midwinter, although an early kick off was necessary to guarantee finishing in daylight.

East Fife started well against the wind and George Wilson put them ahead before half-time with a lovely headed goal. In the second half, with the wind at their backs and their opponents obliged to face the setting sun, East Fife took command, and although they lost a goal, they scored a second with another header from Dominic Currie. Andy Moffat killed Bo'ness' rapidly diminishing hopes with a third goal to take the massive, heavy, Cup back to Bayview, where it was proudly displayed to all those who wished to see it. Its sheer size meant that it was unlikely to be stolen by an opportunistic thief!

Scot Symon, Manager

December 19 1936

The midwinter gloom was well and truly dispelled today at Bayview when East Fife hit top form, turned on their best performance of the season so far and beat Brechin City 7-0.

The extent of this victory would have been difficult for anyone to predict before the game, for East Fife had been a little inconsistent this season, and Brechin did not give the impression of being in any way a bad team.

But today, inspired by the diminutive Tommy Adams, the Fifers simply turned it on and blew away any challenge from the men of Angus.

Joe Cowan had a hat-trick, Tommy Adams had two and George Scott and the "Newman" from Manchester United, a man called McMahon, scored the other, although *The Courier* is of the opinion that he was "cumbersome".

Brechin squandered two chances in the early part of the game. What little chance Brechin anticipated had disappeared. After that, it was all one-way traffic.

The crowd was a reasonable 2,000, possibly reflecting the upturn in industrial production now that the worst of the depression had gone. But the depression had been replaced by real fears of another war with everyone increasingly worried about Hitler. There was already a vicious war going on in Spain.

And all this for a country still reeling from the abdication of its King Edward VIII only nine days ago because he was not going to be allowed to marry his twice-divorced American lady friend Wallis Simpson.

The new King, George VI, was a quieter, more introverted man — and his wife claimed to be Scottish and they had two charming girls!

December 20 1952

East Fife's win at Shawfield guaranteed that they would spend Christmas at the top of the Scottish League Division "A".

They looked a good bet for being League winners at the end of the season. The weather was cold, and there was some snow in the east of Scotland (enough to put off Raith Rovers game at Kirkcaldy) but the further west one travelled the more it turned to sleet and then rain.

East Fife had beaten Clyde 7-1 at Bayview earlier in the season, but on this occasion, they had to work a great deal harder for their win. Shawfield was, of course, a strange stadium, more used for greyhounds than football. The crowd was a reasonable one today (about 10,000 and swelled by the fact that Celtic were away at Falkirk and this game was therefore the only one on in the east of Glasgow), but there was always a slight lack of atmosphere at this ground.

Clyde had some fine players like Harry Haddock, Billy McPhail and Tommy Ring, and it was they who took the lead when Buchanan ran in from a distance and pushed the ball past goalkeeper Curran.

But the small band of travelling supporters cheered when Charlie Fleming equalised with a fierce drive into the roof of the net. That was half way through the first half.

It was an uphill battle for East Fife, who looked as if they would have to settled for a draw until, with five minutes go, Ian Gardiner nipped in to finish off a pass from Fleming.

The last five minutes needed some desperate defending, but the final whistle went and Christmas was spent happily with East Fife on top of the League, one point ahead of Celtic.

December 21 1957

Midwinter's day at Bayview saw attractive visitors in Motherwell. East Fife's grim battle against relegation continued.

It had been a remarkable season so far with Hearts showing themselves to be the team of the first half of the season and they were some distance ahead of the others in the race for the League flag.

Rangers were still reeling from their 7-1 defeat from Celtic in the League Cup final. Raith Rovers were having a reasonable season, but East Fife less so, and they were uncomfortably close to the bottom of the League table.

Today's visitors Motherwell were an enigmatic team with a reputation for playing good football, and still had some great players like McSeveney and McCann.

East Fife had ex-Rangers and Scotland Sammy Cox playing for them now and it was he who started the move which led to the first goal as he sent a long ball to Alex Duchart who threaded it through to Jimmy Bonthrone who ran on and scored just before half-time.

It was Duchart who scored the second goal about halfway through the second half when he picked up a good pass from Robert Leishman. A moment's slackness however cost East Fife a moment's anxiety when they conceded a goal late in the game, but the defence held out to give the home fans a 2-1 victory and a major boost.

There had been a certain amount of dissatisfaction with East Fife's performances so far this season, but, as always, the upcoming holiday fixtures at the New Year would be vital, and then there was the Scottish Cup in which East Fife had been drawn against the runaway League leaders, Hearts.

December 22 1923

East Fife and Cowdenbeath served up a marvellous local derby at Bayview for the midwinter crowd of about 3,000.

The weather was dry and cold, but the pitch was in adequate condition, although it did seem to cut up as the game progressed.

Cowdenbeath were a good team in the days immediately after the Great War. Indeed in 1921/22 (the first season of the Second Division) they had finished second to Alloa, but had not been promoted because only one team was promoted in order to reduce the number of teams in the First Division.

This season Cowdenbeath were going for promotion again and they would eventually achieve it, but today was a serious, if temporary block to their chances.

For East Fife, Andy Cant and Davie Edgar are singled out for their performances (Cant having returned after some time in England with Bradford City) but the two goalkeepers Jock Neish and Brodie of Cowdenbeath were the men of the match and "Neish's lithe form was seen stretched between the uprights in masterly clearances" according to *The Courier*.

Cant scored first for East Fife, but "corn beef" (as Cowdenbeath were then nicknamed) equalised before half-time. But then Cowdenbeath went ahead through an own goal before John Reilly equalised for East Fife.

With only minutes remaining, and the crowd on tenterhooks, Andy Cant ran through to score the winner for East Fife, and to give everyone in Methil a Merry Christmas, even though most Fifers were looking forward to the New Year celebrations rather than Christmas.

Christmas would not even be a public holiday in Scotland until 1958.

December 23 1981

In some ways this was a nightmare scenario, and even those of us who oppose summer football must have weakened a little at this one.

It was midwinter (two days before Christmas), weather dodgy with snow and ice, hardly any daylight at all other than what was reflected off the snow lying at the side of the roads.

East Fife were playing a Scottish Cup tie which had already been postponed more than once. So far so bad, but the game was at Stranraer!

By a quirk of the Scottish weather, Stranraer's pitch at Stair Park was now playable (just, but then it often is as it gets the benefit of the Gulf Stream more than others!) and to the immense distress and disappointment (one imagines) of East Fife's players, the phone call came to say that the game was on.

One cannot have imagined that very many supporters travelled this Wednesday night, but the team did, leaving about lunchtime to reach their distant destination by 7.30 pm. The roads were clear, although there were a few tricky bits south of Kilmarnock, and East Fife arrived to play before a crowd of less than 300, who actually gave them a round of applause as they came out for making the journey!

East Fife went ahead when Davie Miller sent over a high ball for Martin Caithness to knock down for Paul Burt to score. Then East Fife seemed to have resisted all the pressure that the home side applied until with just two minutes left, Stranraer equalised through Harvey. Thus it had all been in vain, for another game now had to be played.

One cannot imagine the Stranraer Directors being all that happy with Mr Harvey, who had thus condemned the team to a journey to Bayview on January 4, where they lost 4-1! But East Fife were not happy either. Did they sing Christmas Carols on the bus home? It was about 3.00 am before they got home! On Christmas Eve!

December 24 1947

Without ever banning the practice outright, the authorities in the late 1940s frowned upon midweek football on the grounds that it encouraged absenteeism from factories and mines where everyone was needed to produce more coal.

However an exception was made at Christmas, and East Fife arranged to play Ayr United this Wednesday Christmas Eve on the grounds that the schools were off for holidays anyway, and that they would attract loads of youngsters, as well as those who worked for enlightened employers who closed at lunch time on Christmas Eve.

So 3,200 came to Bayview this afternoon for the 2.00 pm kick-off before darkness came down. East Fife gave them all a Merry Christmas with an excellent 3-2 win over Ayr United.

Thus Christmas was spent in Methil with East Fife, with three games in hand, a point ahead of Albion Rovers in Division "B".

Davie Duncan scored with a tremendous free-kick and then had extremely bad luck with another two free kicks. It was also he who took the corner kick which found the glancing head of Henry Morris for the second goal.

Then after McGuigan pulled one back for Ayr United, Danny McLennan scored a lovely goal for East Fife, getting the ball about 30 yards out, taking a few steps and hammering home with aplomb.

Ayr United scored at the very death through White, but that was a mere consolation goal. The star man for East Fife was once again "Tantalising Tommy" Adams whose duels with left back Kelly (another small terrier-like man) were a feature of the game.

Santa Claus may have been good to Methil children that night, but the real joy of Christmas came from their team.

December 25 1971

Football used to be played in Scotland on Christmas Day if it happened to fall on a Saturday, but this seems to have been the last time that East Fife played on that day.

Christmas, of course, was only a Public Holiday in Scotland from 1958 onwards, and the dropping of the Christmas Day fixture was a further sign that Christmas was becoming more important in Scotland, almost now as important as the New Year.

There are those who still believe that a game on Christmas Day would be no bad thing to get away from the relentless and enforced happiness of the day!

In fact, in 1971 East Fife were in the middle of a reasonable run of form — they had been unlucky to lose 1-2 to Celtic on December 11 and had drawn 2-2 with St Johnstone on December 18, and today they earned another draw 1-1 with Motherwell.

The crowd was a creditable 4,000, but this would not be 1971 if there was not at least a token and ludicrous attempt at hooliganism — this time a bottle thrown by a nana, hopefully from Motherwell rather than the local area — but it did not disrupt what was a good game.

Heron scored for Motherwell from the penalty spot after a softish penalty was given, but then East Fife fought well and thoroughly deserved their late equaliser from Doug Dailey.

No-one was entirely optimistic that East Fife would avoid relegation in this, their first year back among the big boys, but there seemed little doubt that they would give it a go and not go down without a fight.

December 26 2015

There was a certain score to settle with Stirling Albion at Forthbank today as East Fife, having enjoyed Christmas, returned to their duties.

Stirling Albion had been the team which had put them out of the Scottish Cup — always a sore blow, and with serious implications for the financial side of the running of the club.

It had been a narrow defeat after a replay and relationships had not been great between the teams, but today East Fife got their own back as they won 3-1 with Nathan Austin recording a hat-trick.

The crowd of 645 was not unreasonable for the time of year and the weather was remarkably good. The Binos scored first through Darren Smith, although it was a deflection and some sources gave it as an own goal.

Austin then took a fine pass from Kyle Wilkie to level matters, and then just on the half time whistle, East Fife had turned it all round when Austin scored again with a left foot shot.

The second half was a keen and interesting struggle with Stirling Albion hitting the post, but East Fife put the game out of their reach when Austin headed his third.

In some ways this game, more or less exactly at the half way point of the season, was the turning point for East Fife. Having had a bad run in November and December, they lost to Elgin City on January 2, but lost only another two games between then and the end of the season and won the Second Division by three points.

When they came back to Forthbank in March to play Stirling Albion, they won 6-0.

December 27 1969

East Fife's last game of the year 1969, indeed their last game of the 1960s, was a shocker when they went down 4-1 to Forfar Athletic at Station Park.

The course of the game was inexplicable to East Fife fans for Forfar, now under the influence of ex-East Fife Jake Young, were 4-0 up at half time and the game then fizzled out with East Fife's late consolation goal of little relevance.

It had been a curious season for the team who had started reasonably well under new Manager Bill Baxter, but who had hit a poor spell in December.

Forfar on the other hand were having one of the better spells in their history, and their goals were all well taken, one after the other.

The whole decade of the 1960s had not been great for East Fife. They had now been in the Second Division for well over a decade, and frankly, they had never really looked as if they could get out.

Raith Rovers, on the other hand, against whom East Fife were normally judged, had been in and out of the First Division, and of course Fife's team of the decade were undeniably Dunfermline Athletic who had won the Scottish Cup in 1961 and 1968 and had even performed, not without glory, in Europe.

But the "swinging sixties" had, to a large extent, passed East Fife by, and all the supporters could do now was hope that the 1970s would bring better things. They could also, of course, reminisce about the late 1940s and 1950s, and wonder whether there would ever be another Henry Morris or Charlie Fleming.

December 28 1935

East Fife had now won five games in a row and looked in fine fettle for a promotion push in the New Year, not to mention their forthcoming Scottish Cup date with Rangers.

Today a creditable crowd of 2,800 came to Bayview and saw them beat St Bernards, an Edinburgh team from Stockbridge, 5-2. The half back line of Russell, Casciani and McCartney were very impressive indeed, exerting a domination over the strong Edinburgh midfield.

The star of the show however was Tommy Adams, called "Diddler" according to *The Courier* while The *Leven Advertiser* delivers the verdict that "... he kept the spectators on good terms with themselves. While his tricky footwork and elusive swerve elicited cheers, the sheer impudence of some of his moves brought roars of laughter".

He scored one of the five goals himself and had a direct say in two of the others. Eddie McLeod scored two goals, Joe Cowan one and Billy Downie the other one.

St Bernard's acquitted themselves well — indeed they were still above East Fife in the Second Division — but on this showing there was simply no living with East Fife who thus finished 1935 on a high.

Some indifferent (less charitable supporters said "dreadful") results at the start of the season meant that they were still only eighth in the League table, but they were steadily climbing.

And in Tommy Adams there seemed to be something special in the Scottish tradition of fine left wingers like Alan Morton and Alec Troup. High hopes for 1936 were being nourished in Methil.

December 29 1934

The *Leven Advertiser* is far from impressed by this performance. Granted, East Fife did beat Leith Athletic 5-2.

Leith were described as a "scrappy lot", although they were only a couple of places beneath East Fife in the middle of the table.

George Scott came in for a certain amount of criticism for his selfish play: "he seems to have lost the art of passing once he has beaten his man", a criticism that was to a certain extent true of John Steele as well, even though it is admitted that he showed "dazzling footwork".

Joe Cowan had two good goals, however. One of the Leith goals was an odd one, and should not have been awarded in the opinion of most people in the ground. It was a penalty kick taken by McCormack. It hit the bar and came down on the goal-line before it was smothered by goalkeeper Joe Crozier.

The referee, however, Mr Carruthers from Glasgow awarded a goal whenever he saw the ball hit the bar, and would have none of the justified, and to a large extent, dignified protest by East Fife's captain Archie Pratt.

Not that it mattered in the long run, for East Fife won comfortably enough with two goals from Joe Cowan, one from George Scott (in the first minute of the game), and other from John Phillips and another from Willie Gillies.

Thus ended 1934. Life had not been easy over the past few years since the heady days of the Scottish Cup final of 1927 and the promotion in 1930. The promotion had brought the disastrous 1930/31 season, but there were now beginning to be signs that a good team was gradually emerging under hard working Manager Dave McLean.

December 30 2017

East Fife finished 2017 with a 1-1 draw at Gayfield, Arbroath.

It took them to the very last minute of the 90 to do so, and even then it was a penalty kick! 649 were there to see a reasonable game played by two teams who were just outside the promotion play-off zone.

The weather was not too bad for the time of year, and it was clear from a visit to the pubs within walking distance of the ground that quite a lot of fans were having a double helping of football today for the Celtic v Rangers game (it ended 0-0) on the television was attracting attention as well

But events in Glasgow finished early enough to allow the Arbroath fans to get to Gayfield and East Fife fans were able to listen to it on the car radio on the way up!

Since delighting their fans with a 6-0 drubbing of Airdrieonians at the end of November, East Fife had had a bad December, gaining only one point, and frankly, for a long spell they did not look like getting very much out of Dick Campbell's team today.

Indeed, Arbroath took the lead in the 73rd minute with a fine drive from Leighton McIntosh, something which triggered an exit of the East Fife fans and even some Arbroath fans as well who were clearly fancying some smokies for their tea.

Fouls became frequent as East Fife piled on the pressure and eventually, David Gold of Arbroath committed one in the penalty area, and Mark Docherty finished off the job to the delight of the travelling fans.

The game had still about four minutes of added-on time to run and a ding-dong battle ensued for the winner, but none came. East Fife got a point, but would have earned more if they had played all game as they did in the latter stages.

December 30 2017

Chris Duggan in action at Gayfield, fending off Scott Martin

December 31 1966

East Fife finished the calendar year of 1966 in third place in Division Two after a rather unsatisfactory 2-2 draw against Stranraer at Bayview.

Morton were clear on top, and East Fife were tucked in behind Raith Rovers, who actually lost today.

The weather was cold but dry, and approximately 1,000 turned up at Bayview, some of whom clearly celebrating the New Year rather too early! (Alcohol was allowed in Scottish grounds until 1981).

It was a poor game, but East Fife went in at half-time a goal up thanks to an own goal from Stranraer's left half Logan. The same man then scored in the right goal to level matters, and soon after that Stranraer went ahead and looked like staying ahead, for East Fife's forwards were distinctly feckless.

But then with half the crowd away home vowing not to reappear in 1967, Andy Waddell scored with what was more or less the last kick of the ball in Scottish football in 1966.

Stranraer's players and officials were given "their New Year" after the game, but had to excuse themselves about 6.00 pm because they said they needed to get home "this year". They were not joking either!

East Fife's players would not be able to indulge in a huge amount of revelling however, for they had an important date at Stark's Park on Monday January 2 1967. Sadly it would not turn out well . . . but no-one knew that at the time, and reflections on 1966 probably had more good memories than bad ones.

Some players had enjoyed good years, notably Andy Waddell and Alan Guild. Things seemed to be moving in the right direction.

December 31 1994

East Fife v Meadowbank on December 31 1994

January

East Fife in 1981

January 1 1938

1938 would prove to be a memorable season in the annals of both Fife clubs, and it opened in spectacular fashion before 19,700 spectators at Stark's Park, Kirkcaldy with a 3-1 win for East Fife.

The weather was fine for the time of year, and a huge contingent from Methil made the short journey to Kirkcaldy.

One could sense, however, a certain degree of anxiety in the air, given the tense International situation, although it was also clear that the worst of the economic problems had passed and that we were heading for a situation of more or less full employment.

The Fife Free Press is unstinting in the praise of both teams, East Fife in particular, for a fine game of football. Eddie McLeod, Davie Russell and Joe Cowan scored for East Fife while Raith Rovers' solitary counter came from John Whitelaw.

This was one of the first Scottish League Second Division games to have neutral linesmen (normally in those days, each club would supply a linesman) and *The Fife Free Press* gives credit to Mr James Bogie, the Chairman of Raith Rovers, for arranging this.

It also says that both linesmen did well and were appreciated by the large crowd, but it felt that referee Mr Carruthers from Airdrie did not use them as well as he might have.

Both teams then went on to win their respective games on Monday January 3 leaving them first and second respectively in the Second Division with East Fife at the moment marginally ahead.

January 2 1950

In what is now generally claimed to be the record attendance for Bayview, 22,515 saw East Fife beat Raith Rovers 3-0.

The Courier estimates 21,500 but those who were there say that the attendance was a great deal more than that if one allows for the many who climbed the wall!

New Year's Day having fallen on a Sunday, games were scheduled for both Monday and Tuesday, and the weather, although somewhat cold, was dry and the underlying ground conditions were acceptable.

The Courier laments the decline of an ancient activity called "Bawbee She Kyles", a traditional Kirkcaldy New Year sport in which one tries to roll a cannonball into a hole into the ground.

This bizarre activity, now no longer practised, was struggling even in 1950 and had to be brought forward to 10.15 am to allow the crowds to head along to Methil for the 2.00 pm start.

East Fife were always the better side, and their man of the match was undeniably their inside left, Allan Brown, who fed Bert Aitken for the first goal, and then he scored the other two himself.

There could be little doubt as to who the better team were, but there was to be "no rest for the wicked", as that night East Fife boarded a coach to take them to Dumfries to play Queen of the South tomorrow.

A slight worry was the non-appearance of Bert Aitken who was suffering from concussion. Raith Rovers meantime had to brace themselves for the visit of Celtic to Kirkcaldy.

January 3 1972

In one of the best East Fife performances for many years, the team delighted their 8,217 fans at Bayview with a 2-1 win over Hibs.

There had been some poor Hibs teams in the past, and some good ones, and this was certainly one of the better ones with men like Pat Stanton, Alex Cropley and the two Johns Brownlie and Blackley.

In 1972, Hibs would provide as strong a challenge to Celtic as anyone else, and they had a reputation for playing good football.

But there was an unpleasant side to this game as well resulting in the sending off of Alex Edwards, a correct decision after what the newspapers described coyly as a "tangle" or a "clash" with a couple of East Fife players.

This did not go down very well with the sizeable Hibs contingent in the crowd, some of whom appeared to have been celebrating the New Year rather too well, and the police had to apprehend and remove a few missile throwers.

East Fife had gone ahead in the first half from a free kick hammered home by Billy McPhee, and then had to resist a certain amount of pressure from this strong Hibs team, even though they were hampered by having only 10 men.

East Fife then went further ahead late in the game when Joe Hughes was on the spot to net a rebound after a rare error by Scotland Internationalist Jim Herriot in the Hibs goal.

It looked all done and dusted but then as the game was coming to an end, Hibs were awarded a penalty kick, duly sunk by Pat Stanton to set up an anxious last few minutes before a tremendous cheer at the full time whistle.

January 4 1955

Charlie Fleming was today transferred to Sunderland, a club which had long admired him and which had on at least two previous occasions made an offer for him. This was a move which had been on the cards for a while after being hinted at in the Press for many weeks, but which East Fife supporters had been dreading,

This time the pill was sweetened by the swopping of Scotland International Tommy Wright with a cash adjustment in East Fife's favour. The deal was signed in the Station Hotel, Kirkcaldy soon after Tommy Wright and Sunderland's Manager Bill Murray had arrived at Kirkcaldy Station on the 3.00 pm train. Part of the deal was that both houses would be swopped as well with Tommy moving into the Fleming house in Leven and vice versa.

George Aitken, with whom Fleming had played at Bayview, was already with Sunderland, so Charlie would not be entirely lonely among the Mackems of Wearside. Everyone was sad to see the departure of "Legs" or the "Cannonball".

Although Tommy Wright was no mean performer, he took a long time to settle at East Fife, as the team now began to struggle. Fleming on the other hand had a couple of good seasons for Sunderland, scoring 71 goals in 122 outings, although crucially Sunderland never won anything, and were duly relegated in 1958.

Nor did Charlie ever win back his Scottish cap. It was a shame; it would be hard to argue against the contention that, even in a team which had many great players over the years, Charlie Fleming was the best of them all.

January 5 1952

In a thrilling contest watched by a large crowd, East Fife recorded their first ever victory over Rangers in the Scottish League.

East Fife had not had a good New Year holiday period. A defeat by Raith Rovers on New Year's Day was bad enough, but it was then followed by a 2-1 defeat at Pittodrie. Everyone seemed now to be of the opinion that the East Fife bubble had burst and that all the good work of 1951 had been undone.

Today however reversed the trend and Rangers, who themselves often baffled their fans by their inconsistency (on New Year's Day they had beaten Celtic, but then lost to their bogey team Dundee on January 2) were well beaten, with the 2-1 score line not quite reflecting the run of the play.

The pitch was heavily sanded but seemed to give players a reasonable grip in the icy conditions. Most games in the west of Scotland were frosted off that day, but the weather in the east was a degree or two higher.

The first goal game from Ian Gardiner, although he was lucky to get a deflection off George Young; the second was a delicate flick of the head from Jimmy Bonthrone.

The star of the side, however, was Willie Finlay, the centre half who was given the difficult task of marking Willie Thornton, but he managed it well.

Rangers, for whom Willie Waddell was absent with a chill, scored their only goal though Willie Thornton. It was a nice header from a free-kick foolishly conceded by Danny McLennan.

January 5 1952

Ian Gardiner challenges Bobby Brown and George Young of Rangers at Bayview on January 5 1952

January 6 1923

East Fife today welcomed three times Scottish Cup winners Vale of Leven to Bayview for a Scottish League game.

The men from Milburn Park, Alexandria had won the Scottish Cup in 1877, 1878 and 1879 — astonishingly the 1879 success had come about because Rangers refused to turn up for the Scottish Cup final replay! — but had now clearly passed their peak. Nevertheless the Dark Blues, a small village side just rather too close to Glasgow and unable to cope with the rise of professionalism, were making an attempt to come to terms with post-war football in the Second Division.

Today however, East Fife beat them very comfortably 2-0. The first goal was a fine shot from Peter Barrett.

The second was like a scene from a Charlie Chaplin film. East Fife right winger Murray and Vale left back Browning had been have some rare old tussles on the left wing (*The Sunday Post* tellingly uses the word "bouts"!) but from one of these, Murray crossed. It looked as if the ball was drifting safely into the hands of goalkeeper O'Neill, but the luckless custodian mistimed his jump, and it sailed gently over his head into the net. Cue laughter, before an outburst of cheering, and East Fife never looked back after that.

It was a game much enjoyed by the 3,000 crowd and it moved East Fife into seventh place, but poor Vale of Leven were now heading almost inevitably to extinction. However, the Scottish Cup was now approaching and East Fife were to host Berwick Rangers, a team about whom no-one seemed to know very much.

January 7 2017

In their first game of the calendar year of 2017, East Fife beat Stenhousemuir 1-0 in a competitive game where there was more good football than the score line would have suggested.

The crowd was 635, slightly disappointing perhaps considering that this was one of the two Saturdays on which the Scottish Premier League teams decided to award themselves a holiday called the midwinter shut down which they tried to justify in terms of bad weather etc.

Yet this was a reasonable day, and all the rest of Scottish football seemed to be able to function! When one considers that statistically the worst month of the year is February, the justification becomes even more threadbare.

Today East Fife scored half way through the first half when Scott Robinson picked up a ball from Kevin O'Hara and fired home from the edge of the box. Thereafter play ebbed to and fro with Stenhousemuir belying their lowly position in the League and indeed being very unlucky not to get a draw. A chap with the unlikely name of Willis Furtado came close, and a man with the even less likely name of Carlos Mazana-Marinez (hard to believe that that is a common name in Larbert and Stenhousemuir!) spoiled a promising move at the end with a hand-ball.

The final whistle came as a great relief to the East Fife supporters, and it meant that they were in 6th place in the First Division (third tier), and Stenhousemuir, sadly for them, now found themselves 10th, and that was more or less where they both ended up at the end of the season.

January 7 2017

Ross Brown and Willis Furtado

January 8 2011

Aberdeen had seen better days, it would have to be said. Since they had won the Scottish League Cup in 1995/96, success and the Dons had been strangers to one another.

There had been several constant motifs — a succession of poor managers, a disillusioned support, foreign players who had arrived, failed to deliver and then departed, and a propensity to go out of the national Cups to teams from lower Divisions.

Although form had taken a turn for the better since Christmas, they had still won only five League games, and in November they had succumbed to a 9-0 thrashing from Celtic at Parkhead.

All this gave East Fife encouragement for their rare trip to Pittodrie in the Scottish Cup, although form had been patchy and unpredictable, not helped by the rather severe weather which had affected Great Britain in December 2010.

The weather was still not great today but the game was on, and 6,918 (with 473 in the visitors' section) were at Pittodrie to see what turned out to be a rather one-sided contest with this Aberdeen side, under Craig Brown, determined to allow no slip-up.

Chris Maguire scored a first half hat-trick, Scott Vernon scored another two and Josh Magennis another, as poor East Fife were totally outclassed.

It was however a chance to visit Pittodrie, one of the famous old grounds of Scottish football, and the veteran supporters on the buses took the chance to tell the youngsters about times when East Fife had beaten Aberdeen. You had to go back a bit for that, though!

January 8 2011

Action at Pittodrie against Aberdeen

January 9 1932

This game can only really be described as a "hammering", and only to a point can one make excuses of the wind and the rain.

East Fife and Forfar Athletic were old foes since soon after East Fife's formation, and usually games were tight. Not today however, for Station Park saw a very one-sided game as Forfar won 6-1.

This was one of the best Forfar teams for some time and today they mastered the conditions a great deal better than East Fife did. Yet East Fife scored first through Ted Lowery. This was when they had the benefit of the conditions, but even so, Forfar turned round 3-1 to the good, all their goals coming in the last three minutes of the first half; two of them were from well-taken corner kicks.

John Kirkwood failed to return, having collapsed with hypothermia in the dressing room at half-time. The conditions did not improve in the second half, and Forfar scored another three in the wind and the rain, doing so against 10 men. However a vigorous rub down by the trainers of both East Fife and Forfar restored Kirkwood and he returned to finish the game.

The referee, Mr Grant from Edinburgh stopped the game three minutes early. Those who had watches realised he had made a mistake, and many of the Forfar crowd refused to go home, such was their enjoyment of the game! Mr Grant was adamant and Forfar won 6-1.

Quite a few players, fans and journalists felt that the referee had made no mistake. Self-preservation is always an important factor, and he may also have just decided to be merciful on the East Fife players and supporters!

January 10 1931

This was a very dark day indeed in the annals of the club as they travelled to Celtic Park to be on the wrong end of a 9-1 hammering, confirming the undeniable fact that East Fife's stay in the First Division was to be a very short one indeed.

Frankly they had no answer to a Celtic side who had themselves been struggling for a few years, but were now beginning to show signs of rallying to the standard of what their spectators expected.

The blessing for East Fife was that very few of their supporters were there to see it, for *The Dundee Courier* states that when Phil Weir scored East Fife's only goal following a John Wilson cross "not a cheer greeted the goal, although the point was well taken".

The Parkhead crowd had more reason to cheer the five goals scored by Jimmy McGrory, the three by the excellent Peter Scarff and the one by Bertie Thomson.

Only later in the game did East Fife began to play a little better, with Danny Liddle beginning to show some form, bringing out some good saves from John Thomson in the Celtic goal. *The Scotsman*, on the other hand, states that "(John) Bernard in goal (for East Fife) made some bad mistakes, but he also had some wonderful saves".

As the dispirited East Fife players trudged off, they were hardly likely to be comforted by the thought that next week's opponents were also Celtic, but this time in the Scottish Cup at Bayview.

January 11 1964

It was Scottish Cup day; East Fife had received a bye, and so they played against Hamilton Academical at Bayview in what was the only Scottish League Second Division game of the day.

The season so far had been not too bad, but there had been a tendency to draw games that they really should have won. Nevertheless, in fifth place they were handily placed for a promotion charge.

What was obvious this year in the Second Division was that no-one was going to catch Morton, who had played 22 League games and won every one of them!

East Fife's talking point at the moment was the emergence of Morris Aitken, a talented youngster with the psychological and possibly subliminal advantage of have the same names of two great stars of a decade ago in Henry Morris and George Aitken!

Today it was Aitken who scored the winner with a 20 yard shot after a rather turgid first half in which East Fife had equalised with a penalty kick rather generously awarded by referee Bert Crockett of Dundee. Jimmy Walker converted it, but apart from that there was not a great deal to entertain the 1,500 crowd on this dull, but mild January day.

The Scottish Cup ties had shown a few surprises — Cowdenbeath had earned a draw with Morton, Eyemouth had held Celtic to 0-0 at half time before the inevitable happened, but maybe the most significant was the giant killing of First Division Third Lanark at Stranraer — one of the first nails in the coffin of that great Glasgow side.

January 12 1952

East Fife's form slump continued with a disappointing 2-1 defeat at Fir Park, Motherwell.

Motherwell were a good side in 1952, having won the Scottish League Cup the previous season and then appeared in the Scottish Cup final. Although East Fife had been temporarily boosted with a win over Rangers last week, they had had a poor time of it in the New Year fixtures.

The League this year was dominated by Hearts and Hibs with the two Glasgow sides, Celtic in particular, having a very thin time of it.

Motherwell, before a crowd of about 10,000, started well but it was East Fife who scored first through Jimmy Bonthrone. He proved his value to the side when he latched on to a misplaced clearance, turned quickly and fired home a fine shot.

This was a bad blow for the home side, but in the second half they continued to dominate and to bring out fine saves from goalkeeper Johnny Curran, until about ten minutes after the restart when Archie Kelly of Motherwell got a ball after a great Willie Redpath and Wilson Humphries move to level the score. Ten minutes after that, Kelly scored again, this time a fine header from another Humphries cross.

Now at last East Fife got back into the game, and there were several close things with Bonthrone having bad luck on several occasions.

The reaction of Motherwell's players and supporters at the full-time whistle told its own tale, but it was another defeat for East Fife, a result noted with interest in Eyemouth where East Fife were due in two weeks' time in the Scottish Cup.

January 13 1962

That there was to be no "quick fix" for East Fife in their attempts to regain their First Division status was becoming more and more apparent year by year, and this 0-1 defeat at Albion Rovers probably represented East Fife's last chance of climbing the Second Division table.

Form had been somewhat unpredictable before Christmas, but the last few results had been good, and this was why today's result had been all the more disappointing.

The weather had been frosty in the morning, but had turned milder during the day and more supporters might have been expected than the 500 who turned up with very few coming from Methil.

Lamont of Albion Rovers scored the only goal of the game with a snap shot soon after the interval, but that was all that really separated the teams. East Fife might well have equalised or even gone ahead but for some "profligate finishing".

This game could be looked upon as a dress rehearsal, for the teams were due to meet again at Bayview in two weeks' time in the Scottish Cup. This would be a different competition and different teams, however.

Elsewhere, Scotland lost their first game in the Rugby Five Nations (only five, because Italy did not join until 2000) Championship to France at Murrayfield, and Dundee held on to their lead in the Scottish League Division One by beating Hearts at Tynecastle.

In Dundee itself at Tannadice, there was a remarkable game won 5-4 by Celtic who had led Dundee United 5-1 shortly after half-time, but then United staged a comeback which took a few years off the life of many Celtic supporters!

January 14 1928

The two old rivals East Fife and Forfar Athletic served up a tremendous exhibition of football at Bayview today to make the crowd forget the cold.

Forfar were enjoying a good season and had dumped East Fife 4-0 at Station Park in September, so some revenge was called for.

Today Forfar were without star forward Davie McLean (a man who by chance shared the same name as East Fife's Manager) and this possibly told in the end.

The final result was 4-3 for the Fifers, but there could quite easily have been more goals scored at either end, particularly for East Fife, because Forfar were indebted to a great display of goalkeeping from Jock Bruce (who had previously played for East Fife) to keep the score down.

The Sunday Post talks about a "ragtime exhibition" of football, a reference to the musical craze of the time, but then says that some of the football was "patchy".

Forfar were 2-1 up at half time, East Fife's goal coming from Phil Weir, but then in the second half Paterson and Russell scored for East Fife and Wilson for Forfar, before the final and winning goal came from a race for the ball between Weir and Bruce, and Weir won!

It was generally agreed that the man of the match was Frank Hill, Forfar's left half, a man who would go on to play for Aberdeen and Scotland.

The main topic of conversation in Fife that night however was the performance of Dunfermline at Celtic Park that day. They had lost 0-9 and Jimmy McGrory scored 8 of them!

January 15 1938

There seemed little doubt that storm clouds were gathering over Europe. War was already tearing Spain apart, and Hitler kept making bellicose statements about Austria and Czechoslovakia while Great Britain seemed to prefer to bury its head in the sand and ignore him.

Football in Fife was a welcome distraction, as both Raith Rovers and East Fife strove to earn promotion to the First Division. Today as Raith Rovers beat Dunfermline Athletic to consolidate their place at the top, East Fife stayed in second place after a thrilling 3-3 draw with the Edinburgh side St Bernards.

The large crowd saw end to end stuff at Bayview, but East Fife were bereft of their star man, Tommy Adams, who was ill with flu. It was probably his absence which prevented a victory, although East Fife almost snatched it at the very death when a McLeod shot scraped the post with the goalkeeper beaten.

The Edinburgh side had started better and were soon 2-0 up after defensive frailties had given easy chances, but then McLeod pulled one back to trigger a period of East Fife pressure. But then, just as East Fife looked sure to score, Pinkerton of St Bernards put his side 3-1 up, and so it was at half-time.

It stayed like this for a long time in the second half, but with little over 15 minutes left, Henderson pulled one back. One brings two, they say, and a few minutes later after the ball bobbed about the penalty area for a spell, McCartney poked it home. 3-3 and then a really breathtaking finish when McLeod almost scored. Both teams received a standing ovation at the end for a magnificent game of football.

January 16 1932

The Scottish Cup draw sent East Fife to Rugby Park, Kilmarnock this year.

This was hardly looked upon as a "plum" draw, for Kilmarnock were, then as now, a very efficient but poorly supported club. The likelihood was that there would be a poor crowd and a defeat for East Fife. So it turned out.

Kilmarnock had won the Scottish Cup in 1920 and 1929 and although their legendary Mattha or Matt Smith had now gone to finish off his career at Ayr United, they were still a formidable outfit.

The weather was not all that cold for mid-January, but it was blowing a fierce gale today at Rugby Park. Partly because of that, the attendance was reduced to 5,700 and the receipts were given as £217, something that was not perhaps as much as the Fifers would have wanted.

East Fife won the toss and chose to play with the gale in the first half, but failed to capitalise on the wind, most of their efforts being frustrated by Kilmarnock's Scotland Internationalist Joe Nibloe.

Phil Weir had scored for East Fife, but Kilmarnock had scored twice. Shortly after half-time, East Fife scored through Englishman Ted Lowery but Mr McArthur of Airdrie disallowed it for a foul.

This was a blow from which the gallant East Fife never recovered; two further goals came for Killie, but not before East Fife had earned the respect of the Killie fans — and more importantly, their own travelling fans who had been not a little cheesed off with them after last week's humiliation at Station Park, Forfar.

January 17 1931

9,000 were at Bayview to see what was described as a rollicking Cup tie between East Fife and Celtic.

Played on a dry day, although the pitch was still a little heavy, East Fife did well enough to earn at least a replay at Celtic Park; this was no mean feat, considering that they had lost 1-9 to the same opponents the previous Saturday.

Celtic brought their usual huge crowd of supporters, and their team contained three Fife men — Chick Geatons from Lochgelly, John Thomson who had been born in Kirkcaldy but had played for Wellesley Juniors before joining Celtic, and Buckhaven's own Alec Thomson, commonly known to all and sundry as "Eckie Tamson".

East Fife scored first to a tremendous cheer from the locals after John Thomson had left his goal and collided with a defender, leaving Johnny Wilson with an easy goal. That was the score at half-time, but then Celtic fought back in the second half.

McGrory was not having one of his better days in front of goal, however, and it took a surprise shot from Charlie Napier to equalise for the green and whites. Then late in the game after John Bernard saved an excellent shot form Peter Scarff, Bertie Thomson netted the rebound.

It was hard luck on East Fife, however, a point conceded by Celtic manager Willie Maley. Celtic would go on to win the Scottish Cup that year, and as tough a game as any was the struggle to defeat East Fife at Bayview.

Tommy Adams

January 18 1982

The weather which had been positively Arctic for the past week and a half eased slightly this Monday night to allow East Fife's Scottish Cup second round tie against Forfar Athletic to go ahead.

The Scottish Cup was in total chaos with some of the first round ties not even played yet. East Fife however had managed to play and win their replay against Stranraer on January 4 after a drawn first game on December 23.

The thaw tonight was not yet total and all of the other games scheduled were postponed again, but Bayview's proximity to the east coast meant that the game could go ahead, admittedly in imperfect, but just playable conditions. This game therefore had all of Scotland to itself and thus enjoyed more media attention than it might have expected in other circumstances.

The Glasgow Herald, for example, purrs its pleasure at this game which "swung like a pendulum" and gave great satisfaction to the less than 1,000 fans who braved the cold, including a few from the frozen north of Forfar.

The game did indeed swing to and fro with Gordon Scott opening the scoring for East Fife with a shot that went through the legs of Forfar's one-time Scotland goalkeeper Stewart Kennedy.

John Mitchell then equalised before half-time for Forfar, but early in the second half Gordon Scott put the Fifers ahead from close range in the aftermath of a corner kick.

But then John Clark equalised before Alex Brash (who would go on to play for Raith Rovers) won the day for Forfar with a header. Both teams were well worthy of the applause they received at the end before the crowd braced themselves for the wintry journey home.

January 19 1929

East Fife's supporters had their hearts broken as they exited the Scottish Cup at the first time of asking on a dull but playable day at Bayview.

Their opponents were First Division Partick Thistle, even as early as 1929 known as "the old unpredictables" or the "loose cannons" of Scottish football. They had won the Scottish Cup in 1921, were currently in the top half of the First Division and brought with them a fair support "full of Glasgow friendship and banter" but lacking the unpleasant side of other Glasgow football supporters.

The crowd saw a good game but East Fife supporters were rather led up the garden path at the end. The first half and most of the second half saw some delightful football from the Glasgow men with crisp passing and running, and they really should have put the game to bed long before John Torbet opened the scoring for them.

Then after more Thistle pressure, East Fife came back into the game, and from a breakaway, Sharkey, who had done little else in the game, surprised Thistle's International goalkeeper Jakie Jackson with a fierce shot.

Hopes were now even being entertained of a shock victory or at least a trip to Glasgow in midweek for a replay when inexplicably James Rarity handled in the box when there seemed no need, and Torbet converted.

It was a disappointment for East Fife, but over the piece Thistle were the better side with even *The Leven Mail* conceding that and using words like "artistic" to describe some of their passing. For financial reasons, however, East Fife could have done with a good Cup run.

January 20 2018

Chris Kane heads for goal against Brora Rangers

January 20 2018

By their very nature, it does not happen very often that East Fife are "giant killed" in the Scottish Cup.

They have themselves done their odd bit of giant killing — one thinks of Motherwell in 1967, for example — but today at Bayview they exited the Scottish Cup to Brora Rangers of the Highland League.

In the previous round, Scotland had been stunned by the men from Dudgeon Park who had travelled all the way down to Stranraer to beat the local side in the last minute, and here they did it again.

There were not a huge amount of Brora supporters at New Bayview, but those who were attracted a little attention with their soft Highland accents and the fact that they had left home at about 7.00 am that morning in order to get here.

Their voices were heard and their red colours were seen to advantage when their team went ahead when Colin Williamson was allowed by a static East Fife defence to head home a corner kick in the 12th minute.

This early reverse did not in itself cause a major panic for there was a long time to go, but after half-time came and went, a little anxiety began to creep in to the sea end of the New Bayview Stand, and a few decent chances were missed. There are some times when the ball simply will not run for you in football, and this seemed to be one of those days.

The last ten minutes saw frantic action in that Brora goalmouth, and more or less at the death Chris Kane missed with a header before referee David Munro ended the tie to the incredulous joy of the Highlanders and the boos and catcalls of the Fife supporters.

January 21 1939

Hopes that East Fife could repeat their Scottish Cup success of last year came to a shuddering halt today as they surprisingly went out to Montrose at Bayview.

It was a remarkable day in Fife football when all five (yes, five!) Fife teams were playing in the Scottish Cup, and all of them were at home! Raith Rovers rather unluckily lost to Rangers 0-1, Burntisland Shipyard scored three goals against Celtic, but conceded eight (!) Dunfermline beat Morton 5-2 and Cowdenbeath drew 3-3 with Partick Thistle.

East Fife, who made £8,000 out of the Scottish Cup last year, exited the tournament with £152 this year. A crowd of 4,800 assembled on a dull but dry and mild day to see the East Fife Scottish Cup hoodoo strike again.

In 1927 they had reached the final, but had then gone out at the first time of asking for the next ten years! Now having won the trophy, they lost to Montrose who absorbed a great deal of East Fife pressure, and then nipped up and scored two goals before half-time through Rodi and Adam.

East Fife then piled on the pressure throughout the second half but one solitary goal from Wilkie was all that they could muster, and when Mr Faultless blew his whistle for full time, East Fife were out of the Scottish Cup.

The whistle was about to be blown in another way on Barcelona in the Spanish Civil War as the Nationalists closed in on the beleaguered city, and in Britain, an armed guard had to be put on Chequers following death threats to Mr and Mrs Chamberlain, not so much from Nazis as from the IRA.

January 22 1927

It is not often that Thornhill in the south-west of Scotland come any place close to Fife, but 2,800 were there to see them take on East Fife in the Scottish Cup at Bayview today.

Originally when the draw was made in December, it was Thornhill v East Fife, but East Fife bought the ground rights from them — a wise decision, as it turned out, for Thornhill's crowds numbered in the hundreds normally and there were two other games being played in the south-west that day, one of them being Queen of the South v Celtic.

The £150 raised at Bayview was more than enough to pay the train fares, and gave every one a little profit.

Thornhill shocked the home supporters by scoring first through Halliday, but East Fife soon equalised through Davie Nairn (the first of his hat-trick) and then just close to the interval, Phil Weir scored to put East Fife ahead, and then Jock Wood converted a penalty kick to make the half time score 3-1.

East Fife then ran amok in the second half with Nairn completing his hat trick, and other goals from Weir, Hope and Wood.

The Bayview crowd ended up willing the outclassed southerners to score a consolation goal, but it never happened, and East Fife ended up with the highest score of the round.

When the evening papers arrived in the shops later that evening, the score line that jumped out at everyone was Forfar Athletic 4 Raith Rovers 2, something that caused scarcely less joy than had been seen at Bayview in the afternoon!

January 23 1971

No-one at the time thought that this was likely to be the start of a marathon which lasted three games.

In fact it looked like a good Scottish Cup tie in that East Fife, going strongly for promotion, would have a chance to pit themselves against some First Division opposition in St Mirren.

A crowd of 7,031 including a fair number of "Buddies" from Paisley turned up to see the game on what was a fairly good day in a generally mild winter. Scottish football was still recovering from the horrendous Ibrox disaster of only three weeks previously, and concern was expressed by quite a few fans at the crushing at one of the gates. Fortunately nothing untoward occurred and the crowd saw a very good game.

East Fife were perhaps just a little on the unlucky side. It was the Fifers who took the lead when a move involving Graham Honeyman and Bertie Miller found that old fox, Pat Quinn, who was able to slip the ball through for Billy McPhee to score.

East Fife finished the first half well on top and might have been further ahead, and this state of affairs continued well into the second half until St Mirren struck back through Hamilton after some good work from Archie Knox.

This was in the 80th minute, and the last 10 minutes saw end to end stuff with goals always possible at either end until the final whistle. The 1-1 draw meant a midweek replay at Love Street.

January 24 1970

Before a slightly disappointing crowd of 6,893 (blamed unconvincingly on industrial action which affected some of the service buses) East Fife won the local derby Scottish Cup tie over Raith Rovers by 3-0.

The weather was dull and uninspiring, symbolic perhaps of the Scottish word "dreich" frequently used in football reports.

Most pundits, however, would have been inclined to blame the poor crowd on the form of both sides (which could be most charitably be described as "indifferent") in their respective Divisions of the Scottish League.

Raith Rovers were struggling to avoid the drop and East Fife had pretentions to join Division One but were doing little to enhance them at the moment!

Today however East Fife were well on top. Andy Waddell put the home side ahead in 10 minutes, and they should have gone further ahead when awarded a penalty just before half time. Doug Soutar took it but his first effort was well saved by goalkeeper Whiteside and eventually cleared after a prolonged scrimmage.

1-0 at half-time represented scant reward for East Fife's superiority, but then in the second half it was all one-way traffic with Jim Finlayson scoring two fine goals, one a good finish from a Miller cross and the other a deft lob over the goalkeeper's head.

East Fife thus ran out 3-0 winners, maintaining the record of never having been beaten by Raith Rovers in the Scottish Cup. Most of the Raith Rovers fans, after a few pathetic attempts at hooliganism, had departed the scene long before the final whistle.

January 24 1970

The East Fife team that beat Raith Rovers 3-0 in 1970

January 25 1947

For what was only East Fife's second Scottish Cup tie since they won the Cup in 1938, (for the Scottish Cup had been in abeyance all through World War II) 9,961 fans came to Bayview to see a local derby against Dunfermline Athletic.

The weather was dull but dry and a great game was anticipated. Long queues formed outside the ground long before the game, and anyone who was five minutes late would have fought his way onto the terracing to be told that East Fife were two goals up!

Not only that, but they had actually scored a third to find it disallowed by referee Mr Dale from Glasgow! Douglas Davidson had scored first, and then Scotland's top goal scorer Henry Morris scored the second.

From then on it was completely one way traffic with Dunfermline's defence doing really rather well to keep East Fife down to 2-0 at half-time. Davie Duncan netted early in the second half, and then there was a flicker of a revival when Ellis pulled one back for the Pars.

Then Henry Morris simply took over and scored another three to make the score 6-1 before Kinnell scored an irrelevant consolation goal more or less on the final whistle.

Dunfermline were a poor side with the only challenge coming from Davie Kinnear, who had played for Rangers before the war. He was however well policed by Willie Laird today.

But the toast of all the Burns Suppers in Levenmouth tonight was not so much the Ayrshire Bard as ... Henry Morris!

January 26 1991

A great view of Bayview for the visit of Dundee United in the Scottish Cup on January 26 1991. The game ended in a draw, but Dundee United won the replay

January 26 1935

Since East Fife had reached the final of the Scottish Cup in 1927, they had fallen at the first hurdle every time (although twice they had managed to take the tie to a replay).

This tradition was melancholically maintained at Bayview today when Clyde came to Bayview and won 2-1 before an impressive crowd of 6,250.

"Kestrel" of *The Leven Advertiser* was of the opinion that it was a poor game and had made up his mind at an early point in the proceedings that he was not today watching either of the Scottish Cup finalists.

Clyde had a slightly stronger Scottish Cup tradition (they had been to the final in 1910 and 1912, losing narrowly to Dundee and Celtic) and of course they were a First Division side.

East Fife's Archie Pratt won the toss and decided to play with the bitter east wind behind them, something that meant they were facing the sun in the first half. The weather was still cold but the hail which had disrupted Clyde's journey to Methil seemed to have abated.

Clyde's strength lay in their shooting and Joe Crozier's goal was peppered with shots, two of which went in, scored by Robertson and Mayes. In both cases Crozier was blamed by his supporters for not doing better, but that was perhaps a little unfair.

In addition, Clyde were a little more streetwise than East Fife in that they knew how to keep the ball on the ground when playing against the wind, and how to move it about when playing with the wind. John Steele managed to pull a goal back for East Fife in the second half, but to no avail because the Clyde defence was compact and efficient.

January 27 1951

Season 1950/51 had been a poor season for East Fife so far.

This was always likely to happen to a provincial side after a few good seasons, especially with the departure of some of their star men. The poor form had been reflected in their lowly League position and a few poor home attendances.

Today however was different. This was Scottish Cup day and the East Fife had drawn Celtic at Bayview. The arrival of the green and whites always did bring a special buzz with it, and supporters' buses had been arriving in town since the early morning.

Today 16,000 crammed into the ground to see a thrilling 2-2 draw in which neither side could claim any great superiority on the hard pitch.

The crowd enjoyed the contest though, with East Fife going ahead after Celtic's goalkeeper John Bonnar flapped at a corner kick and left Bobby Black with the easiest of tasks to score. Than after Jock Weir had equalised for Celtic, Davie Duncan put East Fife ahead just on the stroke of half time.

For a long time in the second half it looked as if East Fife were going to win, but a piece of wizardry from Charlie Tully set up Bobby Collins to give Celtic an equaliser.

In the replay at Celtic Park on the Wednesday, Celtic would win comfortably 4-2 and indeed would go on to win the Scottish Cup that year, but East Fife would also rally to certain extent after this game to end up a respectable 7th from the bottom.

January 28 1967

This day is famous in Scottish football history as the day that Berwick Rangers defeated Glasgow Rangers in what is still looked upon as Scottish football's greatest shock.

East Fife supporters consider that this is a shame because on that same day East Fife also pulled off a giant-killing shock by beating Motherwell 1-0 at Fir Park.

They were denied the media attention that this achievement deserved because of the seismic effect that the Berwick result had on all football, even in England where the BBC announcers were astounded.

The day was reasonably mild for the time of year, and Fir Park saw a crowd of around 8,000, just about their average gate. East Fife were doing reasonably well in the Second Division and had brought along a sizeable support from Fife to see the following teams take the field —

Motherwell: McCloy, Whiteford and R McCallum; Campbell, Martis and W McCallum; Lindsay, Murray, Deans, Hunter and Moffatt. Substitute — Thomson.

East Fife: McGann, Brodie and Soutar; Walker, Gilchrist and McLeish; Miller, Rae, Gardiner, Lawlor and Mitchell. Substitute — Watt.

Motherwell were the better team in the first half but missed quite a few chances — one in particular by Dixie Deans (who would be a great success for Celtic a few years later) almost defying belief — and then in the second half John Gardiner scored for East Fife.

After this, it was a question of holding out, and the full time whistle brought great relief. But who was the future First Minister of Scotland who played in this game?

January 29 1936

After an impressive minute's silence at staunchly royalist Ibrox in memory of the late King George whose funeral had taken place on Monday, East Fife this Wednesday afternoon took on Rangers in the postponed Cup tie.

The game should have been played last Saturday but Ibrox failed a late pitch inspection. The size of the crowd therefore was affected by it being a Wednesday afternoon, less than 20,000, whereas something in the region of 40,000 might have been expected on a Saturday. That was a disappointment to cash-strapped Second Division East Fife.

League form had been reasonable since the turn of the year, and there were also a few signs that Rangers were beginning to struggle (they would lose the Scottish League this year to Celtic) so Dave McLean's men were not without hope.

Indeed *The Courier* says that they won many friends in Glasgow by this performance, but it was still 3-1 for Rangers. "The Captain" in *The Courier* says that Tommy Adams was one of the "trickiest wingers I have seen for a while...centred beautifully and showed precision in most of his moves. A promising lad this".

The star of the game, however, was Alex Venters, a Fife man who had joined Rangers from Cowdenbeath, and it was he who set up Jimmy Smith to score twice before scoring himself.

Joe Cowan scored a consolation goal for East Fife near the end. It was a gallant failure for East Fife, who were still very much in the promotion race from the Second Division.

January 30 1960

East Fife's miserable season continued at the hands of Partick Thistle today at Bayview — a 0-2 defeat and therefore an early exit from the Scottish Cup, when a good Cup run might have helped to ease financial problems.

The pitch was described as a "gluepot" or a "porridge dish" and the bad weather was responsible for a low crowd of 4,000, which contained nevertheless more than a fair sprinkling of brightly bedecked Partick Thistle supporters, a pleasant bunch with all the normal Glasgow banter and good nature.

Partick Thistle had throughout the 1950s lived up to their reputation of being the "old unpredictables" — they had reached three Scottish League Cup finals and lost the three of them (one of them in 1953/54 to East Fife).

In addition they had gone out of the Scottish Cup rather too often to teams of the Second Division. Not today however. Sammy Stewart, normally the most reliable of full backs but now coming towards the end of his career, conceded an own goal early on.

Then as the rain intensified and with referee Mr Phillips of Wishaw clearly debating the possibility of an abandonment because of the state of the pitch, Davie McParland scored another for Partick Thistle, and the game limped on to its finish.

It was a bad day for Fife clubs generally, for although Dunfermline earned a draw, Raith Rovers also went down 0-2 to Glasgow opposition in Queen's Park. The score of the day however was St Mirren 15 Glasgow University 0, something that made one question the wisdom of full time professional players playing against students.

January 31 1923

East Fife v Kilmarnock

January 31 1984

One of the best nights in the history of Bayview was when East Fife defeated Hibs 2-0 in a Scottish Cup replay a few days after having held them to a draw at Easter Road.

It was like the "good old days" of Bayview with a crowd of about 7,000 and the kick-off having to be delayed by referee Williamson to allow everyone the chance to get in.

The downside was that there was rather too much overcrowding in some parts of the ground, and at one point some fans spilled over from the enclosure, although whether that was overcrowding or hooliganism, one could not be sure.

What one could be sure of was that it was a great victory for East Fife, and the first time ever that a Premier Division team (the Premier League had only been in existence since 1975) had been removed from the Scottish Cup by a lower division side.

The goals were scored by Tom McCafferty in 15 minutes from a rebound, and then a late header by Steve Kirk. Even that was scant justice to the home side, for a good penalty claim was refused and several chances were missed.

It was a great triumph for the home side, but once again Scottish Cup misery for Hibs whose inconsistent form was driving their fans crazy. Some of the away fans did not take kindly to this defeat and the police were very happy to usher them on to their buses.

But it was nothing but joy for the East Fife fans whose team had once again attracted national attention and now awaited the arrival of Celtic.

February

Team photo taken Christmas 1960 at Station Park.
Back Row, left to right: Stirrat, Morrison, Allan, Moffat, Young, Bryce. Front, left to right: Tran, Scott

February 1 1964

East Fife 3 Morton 1 was the score line that had all of Scotland talking today, putting Dunfermline's defeat of Celtic and Partick Thistle's win over promotion chasing Kilmarnock in their place.

It was in fact Morton's first League defeat in the Second Division that season, and people were beginning to use words like "invincible" to describe them.

Under Manager Hal Stewart and with a great centre forward called Alan McGraw, they had swept all before them (East Fife had been thumped 6-1 at Cappielow on October 5 1963, for example) and it was only a matter of time, it was felt, before they tied up the Second Division.

They were also the beaten finalists in the Scottish League Cup and only a week ago, they had put up a great performance in the Scottish Cup before losing to Celtic, so the very healthy crowd of 5,000 contained quite a few from the west of Scotland with blue and white scarves.

There were also a great deal of locals who wanted to see this team which had set Scottish football alight this season.

Opening with the wind behind them as they attacked the Aberhill end of the ground, Morton scored first with a spectacular 30 yard shot from Campbell which deceived Donnelly and entered the net after taking a late dip.

But East Fife fought hard and Ian Stewart scored in a goalmouth scramble about the half hour mark. The wind seemed to strengthen in the second half and East Fife took full advantage.

George Dewar's goal triggered off a pitch invasion of misguided youths, and then with Morton visibly tiring, Ian Stewart scored a third to give East Fife a famous victory.

February 2 2019

Today several hundreds of East Fife supporters had a day in Dublin.

The Guinness was good, no doubt, and Dublin is a lovely city with loads of tourist attractions like Kilmainham Gaol, Glasnevin Cemetery and O'Connell Street itself, but it was not exactly what East Fife supporters or the team itself necessarily had in mind.

They had gone to the Emerald Isle to see their team play in the Scottish League Challenge Cup against Bohemian, commonly known as "the Boh" or "the Gypsies" and who play at Dalymount Park which was once the home of the Irish national team.

It had seemed not a bad idea either when the Scottish League invited Welsh and Irish teams to take part in the League Challenge Cup. The problem was that when the game was meant to be played in the autumn, Bohemian were in their close season, and February 2 was the earliest possible date that the game could be played.

The other problem was that the day was beautiful but frosty, and there was no undersoil heating or artificial surface at Dalymount Park. The referee thought that the pitch was unplayable at 1.30 pm but delayed a final decision until just before 3.00 pm.

Thus it came about that seven minutes before the start, the game was called off to everyone's intense disappointment. Following this fiasco, Bohemian announced a day later that they were withdrawing from the tournament, as they could not arrange another date.

East Fife therefore were now in the semi-final, something that must have been a great consolation to their fans as they disgorged from their aeroplanes nursing massive hangovers and wearing these silly Leprechaun hats that seem to be *de rigeur* when shopping in Dublin.

February 2 2019

Dalymount Park, Dublin and the game is off!

February 3 1906

Scott's Park, Kirkcaldy, home of Kirkcaldy United, saw a disappointing performance from East Fife in today's Northern League game.

The narrowness of the defeat (3-2 for the Kirkcaldy men) was a little deceptive for two reasons: both East Fife's goals came late in the game, and goalkeeper Bernard was singled out as having an excellent game — often an indication that the rest of the team did not play very well at all!

The weather was wintry with a north-westerly breeze bringing snow showers, but fortunately not enough of them to imperil the game.

Indeed it was only when East Fife had the benefit of the wind that they came into the game, but before then, they enraged the crowd with rough tactics particularly when they were 0-3 down.

But then Horne scored with 25 minutes to go to reduce the leeway, and close to the end, Dewar scored another.

Kirkcaldy United however held out and left the field to a boisterous reception from their fans, while East Fife were booed by some "hotheads". This was a blow for East Fife who had been higher up the Northern League than Kirkcaldy United.

Meanwhile on the broader front, it was now clear that there was going to be a huge Liberal majority in the House of Commons in the General Election which in 1906 was held over a period of weeks.

East Fifeshire had re-elected Herbert Asquith, and Henry Dalziel had been returned in Kirkcaldy. Both of these gentlemen were Liberals, and Asquith could expect Cabinet office.

There was therefore a feeling of optimism in the air that something was going to be done about the appalling poverty that abounded all over Fife.

February 4 1963

It was the middle of the prolonged frost of 1963.

Probably 1947 was worse in terms of snowfall, and 2018's "beast from the East" will be a collector's item as well, but 1963 saw very little football played in Scotland between mid-January and early March.

There were however a few oases of football, and on Monday February 4, three Scottish Cup ties were able to go ahead.

Dundee beat Montrose, Partick Thistle beat Morton — and East Fife drew with First Division Third Lanark at Bayview.

Each of the three games saw newspaper reporters raising eyebrows about the wisdom of playing football on such tricky and even dangerous conditions, but East Fife and Third Lanark deserved praise for entertaining about 1,000 frozen fans. with intermittent snow showers falling in the second half. *The Glasgow Herald* says there was an inch of "powdery snow" which gave the players enough of a foothold to play the game.

Third Lanark were already, in 1963, struggling to survive in the now harsh economic climate of a depopulated Glasgow, hampered by incompetent and perhaps even corrupt stewardship.

Nevertheless, they still had some good players like goalkeeper Jocky Robertson and centre forward Matt Gray. After an even first half, they went ahead through Joe McInnes, but East Fife stuck to their task and earned a late equaliser through Ian Stewart.

Sadly, a month later when the replay could be played, Third Lanark won at Cathkin. East Fife would not meet Third Lanark very often in the future, for Thirds were destined to fold in 1967.

February 5 1927

It was a big day in Methil today.

Aberdeen were in town for the Scottish Cup tie. In those days, Aberdeen wore black and gold, and the custom was for the home team to change strips, on the grounds perhaps that they were likely to have more spare strips handy.

From early in the morning, Aberdeen supporters arrived in town, all mingling happily with the locals in the pubs and shops and speaking in that lovely sing-song accent so characteristic of the North East.

Both teams had been founded in 1903, Aberdeen an amalgamation of three smaller teams, but as yet Aberdeen were under-performers in the Scottish League and Cup, something that was rather surprising for a city of its size.

They tended to do well at Pittodrie, but less so away from home. Today a crowd of 9,000 was at Bayview, the third largest attendance in Scotland below only Rangers v St Mirren and Kilmarnock v Dundee. The ground had problems coping with such a large attendance; the police had to move some of the crowd to less heavily populated parts of the ground.

But everyone was well behaved, and although the weather was dull, they saw a good game. Jock Wood scored first for the Fifers, putting the ball past the goalkeeper with the unlikely name of McSevich, but Willie Wood had a terrible miss after Lawson had equalised for the Dons.

The game finished 1-1, which everyone tended to agree was a fair result, but East Fife were ruing their missed chances. So now it was Pittodrie on Wednesday afternoon. Somehow it was hard to be optimistic about winning there, but you never know!

February 6 2016

East Fife's drive for the Second Division Championship was stalled today at Links Park, Montrose when a 2-0 lead was surrendered more or less in the last minute.

This was distressing for the large East Fife support in the 581 crowd, for Elgin City also drew today and East Fife might have gone top of the table had they been able to hold out.

Arguably, more men should have been pushed forward when they were 2-0 up so that they could kill the game, but in any case a draw was still a reasonable result at an away ground.

It was the old "stick or twist" argument. Should one settle for 2-0, or should one go for more? The supporters certainly felt that they should have gone for more.

The first goal came from a magnificent shot by Kyle Wilkie, and that was how it stayed until half time. Then Jason Kerr's header extended the lead, and things looked quite secure for Gary Naysmith and his men before slackness in defence allowed Gary Fraser to pull one back for Montrose.

Then, heartbreakingly in the last minute, Terry Masson scored with a fierce shot. A statistical peculiarity of today was that all four Second Division games played (Annan Athletic's game with Clyde was postponed because Annan were playing in the Scottish Cup) ended in draws, and thus there was no real change to the League table.

Elgin City thus remained two points ahead and a game in hand, but there was a lot of football remaining to be played. But it was still an annoying, frustrating day for the Fifers.

February 6 2016

Kyle Wilkie scores against Montrose

February 7 1953

It was a bad day for Fife today as the three remaining Fife teams exited the Scottish Cup.

Dunfermline were already out, Raith Rovers at home lost to Hearts, Cowdenbeath flopped against Morton, and most disappointing of all, East Fife, surprisingly went out 0-3 to Airdrie at Broomfield.

It was a result that one would not have predicted from recent form (although with the normal January postponements, "recent form" meant very little) or League positions.

Broomfield was a quaint little ground, down in a hollow, with a cricket-style pavilion behind one of the goals. They had had a proud history, winning the Scottish Cup in 1924 when they had great players like Hughie Gallacher and Bob McPhail.

At the moment, they had one great player in Ian McMillan, a crafty inside forward who would later be transferred to Rangers and would earn the nickname "the wee Prime Minister", at the time when the real Prime Minister was Harold McMillan.

Today, he was largely responsible for East Fife's demise, having a part in the three first-half goals scored, one by Willie Brown and two by Hugh Baird.

East Fife simply never got going. Davie Duncan was out, but Charlie Fleming and Jimmy Bonthrone, East Fife's two potential match winners had chances but the Airdrie defence was always on top.

This result was a particular disappointment to the large contingent of East Fife supporters who had travelled through, for East Fife considered themselves, and were considered by Scottish football at large, a good Cup team.

But it was back to League business. East Fife were destined to finish third, equalling last season's achievement while Airdrie resumed their struggle against relegation.

February 8 1956

East Fife made history tonight by playing the first ever floodlit Scottish Cup match at Bayview.

The floodlights had been in position for some years, but had only been used for friendlies, and official permission to use them in competitions had not been forthcoming.

However, the Scottish Cup tie against Stenhousemuir on the Saturday having been postponed because of bad weather, East Fife applied on Monday for permission to play the game under floodlights. Stenhousemuir, who had been one of the pioneers of floodlit football, had no objections.

Permission was granted; on the same night, Hibs played Raith Rovers at Easter Road under floodlights, although East Fife made sure that they started earlier so that they could claim to be the first!

However at full time, they may have had second thoughts, for they lost embarrassingly 1-3 to Stenhousemuir, a Second Division club, for whom Peter Stewart, who used to play for Falkirk, scored a hat-trick.

The crowd was given as around the 6,000 mark, more than might have been there in the afternoon, but still a little disappointing for such an auspicious occasion.

Journalists however agreed that this was the beginning of something, and that the lights were good, although there were those who objected on the grounds that they dazzled the goalkeeper, made the ball swing, created shadows etc. And of course many East Fife supporters, their team having lost, joined in the moaning!

February 9 1927

Those who had written East Fife off after Saturday, saying that the First Division club on its own ground and in front of its own spectators would be too much, were made to eat their words today.

The Fifers travelled to Aberdeen and in front of a crowd of 10,539 (large for a Wednesday afternoon) beat the home side 2-1, winning the plaudits of *The Courier* but reducing *The Aberdeen Press and Journal* to paroxysms of rage. Their mood reflected the Aberdeen support who wondered if they were ever likely to see their favourites in a Scottish Cup final.

East Fife were compelled to play a Junior called Brown from Wishaw Juniors at centre half and he was outstanding, but the man of the match was once again Jock Wood, who scored the first goal, and led the forward line outstandingly well, spraying passes to both wings in a first half where the home side were described as being "all at sea".

Phil Weir scored brilliantly early in the second half but then late in the game, the full-time side began to rally. Bruce scored for the Dons in the aftermath of a free kick, but goalkeeper Jock Gilfillan held out well, and the small travelling support cheered the final whistle.

As is often the way with Aberdeen supporters, they turned on their team long before the final whistle, but East Fife had now won themselves a home derby game in the next round against Dunfermline Athletic. It was without a great deal of doubt, East Fife's best result of their history so far.

February 10 1965

Aberdeen were generally looked upon as the great under-achievers of Scottish football in the 1960s, and so it turned out here as well when they came to Bayview and lost 0-1 in the replay of the First Round of the Scottish Cup before a large crowd given as 8,001.

They thus continued their melancholy tradition of losing to Second Division teams for the third successive season — Raith Rovers in 1963, Ayr United in 1964 and now East Fife in 1965 this damp Wednesday night.

Truth to tell, they were well beaten — indeed they had been booed off the park by their own supporters at Pittodrie on the Saturday, and the general opinion was that East Fife were unlucky on Saturday.

Tonight, East Fife were worth more than their solitary George Dewar goal, and one often wondered why they defended so deeply when Aberdeen had very little in the way of creativity, with their cult hero Ernie Winchester and Danish import Ole Mortensen very disappointing. Having been tanked 8-0 by Celtic recently as well as this disaster, it was difficult to see where Aberdeen were going from here, with manager Tommy Pearson now under so much pressure.

For East Fife, it was a great triumph and Willie Waddell's Kilmarnock were now expected in the next round. Manager Jimmy Bonthrone expressed himself as very pleased with an understatement to the effect that it was "a good night's work!"

League form had been a little disappointing so far, and an improvement was now expected.

February 10 1965

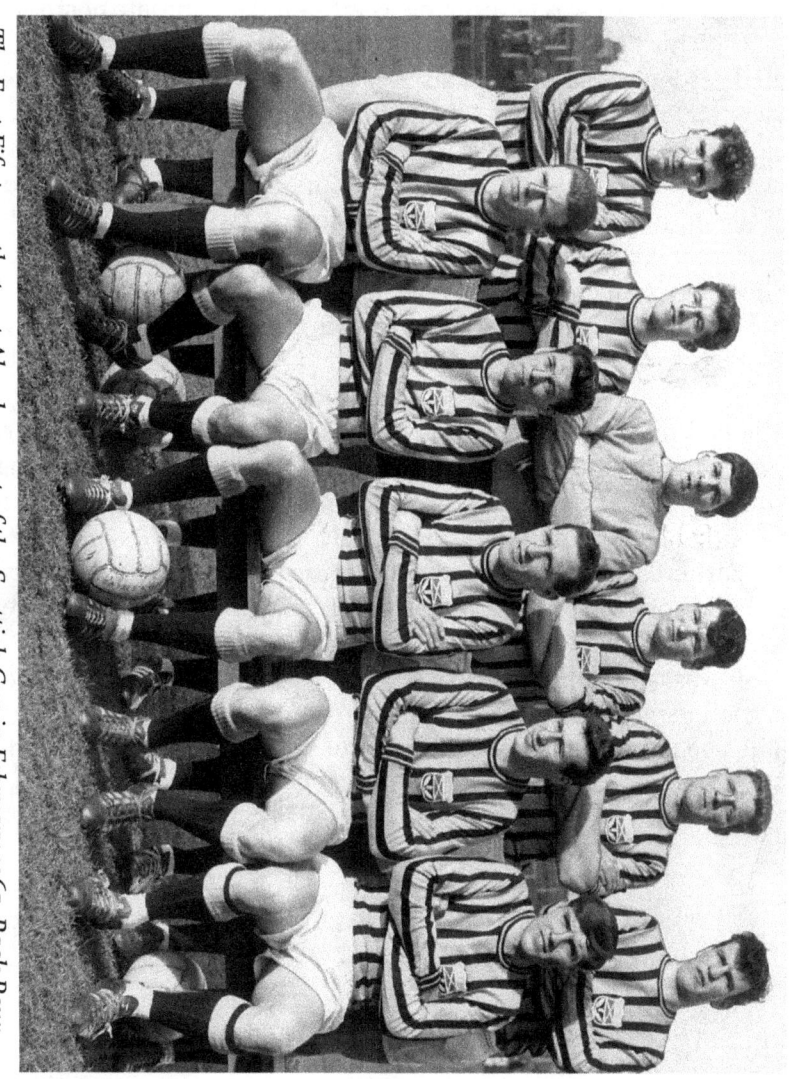

The East Fife team that put Aberdeen out of the Scottish Cup in February 1965. Back Row: Stirrat, Smith, Hamilton, Aitken, Walker, Donnelly; Front Row: Rodger, Dewar, Young, Stewart, Ross

February 11 1950

East Fife won a tremendous Cup tie at a packed Brockville, containing a crowd of about 13,000 fans, to defeat Falkirk 3-2.

The weather was far from pleasant — indeed the late postponement of the Third Lanark v Celtic match at Cathkin led to unpleasant scenes of disorder in Glasgow — and East Fife suffered a blow before the game when "Dod" Aitken had to call off with flu.

The bus had stopped at Crossgates to pick him up; then he said he was not well, and Scot Symon sent him home to bed, and had to make a last minute re-arrangement to the team.

Partly because of this, East Fife, the League Cup holders, struggled; most newspapers were of the opinion that Falkirk were the better team, until an unfortunate goalkeeping error by Bob Carrie gave East Fife what turned out to be the winner.

A low cross from Davie Duncan took a bobble on the hard ground, the ball hit Carrie's arm and the ball rebounded to Henry Morris for the easiest of tap-ins. This came immediately after Falkirk equalised, and even after that, the East Fife defence, minus the powerful presence of Aitken, had to hold out desperately.

Earlier East Fife's two goals had come from a header by Morris, and a hard shot from Charlie Fleming, now fast developing and well worthy of the nickname "Cannonball".

It was generally agreed that the young Falkirk goalkeeper had had a good game apart from his fatal error, and it was noticeable that East Fife's goalkeeper John Niven went out of his way to console him at the end.

February 12 1910

This was East Fife's biggest day in their history to date. The great Queen's Park were drawn to come to Bayview in the Scottish Cup.

Queen's Park had won the Scottish Cup ten times in their history. Although in recent years they had lost out to professional teams, they themselves refused to give up their amateur status. Their apparent contempt for money however did not prevent them from offering East Fife £150 to play the game at their magnificent Hampden Park.

They had more success in this respect with Kirkcaldy United in a previous round, but East Fife laudably turned the money down; the game went ahead at Bayview which had undergone a few hurried improvements for the arrival of the distinguished middle class men from Glasgow.

In spite of the weather not being as hospitable as it might have been, the game attracted a huge crowd to Bayview and East Fife were twice ahead in the game with goals from Patrick Dougan, a man, clearly, of Irish descent but Queen's Park had R S McColl (the famous "Toffee Bob" whose name is still seen on High Streets for his confectionery business) on board and eventually won 3-2.

It was generally agreed that Queen's Park were the better side, but East Fife emerged from the game with a great deal of glory, and of course a great deal of money!

The Queen's Park supporters, including a few ladies wearing fur coats, who travelled with the team were obviously in Methil for the first time in their sheltered, middle class lives, and the day was a bit of an educational experience for them, one feels.

February 13 1937

Telford Street, Inverness was the unusual destination of East Fife for their Scottish Cup tie against Inverness Caledonian, a Highland League team.

(In the future Inverness Caledonian and Inverness Thistle would merge to become the modern team now known as Inverness Caledonian Thistle, but that would not happen until 1994).

When the draw was announced, the East Fife Directors laid on a special train to take supporters, leaving Leven at 8.30 am in the morning. This excellent idea was somewhat spoiled when some supporters turned up and discovered that their fare was to be 11 shillings and sixpence (about 58 pence in modern money) whereas local rumour had it that it would be seven shillings and sixpence (about 37 pence).

In fact the first 120 to book would go at the cheaper rate, but this had not been made clear, and a certain amount of friction developed between the privileged and the less so, with some of those who were being obliged to pay the full fare refusing to join the train and going home.

The weather was not great, but the trip to the Highlands (for many people, their first ever trip there) was made complete by a very impressive 6-1 defeat over the Invernesians.

Eddie McLeod scored a hat-trick and the other goals were scored by Tommy Adams, Joe Cowan and Bobby Scott with newspapers all praising the heroics of Mackenzie in the Inverness goal, an indirect way of saying that the 6-1 score line should have been a great deal more.

February 14 1953

This may have been St Valentine's Day, but East Fife were in no mood for romance; they turned on a splendid performance to beat Aberdeen at Bayview today.

Aberdeen were a team which continually infuriated their supporters. They had fine players like George Hamilton and Jackie Hather, not to mention the man of whom great things were expected, Paddy Buckley, but they never seemed capable of getting together any consistency.

Yet they were always a well-supported team, and their fans arrived early today in Methil to see a ground which had improved beyond all measure in the last 24 hours thanks to a reasonably quick thaw after some frost and snow.

Today the sun was out, and it was a very pleasant day for football particularly if you were an East Fife supporter, for they went in at half-time with the cheers of their supporters ringing in their ears and leading Aberdeen 3-0.

Charlie Fleming had put East Fife ahead slamming a ball through a sea of players to open the scoring, and then he had been responsible for Andy Matthew putting East Fife 2-0 up before Jimmy Bonthrone and Jackie Stewart teamed up to pass the ball to Matthew for a third.

The shell-shocked Dons tried to regroup in the second half, but it was East Fife who went further ahead through Ian Gardiner before Dons at last got a goal through Harry Yorston.

This result proved, if there was ever the slightest doubt, that East Fife were genuine challengers for the League flag. Rivals Hibs won today against Clyde but Rangers were held to a draw by Dundee.

February 15 1947

Almost incredibly, East Fife managed to get Bayview playable for today's Scottish Cup tie against East Stirlingshire.

It was the only Scottish Cup tie played that day, and one of only a handful played in all Scotland, and it was all the more remarkable when it was only the day before the game that Largoward was "relieved" after having been cut off for days!

Parts of Fife and Angus were still snowbound, and the roads of the Highlands were more or less totally impassable. East Fife employed bulldozers to clear the pitch, but they were damaging the pitch so that had to stop, and then a "barrow and shovel" brigade of supporters, players and even Directors got to work.

They got their reward when East Fife won the game 5-1 on what was an almost perfect pitch. They were also rewarded by a reasonable crowd and a certain amount of media attention to record the three goals scored by Davie Duncan, the one by Henry Morris, the other by a lesser known player called Smeaton. But it might have been a different matter if John Niven had not saved an early shot from McCreary.

Immediately after the game, East Fife were able to announce that they were making their next Scottish Cup game against Queen's Park all-ticket, and that they were (optimistically) expecting a 15,000 crowd.

But considerable concern was being expressed about the now huge backlog of fixtures which gave no sign of being played off in the near future, given that there was no great thaw.

February 16 1957

Shearer Borthwick, writer in the *Evening Times*, has an unusual complaint about this 0-0 draw between East Fife and Kilmarnock at Methil in the Scottish Cup today.

The sun was too strong! The sun apparently shone in loads of players' eyes and made them make errors. One can take it that Mr Borthwick would have been no advocate of summer football, then, but the crowd of over 10,000 had few complaints either about the weather or the standard of football.

The game, although goalless, provided excellent entertainment, although shooting was wayward with fingers pointed at Jimmy Bonthrone and Angus Plumb. The closest we came to a goal was one scored by Frank Beattie of Kilmarnock but correctly ruled out by referee Willie Brittle of Glasgow for being offside.

An interesting point about the line-up of this game was that both teams had two men called Stewart, Sammy and Jackie for East Fife and Jimmy and Rab for Kilmarnock. But no-one could provide a goal.

There were two goals in the replay at Rugby Park the following midweek, but sadly they were both for Kilmarnock *en route* to reaching the final this year.

Sadly this 0-0 draw, good game though it was, was overshadowed by two high scoring games on the same day. One was Raith Rovers' 7-0 tanking of Dundee United, and the other was the Old Firm game at Celtic Park which ended up 4-4.

In any case, the Scottish Cup came as a welcome relief for East Fife who were now embroiled in a dogfight to avoid relegation.

February 17 1973

This was one of the best games seen at Bayview for many years.

Celtic came in search of two points as they pursued their 8th League championship in a row on a day when most games in Central Scotland fell victim to a heavy fall of snow.

This was a truly remarkable game and the fact that Celtic managed to miss three penalties taken by three separate players must be some sort of a record.

First Bobby Murdoch "blootered" (as Ian Archer in *The Glasgow Herald* put it) the ball over the bar.

But a retake was ordered and this time Harry Hood had a go but Ernie McGarr got a foot to it.

Then later in the game, Kenny Dalglish had his penalty saved by McGarr as well.

While all this was going on, there were some goals as well — Dixie Deans scored first, then in the second half East Fife came back with a penalty scored by Billy McPhee and then a fine goal by Walter Borthwick.

Given the missed penalties, it looked as if East Fife were going to gain a surprise and by no means undeserved victory, but then virtually in the last minute, Deans scored with a glancing header from a Tommy Callaghan corner. The crowd of 11,000 enjoyed this game, but Manager Pat Quinn stated to the Press that it was the kind of game that could take "years off a Manager's life".

Jock Stein of Celtic, who had himself had a heart scare a few weeks ago sagely nodded his agreement.

February 17 1973

Walter Borthwick scores for East Fife v Celtic on February 17 1973

February 17 1973

Kenny Dalglish of Celtic tries to beat Ernie McGarr

The Bayview

18

Printed & Published by Artigraf Printing Company, Buckhaven. Price 5p.

"50 up" Billy McPhee scores his 50th goal since joining East Fife but this was not enough to keep the Fifers in the cup when they went 4 — 1 down to Celtic.

SCOTTISH LEAGUE
FIRST DIVISION

SATURDAY, FEBRUARY, 17th 1973.

Kick-off: 3 p.m.

EAST FIFE 2

versus

CELTIC 2

EAST FIFE FOOTBALL CLUB OFFICIAL PROGRAMME

February 17 2008

Chris Duggan at Somerset Park, Ayr. Observe the old fashioned terracings.

February 18 1984

This Scottish Cup tie against Celtic, much looked forward to and anticipated, turned out to be a huge anti-climax for the East Fife players and supporters.

Having defeated Hibs in the previous round, excitement "of the kind not experienced over the past 30 years" prevailed all over Levenmouth and the 10,000 tickets sold quickly.

It was also reported that counterfeit tickets were in circulation, and there was certainly a black market with tickets being offered for £30 (a ridiculous sum in 1984). Possibly, one felt, a few more could have been squeezed in, but the East Fife directors deserve credit for not moving the match to a larger stadium like East End Park or Dens Park, for example.

The opponents were Celtic, a club which always generates its own excitement, and although Davie Hay's side were good, they were always vulnerable in defence. Not today however. East Fife held them for the first 25 minutes, but then Murdo MacLeod scored for Celtic.

Even then, East Fife were not entirely out of it, but crucially it was Celtic who got the vital goal just after the restart through Frank McGarvey, and from there on Celtic did not relax their grip, scoring another four goals in the last 20 minutes.

It was reported that Celtic themselves and a few other clubs in both Scotland and England were interested in Gordon Durie. Sadly, Gordon did not do himself any great favours that day.

But oh, things could have been a great deal better for East Fife if it had been they who scored the first goal. They looked sharp in the opening exchanges, and there was a certain comfort to be got from the receipts generated by a large crowd.

February 19 1921

Great interest was engendered in the locality by the appearance of Celtic in the Scottish Cup for this first ever meeting of the clubs.

Ground improvements were carried out in anticipation of this great moment, and 11,000 attended with a large contingent of the "Glasgow Irish" present with their banners and bugles.

From early in the morning, the charabancs had rolled in from the west, and loads more came by train to Kirkcaldy, then tram to Methil. They were loud and noisy, singing their songs about Sinn Fein (the Irish War of Independence was going on at that time) and the landlords of the local hostelries did a good trade.

East Fife were the winners of the Scottish Qualifying Cup and did well against their distinguished visitors, and it was only in the latter stages of the game that Celtic took over, scoring twice through Tommy McInally and once through Patsy Gallacher as distinct from East Fife's solitary counter, a penalty from John McTavish.

Willie Maley, the Manager of Celtic and a key person in the administration of the Scottish League was very impressed by East Fife, and implied that he would not be averse to East Fife playing in the Scottish League sometime in the future.

The crowd were cheerful and friendly but there was a tragic aftermath when a young Celtic supporter from Bonhill in Dunbartonshire was killed when his charabanc hit a tram near the Wemyss Cemetery a few hours after the match. Two others were badly injured.

February 20 1909

Union Park, Berwick was the venue for the first ever game between Berwick Rangers and East Fife.

This was in the Scottish Consolation Cup, the trophy for those teams who had been knocked out of the Scottish Qualifying Cup at an early stage.

There was a certain amount of excitement about this trip which, although distant, was nevertheless practicable given the existence of the railway line; of course, it also offered the opportunity to some players and supporters to go to England for the first time.

Those who made the trip saw a good game, a 2-2 draw on a bright sunny spring like day. The "Magpies" (as Berwick were called) scored first but then Roberts equalised for East Fife, although the writer in *The Berwick Advertiser* was convinced that he was offside.

Even more controversy followed East Fife's second equaliser, for Beveridge's shot seemed to hit the post and then bounce out, but the referee, Mr Nisbit of Edinburgh, was of the persuasion that it hit the stanchion holding the net before it bounced out.

Thus, we came to half-time and there was no further scoring in the second half, although both teams missed chances, and a trip to Methil for the return trip was now necessary.

The writer in *The Berwick Advertiser*, although clearly a lover of his team, was nevertheless highly critical of some Berwick supporters who are "the most ignorant yokels breathing" and "a set of cockle-toed [sic] empty headed nonentities who could not kick a balloon, let alone a football"; a young Berwick player with the unfortunate name of Ersewell was the victim of so many of their vacuous diatribes.

February 21 1948

A crowd of 8,000 paid £480 to see today's Scottish Cup tie at Boghead, Dumbarton.

East Fife, already holders of the Scottish League Cup this season, were now trying to win the Scottish Cup, as they had done ten years ago.

They were top of Division "B". Dumbarton were some distance beneath them but their ground was not called "fatal Boghead" for nothing; they had a fine Scottish Cup tradition which included them having won it in 1883.

Today the Sons of the Rock gave East Fife as good as they got and the Fifers were struggling, with a replay at Bayview on Wednesday afternoon looking a distinct possibility until one moment of magic won the tie for East Fife in the 79th minute.

A Davie Duncan cross was headed out by a tired defender who did not quite put the ball where he wanted to, and Jackie Davidson hit the ball sweetly on the volley. There followed a period of pressure from the now desperate Dumbarton team, but East Fife held out to clinch for themselves a place in the quarter-finals.

Goalkeeper John Niven had a great game but it was the wing halves, Jim Philp and "Dod" Aitken who were the stars of the show, while Tommy Adams, although marked very heavily all game, looked as if he could get more goals for the team.

But 1-0 it remained, and East Fife were joined in the next round by Airdrie, Celtic, Hibs, Montrose, Morton, Rangers and St Mirren. Rather unusually, not a single game was drawn, so there would be no replays.

February 22 1947

Today's 3-1 win over Queen's Park in the Scottish Cup before a crowd of about 8,000 was far more impressive than it sounded.

Indeed, *The Sunday Post* seems convinced that it would have been an awful lot more if it had not been for the brilliance of Queen's Park's young goalkeeper Ronny [sic] Simpson.

"High balls and low balls were all alike to him. His sure handling and cat-like agility stamped him as a 'keeper in the first flight".

Yes indeed, there seemed to be a great future for that boy, although he was still better known in 1947 as the son of Jimmy Simpson, once of Rangers.

But it was East Fife who really sparkled that day with their half back line of Philp, Findlay and Aitken singled out, and of course everyone marvelled at the wizardry of Tommy Adams.

All the goals came in the first half — Davie Duncan scoring twice (one a penalty) and Tommy Adams for East Fife and for Queen's Park a man called A Aitken (Queen's Park players were so designated to indicate their amateur status).

The second half was one-way traffic but East Fife were unable to add to their score past young Simpson. Remarkably in the context of the 1947 winter, seven of the Scottish Cup games went ahead, but this weekend was only a temporary lull and more snow was on the way.

Some teams had not played for weeks but it was a great day for East Fife and news of the draw for the quarter finals was now eagerly awaited.

February 23 1974

Another bad day for East Fife.

Today they travelled to fellow strugglers Morton at Cappielow and lost to the only goal of the game, scored late by Rankin.

"East Fife's eight man defensive set up was no advert for football" said the *Evening Times;* probably the negative tactics got their due reward.

Indeed had it not been for some inspired goalkeeping from Ernie McGarr, East Fife would have received a larger beating. This result represented another turn of the screw in the grim relegation battle and it was all the more painful, for they had earned a point last week against Dumbarton at Boghead.

Most East Fife supporters, however, realised that things were not great, and a return to the Second Division looked likely. What however made things a little better was the knowledge that the Leagues were going to be redrawn for season 1975/76. Although no-one could say that East Fife were likely to end up in the Premier Division, a place in the middle division looked likely, and indeed the natural habitat for teams like East Fife.

East Fife and relegation however were not the only topics of conversation that weekend for there was a General Election in the offing next Thursday, and this one was an important one for it had been called by Conservative Prime Minister Edward Heath in response to the miners' strike.

A three day week had been in operation for large sections of industry and some football matches were consequently played on Sundays. These were interesting and exciting times!

February 24 1965

East Fife went out of Scottish Cup with their heads held high this Wednesday night at Rugby Park, Kilmarnock.

They were defeated 3-0 by the team who would that year become Scottish League Champions, but the game was a great deal closer than that.

The first game at Methil had been a 0-0 draw, and clearly a large number of East Fife supporters believed that they could bring off a major shock this Wednesday night, for they were very vocal in the crowd — and indeed welcomed by the Kilmarnock Directors who, as ever, struggled to persuade their own supporters to come to Rugby Park.

Things looked bad when Jackie McInally scored for Killie in the first three minutes, but after that, East Fife settled, and as half-time came and the second half began, the anxiety of the Kilmarnock supporters was tangible.

Frank Donnelly and Jake Young were superb for the Fifers, and Killie had every cause to be worried, for they kept reminding each other that Jimmy Bonthrone's men had defeated Aberdeen in the previous round.

But crucially East Fife failed to score, and full time training is always likely to make a difference in such circumstances, and when McInally scored again for Kilmarnock in the 75th minute, the show was effectively over.

Ronnie Hamilton scored again before the end, but East Fife were given a great receptions from their own fans and a grudging nod of approval or two from the inhabitants of Season Ticket section of Killie's stand.

After the game, Willie Waddell, Kilmarnock's Manager wondered why East Fife were not in the First Division, for they were clearly better than some of the teams already there.

February 25 1922

East Fife's form in their first season in the Scottish League Division Two had been patchy and inconsistent, but today they gave themselves and their supporters a certain amount of happiness by beating local rivals Cowdenbeath 2-0 at Bayview.

Cowdenbeath had had a far better season than East Fife and indeed were challenging for the Second Division Championship. (They would lose out, however, to Alloa).

Today however, East Fife were undeniably the better team but the Cowdenbeath supporters (a considerable amount of them had travelled through from West Fife) argued that it all hinged on a bad injury to their goalkeeper Falconer just before half-time, necessitating the introduction of Birrell as goalkeeper and Cowdenbeath playing with 10 men. (To modern eyes, it seems inconceivable that this was simply part of the game until substitutes were allowed in 1966!)

By this time however East Fife were 1-0 up, the goal coming from the ever popular Philip Weir, and then in the second half, Jimmy Neish added a second after some fine work from Dom Currie.

Newspaper opinion sympathised with Cowdenbeath for the loss of their goalkeeper, but also agreed that East Fife were so far ahead that they would have won anyway.

The news today however was dominated by the Scottish Cup ties in which Hamilton Academical had shocked Celtic at Parkhead, and Dundee had gone down to Aberdeen at Pittodrie.

Meanwhile the country was still struggling to cope with economic problems in the aftermath of the Great War, and Lloyd George's Coalition Government was beginning to crumble, rocked by repeated rumours of financial scandals.

February 26 1966

Today's game at Bayview against Stranraer did not on the surface seem to have all that much going for it.

East Fife's 2-1 victory made them 12th in the 19 team League and pushed Stranraer down to 13th. It was the sort of fixture than made people ask the question about how long the Second Division could actually last in its current form.

However, there were still almost 1,000 at Bayview to see what turned out to be a good second half after a dull goalless 0-0 first half. Watt and Rae scored for East Fife and Hanlon for Stranraer, something that engendered at least a little excitement.

East Fife had been suspected by their fans of still being in shellshock after their 9-1 hammering from First Division Dundee at Dens Park on February 9 in the Scottish Cup, and of course the bad weather had prevented any other games since.

But at least this was some sort of a victory, although there was little really for East Fife to get excited about in the long "fizzle out" until the end of the season.

The weather had caused a large number of problems with the tie between Ross County (then in the Highland League) and Rangers, but there were now signs that the game could be played off in midweek.

The big topic of conversation at the moment was when Harold Wilson with his small Labour majority was going to call a General Election. Hints had been dropped all week, and a spring General Election seemed a certainty. March 31 would indeed be the date.

February 27 1937

Great was the excitement prevailing in Levenmouth in the fortnight leading up to this game against Celtic in the Scottish Cup.

The visit of the green and whites always did something to build up the atmosphere, but on this case East Fife were on a high as well. League form had been good, and the club were enjoying a good run in the Scottish Cup having beaten Forfar and Inverness Caledonian.

Celtic were of course the League winners the previous year and the appearance of the great Jimmy McGrory could always be guaranteed to add an extra couple of thousand to the gate any way, such was his goal scoring prowess.

Sadly, this game was accompanied by dreadful weather, which saw a crowd of only 12,000 when more might have been expected. In any case, the game was lucky to survive; couple of the other Scottish Cup ties scheduled that day were a lot less lucky in the wind and the snow.

As often happens, Methil was a little more sheltered from the blast than other parts of the United Kingdom; even so Celtic, having won the toss, elected to play towards the Aberhill end of the ground to take maximum advantage of the wind.

In fact, they did not really need any other help for in the first quarter of an hour, they had scored twice through McGrory taking advantage of "crisp attacking play". Joe Cowan came close for East Fife, but that was all that they had to offer.

In the second half, Celtic gave an object lesson in how to play against the wind — namely keep the ball on the ground and short passes to each other and remained in total control, even adding another goal from Willie Buchan.

I wonder how many of the crowd could have guessed however that the teams they were watching were destined to be the next two winners of the Scottish Cup?

February 28 1914

The Fife Free Press is far from enthusiastic about this game played on a dull but fair day at Scott's Park, Pathhead, Kirkcaldy.

"Throughout the game the football played never rose much above the average and occasionally did not even reach that" was the scathing verdict of the scribe.

The fair-sized crowd saw East Fife beat Kirkcaldy United to consolidate their place as third in the Central League over a Kirkcaldy United side who were already beginning to struggle, having long ago lost out in the battle for local supremacy against Raith Rovers.

The two best men on the field seem to have been the goalkeepers — Dorward of Kirkcaldy and Bernard of East Fife. East Fife kicking "down the incline" in the first half scored first through Thorburn, after Dorward had defied the Bayview men for some time. Then East Fife won a penalty, and it was duly taken by goalkeeper John Bernard (possibly not as unusual a phenomenon then as it would be now) and East Fife turned round 2-0 up.

It was a different game in the second half, however, although Kirkcaldy scored only the one goal, with Bernard up to anything that the Kirkcaldy men could throw at them. *The Fife Free Press* states that East Fife were "out of the hunt" and "lucky to retire with both points" but one feels that there was a certainly amount of local prejudice here, for *The Leven Mail*, although admitting things were "even" gives a different impression.

Today was a historic day for the town of Kirkcaldy, for Harry Anderson became the first ever Raith Rovers man to earn a cap for Scotland. Sadly, it was a desperately awful 0-0 draw against Wales at Celtic Park, and Harry was never invited to play for Scotland again.

February 28 1953

Ian Gardiner scores v Partick Thistle in February 1953. Thistle would eventually win 3-2

February 29 1964

East Fife do not play many games on Leap Year's day (when you think about it, it is only every four years; only every 28 years, in theory, that it would occur on a Saturday).

This was one of them, and a miserable undistinguished affair it was as well, at Recreation Park, Alloa.

It was a fixture that did well to attract 400 people to see it. Alloa were having a poor season towards the bottom of the 19 team League and as there was no relegation and only a theoretical chance of not being re-elected even if you were bottom, there was little motivation.

East Fife, on the other hand, were having a better season but the Second Division was dominated this year by Morton, who had lost only the once this season and that was to East Fife!

Today in fact Morton gained promotion from the Second Division by beating bottom team Forfar Athletic 6-1 at Cappielow. East Fife however lacked the consistency to challenge them and were now fourth. In fact, it would be Clyde who would go up with Morton.

Today East Fife were clearly the better team against Alloa, going in 3-1 up at half time with a goal from Morris Aitken and two from Ian Stewart, and then surviving a late fight back after Alloa had scored with a penalty kick.

In spite of everything, there were signs of a gradual recovery under the managership of Jimmy Bonthrone. Whether he could ever hope to take them back to the great days of ten years ago when he himself had played for them remained to be seen, but it was certainly what the fans were expecting. They were reluctant to settle for less.

March

Taken on 18th January 1964 at Glebe Park. Back row, from left: Stirrat, Orphant, Donnelly, Walker, Young, Wright. Front row, left: Meacham, Aitken, Devear, Stewart, McWatt.

March 1 1947

The worst winter of the 20th century was still in full spate — indeed it had a good few weeks to run, with serious shortages of food in remote parts of Perthshire, Angus and the Highlands — but all four Scottish League Cup quarter final first legs were played today.

East Fife and Hearts attracted a crowd of almost 20,000 to Tynecastle to see the "B" Division team getting the better of Hearts by 1-0, the goal coming from a Tommy Adams "tap in" from a Duncan cross.

The Sunday Post writer, clearly affected by the bad weather, and with a hint of the still virtually omnipotent Winston Churchill, talks of East Fife's defence in glowing terms "In the height of the storm, they never faltered ... the better football machine, a calm, controlled, purposeful lot with a victory blueprint to which they stuck all through".

The Courier talks about them being in "1938 form" — a reference, of course, to the Scottish Cup triumph of that year.

The man of the match was wing half Jimmy Philp who controlled the game with his fine, accurate distribution and ability to break up opposition attacks.

The main topic of conversation however was still the weather, although the longer hours of daylight were now encouraging people to believe that it would soon be over.

Trains were more or less back to normal, but road transport was still fraught, particularly in rural areas. Hearts would be able to come to Bayview on Wednesday for a League match, but the outcome would be a lot less pleasant for East Fife and their supporters.

March 2 1957

East Fife suffered a bad 0-1 home defeat at the hands of Queen's Park at Bayview to-day.

1956/57 had not been great with the really good players of a few years ago having moved on and some others visibly ageing.

They were closer to the relegation battle than where they would have liked to have been, and today they played host to Queen's Park, a team in the same boat.

Queen's Park, in some ways a quaint anachronism form bygone days (they had won the Scottish Cup 10 times in the 19th century) were amateur in name, but just as committed as any other team.

The referee was the famous Tom Wharton of Glasgow whose huge bulk was already a feature of the Scottish scene. East Fife really should have scored in the first half. Jimmy Bonthrone and Andy Matthew on at least two occasions tangled with each other and got in each other's way; East Fife continued to exasperate their fans with their persistence of trying to walk the ball into the net rather than trying a shot, as Charlie Fleming would have done a few years ago.

Such profligacy was punished when Queen's Park went ahead early in the second half when G Herd (as amateurs were denoted in the newspapers) was on hand to hammer home a drive after a back header from R Cromar.

East Fife then redoubled their efforts but to no avail, and the full-time whistle brought the realisation that East Fife were in deep relegation trouble.

The mood of their supporters was hardly helped by the news that in today's Scottish Cup quarter finals Raith Rovers had defeated Dumbarton 4-0 at Boghead, and were now in the semi-finals along with Celtic, Falkirk and Kilmarnock.

March 3 1934

East Fife and Forfar Athletic served up a classic thriller for a disappointing turn-out of fans at Bayview today.

If anything, Forfar's performances had been better than those of East Fife of late, but today it was East Fife who edged home in a close 4-3 encounter.

The game was described as "strenuous stuff from the outset". Dunsire scored for the visitors in three minutes, but then Scott equalised. Forfar scored through Gabriel, East Fife equalised through McCartney, then Gabriel scored again. All this before half time!

The game settled down a little in the second half as both teams tired, but East Fife had a definite advantage in the second half with the wind blowing towards the Aberhill end. The Forfar defence held out, with Collie and Ramsay both outstanding, until late in the game when the old reliable Phil Weir popped up to score the equaliser.

With only minutes left, Walker grabbed what proved to be the winner. It was tough luck on Forfar, a point accepted by East Fife's Manager Dave McLean, and tacitly agreed with by Forfar's ever genial supremo Jimmy Black.

Today was Scottish Cup quarter final day and the talking point at the end was the defeat of Celtic by St Mirren at Love Street, for St Mirren were gradually becoming Celtic's bogey team — having beaten then in 1930, and of course in the Scottish Cup final of 1926.

The Love Street Saints would actually reach the final this year but would be defeated by Rangers.

March 4 1972

The country was still coming to terms with the astonishing victory of the miners in their strike which had seriously disrupted electricity supplies and seen some appalling sights of violence on picket lines.

East Fife, however, still had their battle against relegation to win in this, their first year back in the First Division for over a decade. Today on a reasonably bright but still slightly cold day,

Hearts came to town. Hearts had not had a great season, but were still a force to be reckoned with and a crowd of 5,915 were at Bayview to see Bobby Seith's men.

It was a tough game, with East Fife playing with the desperation that danger of relegation inevitably brings. It was they who went ahead when Walter Borthwick managed to get his head to another header from Billy McLaren.

In the second half East Fife went further ahead through Borthwick again, who this time forced his way through the defence to score a second.

That seemed to settle matters, but there were reasons why East Fife were near the bottom of the First Division.

Almost as soon as the game had been apparently won, it was immediately thrown away again; Hearts came back and scored through the hitherto rather profligate Harry Kinnear. Soon after that, centre half Alan Anderson scored another.

The last half hour was then hammer-and-tongs stuff, but the 2-2 draw was probably a good result for East Fife, as most of the other relegation candidates lost today, with Dunfermline Athletic now in a particularly bad way.

March 5 1938

An odd incident. It appears that a woman spectator (and a well dressed, middle class lady at that!) has been carried away by her own enthusiasm and is being escorted back to the crowd by a policeman. This happened at Bayview in a Scottish Cup tie against Aberdeen on March 5 1938.

March 5 1927

Dunterlie Park, Barrhead was the scene of a triumph almost as great as the winning of the Scottish Qualifying Cup in 1920.

East Fife became the first team from the Second Division to reach the semi-finals of the Scottish Cup.

They did this by beating Arthurlie, another Second Division club, on their muddy pitch after so much heavy rain. Arthurlie had of course made history in the Scottish Cup some 30 years previously by beating Celtic on the first Dunterlie Park with its famous slope, but this newer Park (the third version) was little better, being notoriously small and narrow.

East Fife were the better team throughout, even though Arthurlie missed several chances in the first half when the conditions were in their favour.

For East Fife, Jock Wood missed a penalty kick but then they had the luck to get an own goal when the luckless McMeekin diverted a cross from Edgar past his own goalkeeper.

Arthurlie had also lost the services of Malloy through injury and that was vital on the heavy ground. In the last fifteen minutes Peter Barrett scored before Bobby Russell rose like a bird to head home a corner kick.

Some supporters had gone in a special train to support the team, and they were delighted by the outcome. When they and the players came back to Methil later than night, large crowds had gathered to meet them.

The other teams in the semi-final were Celtic, Partick Thistle and the winners of the replay between Falkirk and Rangers.

March 6 1965

Queen's Park are an interesting team, and even in 1965, were considered as such.

Supported by the Glasgow middle class (with *The Glasgow Herald* in particular finding it hard to hide its love for "the Spiders") Queen's Park had remained staunchly amateur even after professionalism had been legalised in 1893. They were one of the few clubs who had a Latin motto "ludere causa ludendi" — to play for the sake of playing.

They were the owners of Hampden Park, and today they played East Fife at a near-deserted home ground in front of a crowd of about 300 in a stadium which, in 1965, frequently housed six figure crowds.

Queen's Park were having a good season and indeed were pushing for promotion whereas East Fife were in the middle of a run of mediocrity with no real prospect of any speedy return to the First Division.

East Fife had had one moment of glory about a month ago with a victory over Aberdeen in the Scottish Cup but, frankly, it now seemed like a flash in the pan and the team had gone out in the next round to Kilmarnock.

Today was the last day that Eddie Turnbull would be the Manager of Queen's Park — he had been appointed Manager of Aberdeen — and frankly East Fife put up little resistance with goals from P J Buchanan, N MacKay and W Neil (as amateurs were so denoted in the newspapers).

East Fife, admittedly hit with chronic injury problems, had no answer, as the 1964/65 season drifted off into historical obscurity.

March 7 1936

The world was today plunged into uncertainly as Hitler, in clear breach of the Versailles Treaty, marched his troops into the demilitarised Rhineland.

This was a threat to the security of France, and although some politicians talked rubbish about "Hitler merely moving some furniture from one room to another in his house", Foreign Secretary Anthony Eden and most sensible people were very worried indeed.

With this in the background, East Fife travelled to Marine Gardens, Edinburgh to take on Leith Athletic, a club who, although playing consistently well in the Second Division, were rapidly losing support, mainly to Hibs.

Today, only 500 turned up to see what *The Scotsman* described as a "rousing match". It was Leith Athletic's sixth successive victory, but "for skill and style, the honours were with East Fife, who, however, were erratic near the goal and counted a penalty-kick among their missed opportunities".

To be fair, the penalty kick was awarded in the last minute when Leith Athletic were already 4-2 up. Joe Cowan smashed it against the bar, thus depriving himself of a hat-trick, for he had already equalised twice for East Fife.

This result finally killed off what little chance East Fife had of promotion, but the general opinion was that East Fife were going in the right direction.

Certainly things were a great deal better on the economic front in Levenmouth, but the events of this weekend in Germany clearly highlighted another major problem. The world, like it or not, having allowed Germany to fall into the hands of a dangerous and ruthless demagogue, was heading towards another war.

March 8 1930

Sometimes to gain promotion, a team has to be lucky.

Another way of putting that is to say that the team has to be professional enough to deal with all eventualities, in this case, a very good team in King's Park of Stirling, and also a very heavy pitch after a week of fairly incessant rain.

Forthbank had absorbed most of the water, though, and the hard work of the ground staff was rewarded. The game went ahead in front of its largest crowd of the season.

King's Park themselves were far from out of the promotion race and had a great forward in Jim Dyet who had put eight (some sources say ten) past Forfar Athletic the day after New Year.

King's Park had played a game on Wednesday afternoon (beating Montrose 5-1) and that too had been on a heavy pitch, so East Fife had a slight advantage in terms of being just a little less tired.

Half-time saw a 1-1 draw with a goal from Weir for East Fife and a penalty from Dyet for King's Park. The penalty was dubious and indeed some of the other decisions of Mr Holland from Glasgow caused puzzlement, not least when he chalked off what seemed to be a good goal from Dyet.

But East Fife took advantage of this with two goals from Rarity, which made it 3-1; the Stirling men were not yet finished. Dyet reduced the leeway, then, in the last minute, the referee seemed to award them a penalty, but then changed his mind and gave a free-kick for East Fife.

Thus the game finished 3-2, with East Fife's best man being goalkeeper Bernard, and Mr Holland being a far from popular man in Stirling.

March 9 1963

The long winter freeze-up of January and February 1963 was at last over.

East Fife had been luckier than most in that they had had some games played recently — sadly disappointing defeats at home to Ayr United and a financially disastrous exit from the Scottish Cup in midweek to Third Lanark — but today most Scottish games went ahead, despite a couple of casualties.

The problem was that the thaw had come too quickly and there had been, for example, a landslide at Gleneagles which affected the railway line, and some major flooding, not helped by today's heavy and persistent rain.

At Bayview possibly 1,500 hardy souls, (although that looked like an over-estimate) gathered to see Dumbarton, a team struggling at the bottom of Division Two, who had suffered dreadfully with the weather.

East Fife themselves were about halfway up the Division Two table and were today good enough to beat Dumbarton 3-0 with two goals from Ian Stewart and one from George Dewar in the glaur and mud of Bayview.

Full time came as something of a relief, and many a supporter would have had his sanity questioned by his wife or mother in the context of why he had gone to such an insignificant game in such awful weather.

But of course, the answer was that football was back! The game that had such a hold on the Scottish population had returned after a prolonged and enforced winter break.

Away to East Stirlingshire next Saturday! Can hardly wait!

March 10 1934

"Bleak" is the word that one finds frequently to describe 1934.

The economic outlook was bleak, football generally was bleak, and East Fife were certainly having a bleak season, typified in some ways by today's 1-3 defeat at Ochilview against the "Warriors" of Stenhousemuir.

In addition to everything else, today's weather was certainly bleak with wind and rain, and East Fife with a few youngsters on board, decided to take advantage of the strong wind in the first half.

The crowd was miniscule and huddled under what cover there was in the stand. This meant that large swathes of the terracing were totally uninhabited; the players had to go and get the ball themselves when it went out of play!

The standard of play was "fast" in the opinion of the writer of *The Falkirk Herald* who was also impressed by East Fife whom he described as "plucky losers".

But their star man was left winger "Junior", which possibly says something about the set-up at East Fife in 1934, and it was he who set up Phil Weir for East Fife's only goal of the game.

The three goals lost however were all well taken, but East Fife also had bad luck on various occasions throughout the game, a point conceded by the honest writer of *The Falkirk Herald*.

This would turn out to be one of the better seasons in Stenhousemuir's under-performing history, for they finished fourth, not all that far behind the teams who gained promotion, whereas East Fife, who had been in the First Division in season 1930/31, had one of their poorer seasons and finished sixth from the bottom.

March 11 1950

Scottish Cup quarter final day, and East Fife were at Stenhousemuir where they attracted an astonishing crowd of 12,525, who paid £937 for the privilege.

The crowd, with more away supporters than home ones, remains to this day the record attendance for Ochilview.

The crowd saw what became, in the end, a comfortable victory for First Division East Fife although the Warriors (currently towards the bottom of the Second Division) put up a brave fight.

Two Fife teams were still in the Cup at the end of this day, for Raith Rovers had drawn 1-1 with Rangers at Ibrox, but East Fife had no need of a replay.

The problem today was the wind, "a biting, snarling wind that blew at near gale force", according to *The Sunday Post;* while East Fife were playing against it, they could make no headway.

Indeed, they were quite lucky to be going in at half-time with the score at 0-0: they had goalkeeper John Niven to thank for keeping them in the game. After the turnaround, Davie Duncan put East Fife ahead, and then came drama in the shape of a penalty kick awarded by referee Mr W Livingstone of Glasgow. The game hinged on this but it was well saved down at his right hand post by Niven.

That might have brought Stenny back into the game, but two goals from Henry Morris settled matters and saw East Fife into the semi-finals with a 3-0 victory.

Man of the match, however, was Allan Brown who entertained the crowd with several long, mazy dribbles.

March 12 1910

East Fife played a terrible game at Mill Park, Bathgate and lost 1-4.

This was a Central League game, and it did little for any chance that East Fife might have felt that they had of moving up the table from their mediocre position.

It was a fine day, described elsewhere as "the first day of spring" and *The Courier* is quite thrilled about the fact that Dundee are still in the Scottish Cup, having drawn with Hibs in the semi-final.

It is also quite scathing about the standard of play at Bathgate using words like "hum-drum" and "third rate", and even though Bathgate's defenders were out with injury, the "make-shift" was "all right".

Such damning with faint praise of the winners does not say very much about the losers, and the only men who earned any sort of praise were Ross in the defence and Mitchell in the forward line.

East Fife's season was now quite clearly fizzling out. They had had their big moment a month ago when Queen's Park came to Bayview in the Scottish Cup; now interest transferred to other matters, not least the politics of this country where a major battle was brewing between the Liberal Government and the House of Lords.

A General Election in January had given the Liberals a narrow majority but with the help of Labour and the Irish Nationalists, they had been able to pass their Budget. Now Asquith and Lloyd George were wanting to severely emasculate the House of Lords, or even to abolish it altogether!

March 13 1948

It was hardly East Fife at their best, but nevertheless it was a valuable victory today at Boghead, home of Dumbarton.

Far from the "fatal Boghead" of old when Dumbarton used to beat Celtic and Rangers regularly, it was nevertheless still a tough place to visit.

East Fife, whom everyone agreed were unlucky to lose to Rangers in the Scottish Cup last week, simply had to get their Division "B" challenge back on the rails.

They were now behind, but still had five games in hand, and their 4-2 victory today put them well back in contention. East Fife were two goals up at half time with counters from Dougie Davidson and Henry Morris, but then Dumbarton came back strongly at them in the early part of the second half with several close things.

Then a strange goal for East Fife eased the pressure. A cross from Tommy Adams was gathered by goalkeeper McFeat who then crossed the line with the ball in his arms under pressure from Henry Morris.

The Dumbarton fans thought this was a foul, but referee Willie Webb from Glasgow was convinced that nothing illegal had occurred and it was 3-0 for East Fife.

Another strange goal followed when Davie Duncan scored direct from a corner kick; from that point, Dumbarton scored two late, irrelevant goals, as if to underline the fact that nothing can be taken for granted. East Fife's biggest enemy was one called "complacency".

A glance at the League table showed that there were nine games left (their two Cup runs having caused disruption to League fixtures) and that they were one point behind both Hamilton and Albion Rovers.

March 14 1931

With East Fife now almost certainly doomed to relegation from the First Division, they nevertheless today went to Cappielow and played some good football but lost 0-3.

Sadly, this was typical of so many days in this First Division season when they started brightly, possibly missed a few chances, then the opposition took over and seized theirs.

Today a crowd of about 4,000 were at Cappielow to see Morton do just that. *The Courier* was of the opinion that East Fife needed more than "ornate football". They needed a "strong leader" as well.

Morton were no bad side (they had been Scottish Cup winners in 1922) but like everyone else they were suffering from the effects of the worldwide depression.

They were, however, one of the teams that East Fife simply had to beat if there were to be the slightest chance of avoiding the drop. McGachie and Herbert missed chances early on, but Morton were able to take theirs, even though the midfield play of the Fife men impressed the crowd who gave them a sporting ovation at the end.

It did however now look near the end of East Fife's First Division career, at least temporarily, for they were now several points behind Ayr United and Hibs, and Ayr had games in hand.

Today was a big day in Scottish football, as it was semi-final day in Glasgow with Celtic beating Kilmarnock at Hampden and Motherwell beating St Mirren at Ibrox. The Morton fans at Cappielow were far from broken-hearted with the news of the defeat of their rivals from Paisley.

March 15 1977

It was like old times again at Bayview as 8,568 crowded in this wet and windy Tuesday night to see a pulsating Scottish Cup replay between East Fife and Hearts.

The prize at stake was a semi-final tie against Rangers. The first game had been an honourable, if occasionally boring, goalless draw at Tynecastle. Tonight was a game in which *The Glasgow Herald* states that you needed "bionic nerves". (1977 was the heyday of a TV series called The Bionic Woman who had overtaken Superman in the fantasy stakes!)

The weather had been so bad with wind and rain that the game had been in doubt, but by kick-off time, the worst had passed and there was the pleasing sight of long queues, and indeed a little dangerous crushing, for entrance.

Bayview was at its best on such nights, and it was the home team who went ahead through a John Love header from a Cutty Young free-kick.

Hearts then scored through Willie Gibson and Bobby Prentice to put themselves into a rather undeserved lead before Harry Kinnear headed an equaliser.

The winner could have come at either end, but it was John Gallacher of Hearts who scored it six minutes from time.

It was hard luck on East Fife but visiting journalists left full of praise for the team. As for Hearts, it was one of the few pieces of good news of that season, for they duly lost to Rangers in the semi-final and ended up relegated from the Premier League at the end of the season.

March 15 2008

"We've won the League!" The very early date of March 15 2008 saw this triumph, and Greig McDonald is chaired off the pitch at East Stirlingshire

March 16 1912

Fife miners were on strike, and things were tough in the homes of the vast majority of the East Fife support.

The problem seemed to be the refusal of the coal mine owners to pay the recommended minimum wage as laid down by the Asquith Government. As usual in such times, there was much hardship in miners' families, and the disruption to transport services throughout Fife was severe.

East Fife were reasonably well placed in the Central League, in fact they were second, but they did not seem likely to catch Dunfermline Athletic. However today's game in the Penman Cup against King's Park went ahead at Bayview, in spite of the transport problems, and East Fife won 3-1.

The turnout was low, unsurprisingly, for quite a few local supporters could not afford the entrance charge, and the King's Park supporters could not easily get there from Stirling.

It was a good win for East Fife though, and indeed it was a very good day for Scotland because the football team beat Ireland 4-1 in Belfast and the rugby team beat England 8-3 at Inverleith.

Attention now turned to next week's projected Scotland v England football International at Hampden Park with serious questions being asked about whether the game would go ahead, in the view of the coal strike. Although rail communications in Fife were poor, they were a great deal better in the rest of the country.

The strike was eventually settled in early April when the Government managed to enforce the national minimum wage, something that the coal owners said that they could not pay, but nevertheless managed to do so.

March 17 1906

This was East Fife's third year of existence, and it was a mark of how far they had come that they were invited to take part in the newly set up Penman Cup for teams in Fife, the Lothians, Clackmannanshire and Stirlingshire, but excluding the big city teams like Hibs and Hearts in Edinburgh. Indeed East Fife had taken some of the initiative in inaugurating the tournament.

East Fife were drawn at home to Cowdenbeath, but sadly exited the tournament at the first stage by losing 0-2 on a pitch that was generally held to be rather soft after recent rain, although the more chivalrous of East Fife fans admitted that Cowdenbeath were the better side.

The ground was in the throes of major improvements and renovations as it was gradually becoming the Bayview that we all knew and loved. The intention was there to apply one day for admission to the Second Division of the Scottish League on the grounds that Raith Rovers were doing quite well there and with a ground, Stark's Park, that was hardly of the best.

In the meantime Scotland were in Dublin today (St Patrick's Day) to play an International.

1906 saw a lull in the troubles with everyone confidently expecting the new Liberal Government (recently elected with a huge majority) to deliver on Home Rule.

Nevertheless the Scotland team did see a massive police presence and a few troops stationed at key points in case of trouble. The precautions were not necessary and Scotland won 1-0, their goal coming from Tommy Fitchie, an eccentric amateur who played for Woolwich Arsenal.

March 18 1939

War now seemed inevitable after Hitler had seized all of Czechoslovakia a few days ago. When the Munich Agreement last autumn allowed Hitler to have the Sudetenland, there was a certain relief, and even in a few quarters, understanding for the German position.

Sadly this was no longer possible, and it was now clear that we were dealing with a madman keen on nothing other than world conquest for his seizure of Czechoslovakia now gave him potential access to the Rumanian oil fields.

Football was difficult in these circumstances, but today East Fife travelled to Firs Park, Falkirk, the home of East Stirlingshire. They duly won 3-2, a result that certainly kept them well in the promotion race, but newspapers were keen to stress that this wasn't "promotion form", or if it was, it wasn't the form that would keep them in the First Division for any length of time.

Wingers Adams and McKerrell both had off days, and although McCartney scored twice, he really should have bagged more. Inside right Milne scored the other goal, but supporters were concerned at the panic that occurred in the defence whenever the Shire (with three trialists on board!) put them under any pressure.

The position at the top was that, although Cowdenbeath seemed certain to win the Second Division, three other teams, East Fife, Alloa and Airdrie were locked together with the same points, and with four games left to play. So it was all to play for, but what would season 1939/40 bring? Would there even be a season 1939/40?

March 19 1938

It was Scottish Cup quarter final day, and excitement could hardly have ever been more intense, for Raith Rovers (enjoying a great League season) were drawn to come to Methil.

In a move which did them little credit, East Fife raised the prices of admission — almost doubling them in fact! There was a certain amount of specious cant about "in the interests of public safety" but in fact it was simply to make money!

Not that it mattered, for 18,642 (with many from Kirkcaldy) happily coughed up to see what turned out to be a rather controversial draw which East Fife really should have won.

It did not escape anyone's attention either (with even a hint or two about this in the Press!) that there was even more money to be made at Stark's Park on Wednesday!

Be that as it may, although Raith Rovers had had the better of the first half, East Fife were two goals up late in the second half through Larry Millar and Eddie McLeod, but then Francis Joyner pulled one back for Rovers through a swirling corner kick.

Even so, East Fife looked home and hosed until late in the game when Raith were awarded a somewhat dubious penalty kick, duly converted by John Whitelaw.

Both Managers Davie McLean of East Fife and Sandy Archibald of Raith Rovers expressed themselves as disappointed that they did not win, but of course another date awaited soon at Stark's Park next Wednesday afternoon! And most of the crowd started to figure out ways and means of getting off their work to go there!

March 19 1938

A section of the crowd at Bayview for the Scottish Cup quarter final against Raith Rovers on March 19 1938

March 20 1948

"The wind-swept plain" of Bayview certainly lived up to its reputation today, but East Fife now took a firm grip upon things at the top of the "B Division".

It was a most curious looking League table for East Fife were third, one point behind the Lanarkshire pair of Hamilton Academical and Albion Rovers.

The Lanarkshire duo had only three games to play, but East Fife, thanks to their involvement in both Cup competitions, had eight games left and unless they did something absolutely stupid, it was hard not to imagine them winning the "B Division".

They certainly did not do anything stupid here, as they beat Arbroath 3-0, and but for a great performance in the goal from John Bonnar (who would go on to have a great career with Celtic) it would have been a lot more.

East Fife faced the wind in the first half and managed to control it by the simple device of short passing along the ground, something that George Aitken and Jimmy Philp could do to perfection.

They also had of course up front Henry Morris, who managed to notch a goal against the wind in the first half, and then scored another two in the second half when the wind was in his favour.

A good day for East Fife was made even better by the news that the reserve team had beaten Leith Athletic 3-0 as well and that the three goals had all been scored by a youngster who was really demanding first team selection. His name was Charlie Fleming.

March 21 1953

That East Fife were certainly League flag contenders was proved in this fine performance at a packed Bayview when they beat Celtic 4-1.

It was possibly not the best Celtic team there had ever been — they had gone out of the Scottish Cup the week before by losing 0-2 to Rangers at Ibrox. East Fife's best ever performance against the green and whites was marred, perhaps, by a little crowd trouble and a bad injury to the famous Celt, Charlie Tully, who was barged into the fence by the burly frame of Don Emery.

The opening goal came from Ian Gardiner, then Jackie Stewart scored. 2-0 up and approaching half time but then two penalties settled the issue, one missed by John McPhail of Celtic and the other scored by Don Emery of East Fife.

The best goal came after the interval when Charlie "Legs" Fleming scored a great individual goal, and at this stage it looked as if we were heading for a record score, but Celtic settled a little and even managed to pull one back through John McGrory (no relation to his manager Jimmy) following a goalmouth scramble.

The game finished in a tense atmosphere with some in the brooding, sullen ranks of the green and whites apparently intent on trouble, but the police did a great job of getting everyone on their buses and sending them home.

East Fife were now on the crest of a wave, and it seemed that if they kept playing like this, they would indeed win the Scottish League. Many games remained however, and Rangers and Hibs were still strong opposition.

Henry Morris

March 22 1930

East Fife continued their push for promotion with a very good 4-1 win over Queen of the South at Bayview today.

The victory was all the sweeter because it had been the Doonhamers who had put them out of the Scottish Cup at Palmerston Park in Dumfries in January. The contrast could hardly have been greater both in terms of weather and indeed performance.

It was a pleasant spring day and the four goals meant that East Fife had now scored 103 goals this season. It might have been an even bigger margin as well but for a great performance by Coupland in the Queen of the South goal and the East Fife forwards themselves who often seemed slightly over eager to atone for their Scottish Cup defeat.

Goals however came from Gabriel, Liddle, Mitchell and Weir and they were all good ones, much enjoyed by the 3,000 crowd. Only later in the game did East Fife tire and allow Queens back in to score a consolation goal.

East Fife were now second in the League behind Leith Athletic, who had been rather lucky to get the better of Forfar Athletic that day, and the next game was a meeting between the two of them at Marine Gardens, and already the supporters were making plans to get there to see that one.

Enthusiasm was certainly in the air. Today also saw the semi-finals of the Scottish Cup, and it was going to be an all-Glasgow affair in the final between Rangers and Partick Thistle.

March 23 1938

The country may have been slowly sliding into another war now that Hitler had organised his Anschluss (union) with his native Austria, and the war in Spain continued to horrify with its casualties, but the big talking point in Fife this Wednesday afternoon was who was going to win the Scottish Cup replay!

Raith Rovers and East Fife had drawn 2-2 at a packed Bayview on Saturday (and had not been above doubling the entrance prices!) and now the game moved on to Stark's Park.

Possibly fearing a backlash from their supporters, Raith Rovers, to their credit, pegged their prices to the normal. They also, like Saturday, took the precaution of making it an all-ticket game lest there was an influx of supporters which would be too much for the ground.

Even though it was a Wednesday afternoon, the crowd was an astonishing 25,500. It was half-day in some shops in Kirkcaldy, and some local firms simply bowed to reality and gave their workers the afternoon off, or at least made a public statement that, although they would not be paid, they would be exempt from the possibility of dismissal! Or they could make up their hours some other time!

Norman Haywood scored for Raith, then Bob McCartney equalised in the first half. The second half was a thriller with East Fife just edging it 3-2 thanks to couple of penalties, one them very late in the game scored by Andy Herd.

Both teams went on to greater things that season — East Fife won the Scottish Cup but Raith Rovers won the Second Division championship establishing a British record for goal-scoring in the process.

March 23 1938

A "near thing" from the quarter final replay of the Scottish Cup at Stark's Park in 1938

March 24 1990

The "doldrums" seemed to sum up East Fife at the moment.

One would have to give the writer of the *Evening Times* a little credit for at least trying to drum up some interest in this game when he says of today's game against Queen of the South that "Both sides needed a win to maintain any hope of creeping back into the promotion race".

The 1980s had not been a great decade for East Fife and since relegation from the First Division (now the second tier, of course) in 1988, even more depression had set in.

There was no greater place for atmosphere than the old Bayview in the 1950s when East Fife were playing Celtic, Rangers or Raith Rovers, Conversely, the lack of atmosphere or bite was apparent on a day like today when the crowd struggled to reach 500, although there were clearly a few carloads of Queen of the South supporters to back up the Doonhamers.

Queen of the South were arguably the biggest under-achievers of the lot in Scottish football, and now like East Fife were languishing in the middle to lower regions of the bottom Division.

Today, however, both teams served up some sort of a game for the fans — Ian Brown scored first for the home side but then referee David Syme awarded a controversial penalty when goalkeeper Ray Charles seemed to have gathered the ball cleanly without touching an opponent.

Queens scored from the resulting spot kick and then went on to take full advantage of a dreadful clearance by Paul Taylor. Hard though the Fifers tried, they could not get back into the game.

March 25 1972

East Fife's grim rear-guard action to ward off relegation in their first season back in the First Division was given a boost today with a creditable 2-2 draw against fellow strugglers Dundee United at Tannadice Park.

The weather was bright but cold, and Joe Hughes scored the two East Fife goals which earned a point, his last coming late in the game, to the noisy relief of the East Fife supporters.

His first had been scored early in the game and was the result of a "Keystone Cops" moment in the Dundee United defence when right half Copland and goalkeeper MacKay collided and left Hughes with the easiest of tasks to prod the ball home.

The crowd was a rather disappointing 4,000 — something that said something about the current disillusion of the Dundee United support even with a rather ebullient new Manager called Jim McLean.

The bottom of the First Division was quite exciting with as many as nine teams involved in the struggle. The race for the flag was less so, for Celtic looked like winning their 7th title in a row — and there were still quite a few games to go. The country was now recovering from the 1972 Miners' Strike — won fairly convincingly by the miners — and the day before, the Conservative Government had suspended the Northern Ireland Parliament in Belfast and had taken over the governing of the province themselves, something that would lead to unrest in the Orange community. And of course, the war in Vietnam was still rumbling on.

But Scottish football was on a high with both Celtic and Rangers having qualified for semi-finals in European competition.

March 26 1927

To the amazement of all Scotland, East Fife became the first Second Division team to reach the final of the Scottish Cup.

Even more surprising was that they were only admitted to the Scottish League a matter of six years ago in 1921, and the most creditable thing of all was the pick-up that they gave to their community now suffering in the vindictive aftermath of the Miners' Strike which had finished in the autumn of 1926.

But they reached the final today in the semi-final at Tynecastle Park when they beat First Division Partick Thistle (who had won the Cup in 1921) by 2-1.

The crowd was 40,000, remarkable because only 1,500 came from Fife, and Partick Thistle were by no means the best supported team in Scotland. But a vast number of neutrals turned up, and most of them lent their support to the Black and Golds of East Fife.

It was a hard fought game — but the team played well as a unit, covering for each other, something that says a lot about a mining community, perhaps.

The first goal was scored through a header by a man with the unlikely nickname of "Pasha" Patterson (possibly he had served as Passchendaele a decade earlier?) and the score was 1-1 at half-time when Grove equalised for Partick.

But it was the legendary Jock Wood who seized on a moment's hesitation in the Thistle defence and fired in the winner in the second half. The only thing that slightly spoiled a perfect day for East Fife was the news that Celtic had beaten Falkirk in the other semi-final. Celtic would be a little more difficult than Falkirk in the final!

March 27 1909

1909 was a great time for people who believed cynically that football matches could be fixed.

A draw in the Cup-tie would result in another big crowd and more money. The riot after the second drawn Scottish Cup final a month later between Celtic and Rangers was emphatically not a sectarian or religious one. It was caused by the perception that the reason why there was no extra-time was because both teams wanted yet another big gate.

In this context, quite a few of the 2,500 people at the 2-2 draw of the replay between East Fife and Arbroath in the Scottish Consolation Cup semi-final "wondered" about this result. The gate was £57, believed to be the biggest gate yet drawn at Bayview in the first 5 seasons of its existence.

The first game at Gayfield had been a 1-1 draw, and today East Fife, having been two goals down at one point early in the game, scored through Roberts and Horne to level before half time, and from then on were totally in command but failed to add to their tally, Horne in the last few minutes of the game shooting wildly over the bar to the intense anguish of the crowd.

A third game, also drawn, was then played in pouring rain at Cowdenbeath (this time earning £70!) the following Saturday before a fourth game finally decided the issue in favour of Arbroath at Recreation Grounds, Perth in front of a far smaller crowd on a Wednesday afternoon.

There could be little doubt that this had been a "tidy little earner" for both teams, and the local press of both towns, the *Arbroath Herald* and *The Leven Mail*, while not saying anything overtly, are not above making a few insinuations about "the swelling of the coffers" of both clubs.

March 28 1964

A good crowd of about 2,000 spectators turned up at Bayview today to see attractive visitors in Clyde, a side who had strong pretentions to reach the First Division.

On the previous Wednesday night, Clyde had been considered unlucky to lose the Glasgow Cup final to Celtic. The first promotion spot had long ago gone to Morton, and Clyde had a substantial lead in second place over potential rivals Arbroath, East Fife and Dumbarton.

East Fife had only a very slim chance of promotion, and the reason was that they had had too many draws this season and were known as "the Treble Chance" team, a reference to the money that could be earned off the football pools in those days if a punter could forecast eight draws.

Today was yet another draw, but that was not bad news for the sizeable minority from Glasgow who cheered at the end as if it were a victory. Ian Stewart had put East Fife ahead early on, but Clyde pressed and pressed and then Harry Hood robbed Stirrat and drove through a ruck of players to equalise.

It was a fine piece of work from Hood, and it was little wonder that he was attracting the attention of Sunderland and Celtic. This result now meant that with only five games left, East Fife were still six points behind Clyde, so it would now be very difficult to imagine East Fife being promoted.

Elsewhere, Dundee and Rangers both won their Scottish Cup semi-finals and would now contest the final at the end of April, and in the Second Division, Dumbarton hammered Cowdenbeath 8-0!

March 29 1930

It is not often that a 0-0 draw is greeted with any great enthusiasm by supporters, but this game at Marine Gardens, Edinburgh was an exception.

In the first place it attracted a 20,000 crowd — surely a record for a Second Division game — and it was between 1st and 2nd in the League. At the end of the game, both teams were on 53 points, but the advantage lay with Leith who had four games left to play whereas East Fife only had three.

As significant an event as any today was that Albion Rovers could only draw with Queen of the South when they would have been expected to win, and other challengers Third Lanark lost to St Bernards.

The game is described as a "titanic" struggle, and took place on the same day as the Grand National, so metaphors about "hurdles" "the home straight" and "the winning post" abounded.

Both teams could have won, never more so than at the very death when Marshall of Leith rose in splendid isolation and got his head to a cross but nodded it safely into the arms of Bernard.

Indeed it was Bernard who earned most of the plaudits in the Press for his anticipation and his clutching. The Press is also unanimous in its opinion that it would have been unfair if either team had lost, and that both teams "will grace next year's First Division".

This was somewhat premature, but another three points from their last three games would do the trick for East Fife, and supporters were already looking forward with relish to their first ever appearance in the First Division.

March 30 1955

East Fife plunged further into relegation trouble after an error-strewn but basically unlucky defeat by Celtic at Bayview this Wednesday afternoon. (Celtic had been involved in the Scottish Cup semi-final on Saturday when the game should have been played).

The crowd was a little disappointing at 8,700 (with a lot fewer from Glasgow than one would have expected on a Saturday), but there were clearly quite a few "auntie's funerals" and "dentist's appointments" this afternoon!

Celtic were going for the League Championship in a two-horse race with Aberdeen, and as for the relegation battle, although Stirling Albion were doomed, the other place could have gone to any of half a dozen teams, including East Fife and Raith Rovers.

East Fife goalkeeper John Curran had a nightmare, allowing an easy Jimmy Walsh shot to squirm under his body and then throwing the ball out to Celtic's Bobby Evans who slipped it to Neil Mochan to score.

For East Fife Angus Plumb scored twice, opening the scoring, and then after Celtic had gone 3-1 up, bringing it back to 3-2. Even after Celtic went 4-2 up, East Fife kept fighting and Jackie Stewart pulled another one back, but Mr McKerchar's final whistle saw scenes of relief in the Celtic camp and a great deal of sympathy for East Fife at the 3-4 score line.

There was, however, a little consolation in that Kilmarnock and Falkirk (both potential relegation candidates) had also lost, but Celtic were disappointed to hear that Aberdeen had also won and remained three points above them.

But now attention began to focus on the International at Wembley on Saturday. Sadly it would not turn out well for Scotland!

March 31 1962

One of the disadvantages of the old League system was that Division Two had 19 teams in it and there was no relegation (there was of course promotion from Division Two to Division One).

This meant that there was a certain familiarity and "old pals" attitude, but it also meant that unless you achieved promotion, you tended to get the same opposition year after year — Albion Rovers, Forfar Athletic, Stenhousemuir, Brechin City, for example — and it also meant that there were a lot of games, particularly towards the tail end of the season, which really had not very much at stake.

The season was now meandering gently towards its end. Today for example East Fife travelled to Somerset Park, Ayr for a less than totally mouth-watering tussle between eighth and tenth in the Division.

There was a little money involved in the "pools money" (you got so much for every point) but hardly enough to entice more than 400 to attend. (That was the figure given). They saw a 1-1 draw which was not as bad as it sounded, Brown scoring for East Fife in the first half and McMillan for Ayr United in the second half.

For many reasons, this game was not the major topic of conversation in Scottish football circles that weekend. That honour, if that is the right word, belonged to the semi-final at Ibrox when with St Mirren leading Celtic 3-0 and only ten minutes left, some misguided youths entered the field of play in a criminal attempt to get the game stopped and replayed some other time.

Fortunately, they did not succeed.

April

Team Photo 1967. Back row, from left: Brodie, McLeish, McGann, Guild, Gilchrist, Nelson, Stewart. Front, from left: Miller, R. Waddell, Dewar, Kinsella, A. Waddell.

April 1 1950

April Fool's Day or not, East Fife reached their third Scottish Cup final in a rather strange victory over Partick Thistle in the Ibrox rain before a crowd of 42,000.

East Fife, of course, were the League Cup holders and hopes grew that a Cup double could be secured, especially with the news that the other semi-final between Rangers and Queen of the South had ended in a 1-1 draw with neither team distinguishing itself.

At Ibrox, the game all seemed to depend on one minute in the second half. East Fife were 1-0 up at half-time thanks to a lovely goal from Charlie Fleming, who showed why he was called the "Cannonball" after he rounded a defender and scored from outside the box.

This seemed to be enough, for East Fife were defending stoutly until, with quarter of an hour remaining, Jimmy Walker of Partick Thistle got through the defence and flicked the ball past John Niven.

But then, as often happens, the team who has just scored switched off. Immediately after the restart an anodyne half-hit cross was sent over by Bobby Black. The Thistle defence all decided to leave it to each other; in nipped the mercurial Henry Morris to score a rather easy goal, but one that was sufficient to get East Fife into the Scottish Cup final.

Thus the score had changed from 1-0 to 2-1 in the space of time that it takes someone to go to the toilet!

Partick Thistle, the stuffing clearly knocked out of them, were unable to mount another fightback.

April 2 1938

Action from the Scottish Cup semi-final against St Bernards in 1938

April 2 2016

That grand old ground of Gayfield, Arbroath, probably the only ground in Great Britain that is closer to the sea than New Bayview, saw East Fife beat Arbroath 1-0 today.

This result consolidated East Fife's position at the top of Division Two, as Clyde, Elgin, Annan Athletic and Queen's Park all drew. The position was now that East Fife were four points clear with four games to go, and all the postponed games were now played off.

Elgin City, in particular, had had a bad March; East Fife had beaten them at Borough Briggs on March 5, and the opinion generally expressed in buses and cars going home from Arbroath was that the only team that could now beat East Fife was East Fife themselves.

Things had been strengthened since their bad spell in midwinter, and the team was clearly focussed on reaching the First Division. Not that they made things easy for their supporters! East Fife scored in the 26th minute through Jason Kerr, but then were unable to add to their total.

The second half therefore passed slowly. Arbroath, hard-working but agricultural and lacking in sophistication under new boss Dick Campbell, who had served Forfar Athletic so well for many years, pressed and pressed.

But goalkeeper Kelly was in good form, and the rest of the defence coped with a degree of comfort. East Fife's supporters in the crowd of 810 gave their team a loud cheer at the end, although the cry of "Campeones" was possibly a little premature.

April 2 2016

Gary Naysmith in action at Gayfield

April 3 1982

After a moment's silence for Tom Pearson, one time Chairman of East Fife and President of the SFA who died earlier in the week, today's game against Alloa at Bayview kicked off before a paltry attendance.

The weather was sunny but a little windy, and the standard of play was not great, certainly not from East Fife.

Murray and Paterson scored for Alloa before half-time, and that was the score at full time as well, a result which did no good at all to East Fife's chances of promotion. It was, however, a great result for Alloa who would indeed earn promotion at the end of the season.

Supporters and players however would be forgiven for not paying 100% attention to the game, for political and international affairs had taken over yesterday with the news that the Argentinians had invaded and captured the Falkland Islands in the South Atlantic.

Today the issue was being debated in the House of Commons (most unusually in session on a Saturday afternoon, although it had happened at the time of Suez in 1956 and on the day before the declaration of war in 1939) and it seemed likely that the government would decide to send a "task force" of ships and aircraft to win back the islands.

It was a matter which created a great deal of interest, but elsewhere in the world of football, just as if to prove that there was no real excuse for East Fife and others, another "small" team, Forfar Athletic were engaged in a Scottish Cup semi-final against Rangers and earning an honourable (and unlucky!) 0-0 draw.

April 4 1953

Everyone else was focussing on the Scottish Cup semi-finals being played today (Rangers beat Hearts, and Aberdeen drew with Third Lanark).

East Fife moved to the top of the Scottish League today with a comprehensive 7-0 hammering of St Mirren.

The obvious star of the show was Charlie Fleming, who scored five while Gardiner and Bonthrone scored the other two. The ever-modest Fleming would say that it was a team performance, as indeed it was, but the five goals from the "Cannonball" were all first class.

St Mirren, who were two goals down within the first three minutes, were frankly swept aside by a first class performance by the Fifers. A few weeks ago, East Fife had more or less given up on any belief that they could win the League flag, but now with Hibs and Rangers both having dropped a few points, they were right back in the hunt.

The position was that they had three games left to play. Both Hibs and Rangers who had games in hand could equal East Fife, and if that happened it went down to the complications of goal average.

It followed however that it all really boiled down to the last three games, but they were all away from home and they could hardly have been more difficult — Hearts, Hibs and Celtic. Nevertheless it was great at this late stage of the season to be thinking of the possibility of East Fife becoming the champions of Scotland. Now that would be some achievement, and some way of commemorating the 50 years of the club!

April 5 1930

There are times when one "wonders" about results, and today was one of them.

We are now in the very murky waters about potential match fixing. It is often believed by cynics that a club does not really want promotion for financial reasons (the First Division was a very expensive place for a provincial side) and the belief is often current that a game is "thrown".

Such allegations are difficult to prove, but one would have to be rather naïve to think that it couldn't ever happen.

Today's result, a 3-5 defeat by Stenhousemuir at Ochilview seriously weakened East Fife's position in the promotion race, and the hundreds of travelling fans were more than a little concerned by the goalkeeping errors of John Bernard, and the amount of chances passed up by the East Fife forwards.

Fingers were also pointed at the referee Mr Robertson of Glasgow for an extremely soft penalty kick awarded to the home side, and *The Courier* may well be trying to say something when it says "numerous opportunities which cropped up were not taken advantage of" and that Stenhousemuir "held the mastery for only a short period".

And yet, there was no evidence of anything untoward, and it may simply be that East Fife had a bad day and that Stenhousemuir (fifth from the bottom) had a particularly good day.

Two games remained. East Fife's future was still in their own hands but it was still a disappointment and a source of worry to the fans. Their mood was hardly helped by the news from Wembley that Scotland had lost 2-5 to England.

April 6 1929

East Fife had had a respectable season, but today proved that they were just as yet a little short of what was required to achieve promotion.

Today's visitors to Bayview were Albion Rovers, a team who had also had a respectable season and might just be considered to have an outside chance of promotion.

Albion Rovers scored first, Quinn passing to Brant to do the needful. But then in a purple patch, East Fife showed what they could do and by half-time they were 3-1 up with McGachie scoring twice and playing a part in the other goal.

But then in the second half, what happened? Goalkeeper Garth had an absolute shocker and the two full backs McGeechan and Gowdy were little better as Albion Rovers scored three to win the game 4-3, one from Quinn and two from Weir (not to be confused with Phil Weir who was playing for East Fife).

It was a shocker of a second half performance, and East Fife's 2,000 fans left the ground in a state of numbness rather than anger. The cries of "Ah'm no' comin' back" probably had a little more meaning in this context, for it was the last home League game of the season.

Meanwhile, congratulations went out to Kilmarnock who won the Scottish Cup for the second time this decade, by deservedly beating Rangers 2-0 at Hampden before a six-figure crowd, and Jock Buchanan of Rangers earned the dubious distinction of being the first player to be sent off in a Scottish Cup final.

April 7 1948

A 4-0 over Stenhousemuir this Wednesday night was enough to guarantee promotion to Division "A" of the Scottish League for next year.

A win on Saturday against Stirling Albion on Saturday would now bring East Fife the Championship.

This represented a great triumph for Scot Symon and his men, for the team were already holders of the Scottish League Cup.

East Fife had been in the top tier before in season 1930/31, but they didn't last long. This time, however, there was clear talent in depth in the squad and although no-one would underestimate the gulf between the two Divisions, East Fife did now seem to have the ability to stay there.

Tonight's game, played in a mixture of sunshine and showers, saw East Fife go in at half time 2-0 up, both goals coming from Charlie Fleming from set pieces taken by Davie Duncan.

Jackie Davidson then scored early in the second half, and the scoring was completed by Henry Morris taking advantage of some defensive hesitancy.

The team was cheered off the park at the end and everyone was making plans to come back on Saturday to see them win the Championship.

Not everyone would be there, though, for it was also the day of the Scotland v England International at Hampden, an event that would turn out to be quite disastrous for Scotland.

But there was a great deal to be happy about in East Fife that season. They had gone through the season and had only lost twice so far in the League, once to Kilmarnock at home, and once to Dundee United at Tannadice.

Charlie Fleming

April 8 1929

For the second time in three days, East Fife went down 4-3.

They had lost by that margin to Albion Rovers on Saturday, and today they went down by the same score to Dundee United at Tannadice Park.

The circumstances, however, were totally different. This was the Holiday Monday (or the "fast" as it was called in Dundee) fixture and it attracted a large crowd, because Dundee United could (and duly did) gain promotion to the First Division if they won this game.

Indeed they would go on and win the Second Division Championship, as they had done in 1925. It was a great triumph for the side still happy to be described as the "Dundee Irishmen" even though they had changed their name from Dundee Hibs to Dundee United in 1923 to try to shake off their Irishness.

Today East Fife put up a good show with two goals from Sharkey and one from McGachie, but Dundee United were the better side and East Fife's players and officials were unstinting in their congratulations.

This achievement by the team of the undeniably under-privileged of Dundee raised the interesting question of why East Fife could not do likewise.

But there was a fly in the ointment. *The Dundee Courier* reported a legal case being prepared to challenge the Scottish League on the issue of promotion and relegation this year saying that it was "ultra vires"; Bathgate had gone bankrupt in the middle of the season and had withdrawn from the Scottish League but their results had been allowed to stand. It was a bizarre case, and fortunately, it came to nothing.

April 9 1955

East Fife today eased their relegation worries (although things were still a little perilous) with a fine 6-1 win over St Mirren at Bayview this Easter weekend.

For a spell, relegation had looked more or less inevitable as the players tried to cope with the psychological blow of losing Charlie Fleming to Sunderland in January, but with the weather slowly getting better, the team had turned over a new leaf.

Today it was fine to note that Tommy Wright, Fleming's replacement and inevitably compared unfavourably with him, was the man who scored a good hat-trick, two other goals coming from Jackie Stewart and the other one from another recent arrival called Angus Plumb.

It was the manner of the win that was as pleasing as the actual result against a St Mirren team which would end up sixth in the League. The position was still complicated, but East Fife were now in third bottom place (two were due to get relegated in 1955) marginally ahead of Motherwell on goal average, and well ahead of the doomed Stirling Albion. Four games remained.

Today was also a historic day in Scottish football for it was the day on which Aberdeen won the Scottish League for the first time ever, and the only team other than Celtic, Rangers, Hibs, Hearts, Motherwell, Third Lanark or Dumbarton to have done so.

East Fife supporters were probably glad to see this, but it was of secondary importance. The Fifers had enjoyed First Division football since 1948, and would be reluctant to drop down into the Second Division again.

April 10 1971

East Fife regained First Division status for the first season since 1958, but they did so in bizarre style without kicking a ball!

The Second Division had 19 teams, so there was always a team having a Saturday off, and it so happened that this was East Fife's day!

Player-manager Pat Quinn decided to keep his players active by taking them to play a couple of games in the Highlands; they were playing a friendly at Victoria Park, Dingwall against Ross County when the radio told them that they were back in the First Division.

This came about when Partick Thistle and Arbroath drew at Firhill, meaning that Thistle were now level with East Fife's total but that Arbroath could not now catch East Fife.

This unorthodox method of gaining promotion must not detract from some of the fine football played by East Fife this season in which they won 22 games out of 36, and drew and lost 7 each.

The following week saw a huge crowd at Bayview to greet the team when they came out to beat Queen of the South 2-0. Amidst all the deserved and justified euphoria, however, came the realisation that next year would be very different indeed, as they were now among the big boys.

Partick Thistle duly won the Second Division Championship, but that was of little significance compared to the prospect of Celtic, Rangers, Aberdeen and Hearts all coming to Bayview next season.

It was a pity that Raith Rovers weren't there as well, said someone with his tongue firmly in this cheek.

April 11 1908

North End Park, Cowdenbeath, (the home of Cowdenbeath before they moved to Central Park in 1917) was the venue for East Fife's first appearance in the Fife Cup final against Lochgelly United.

The venue, considerably closer to Lochgelly that it was to Methil, seemed to favour Lochgelly, but as great excitement prevailed in Levenmouth, East Fife were able to take a very large support with them.

It is important to realise that in those pre-Scottish League days for East Fife, tournaments like the Fife Cup were very important indeed, as were the other local tournaments.

Surprisingly, too, to modern eyes was the transfer back from Hibs (for this one game only) of Jimmy Peggie who had joined Hibs a few months ago. Lochgelly United, in similar circumstances, were allowed to field Scott of Falkirk.

The game, delayed for a few minutes to allow the crowd in, was a fascinating one with East Fife going ahead first, but then Lochgelly scored three times and only a late surge by East Fife managing to gain an equaliser.

There was thus an element of anti-climax, laced with the ever-present motif of Edwardian football in Scotland, namely the suspicion that a draw was all a fix for another big gate.

If this was the case, it was certainly a success, for another large crowd appeared the following week at the same venue (East Fife had rather hoped for Stark's Park, Kirkcaldy) and this time East Fife, to tremendous local acclaim won the game 4-2 and thus lifted their first ever Fife Cup.

April 12 1930

East Fife were clearly irked by some of the things said to them (in a subtle way in the press, but rather more overtly in the street) about last week's game against Stenhousemuir

They came out today to play Forfar before a large crowd with a point to prove, and duly won 5-2, breaking the record for team goal scoring in the Scottish League in the process.

It was a fine day, although a little blustery, and both teams came to attack, but veteran Irish Internationalist Joe Gowdy was the star of the show, for the way in which he tamed (most of the time at least) the twin Forfar attackers of Davie McLean and Davie Kilgour.

But Forfar suffered a bad blow when they were reduced to 10 men when centre-half Cameron had to go off with a twisted foot, thus compelling McLean to take up the centre half role.

Forfar scored first but Weir, Liddle, Mitchell and two goals from McGachie won the day for East Fife in what was a very good football match from which Forfar emerged with credit as well.

This result, coupled with Albion Rovers only earning a draw at St Bernard's meant that East Fife were three points ahead of Albion Rovers, but the Rovers had two games in hand.

It was all very exciting, but East Fife had only one game left — against Armadale at Bayview next Saturday. If they won that one, Albion Rovers would have to win all their three games to pip them.

There had certainly been more excitement at Bayview than at Hampden that day for the Scottish Cup final between Rangers and Partick Thistle had ended in a 0-0 draw with journalists in all newspapers struggling to find anything nice to say about the game.

April 13 1938

Dan McKerrel scores the winner in the second replay of the Scottish Cup semi-final against St Bernards at Tynecastle in 1938

April 13 1938

At last, and at the third time of asking, this Scottish Cup semi-final was put to bed.

East Fife scraped into the final winning 2-1 at Tynecastle this Wednesday afternoon. The previous two games had been 1-1, and in all three games it was difficult to argue against the contention that St Bernards (a now defunct team from Stockbridge in Edinburgh who had actually won the Scottish Cup in 1895) were the better side.

The Scotsman, an Edinburgh newspaper, is certainly sympathetic to their cause. But lucky or not, there was no disputing the enthusiasm of the Fife fans who swarmed across the field "like a column of black and gold ants" to congratulate their team.

Cynics were not slow to point out however that three games with crowds of about 35,000 on each occasion were not necessarily "disastrous to the finances" of both clubs, and East Fife were now definitely in the money.

It was Tommy Adams who made the first goal sweeping across a great ball for Larry Millar to finish things off. But St Bernards hit back with a penalty scored by a man called Jerry Kerr who would in future years become Manager of Dundee United and Forfar Athletic.

East Fife however were not to be denied. The winner came from Dan McKerrell, who had just joined the club on a loan from Falkirk, (this was allowed in 1938 as long as the man was not Cup-tied) and East Fife for the second time in 11 years were in the Scottish Cup final.

The Scotsman describes the game as "tremendously hard".

April 14 1954

East Fife had a good win at Bayview this Wednesday night, beating Scottish Cup finalists Aberdeen 2-0.

Charlie Fleming scored both goals in a welcome return to form. They were the first goals he had scored for some time.

In some ways this was an astonishing game, for Aberdeen had beaten Rangers 6-0 in the Scottish Cup semi-final on Saturday.

It raised interesting possibilities about what could have happened for East Fife in the Scottish Cup this year, had they not unaccountably gone down to Queen of the South in January.

Tonight, the weather spoiled the game to a certain extent with a strong wind and a difficult setting sun in the west, but there could be little doubt about the quality of Fleming's two goals.

The first was a snap shot on the turn which caught goalkeeper Fred Martin unawares.

The second was a piece of sheer intelligence where he dummied a Willie Finlay clearance and allowed the ball to go to Ian Gardiner, but was then in position for the return pass to hammer home a trademark goal. Little wonder that he was called "Cannonball"!

The 6,000 crowd were less than totally impressed with Aberdeen, who nevertheless mounted a late rally to get back into the game, but the Fife defence, with Sammy Stewart outstanding, held out.

Tonight at Brockville, Celtic took a major step to winning their first Scottish League since the war with a 3-0 win. East Fife were fated to end up sixth in the League, but as they had won the League Cup in the autumn, it was looked upon as a very successful season.

April 15 1972

It was nice to be part of history, even if it was someone else's!

Today at Bayview, Celtic won their seventh title in a row, beating their own record set between 1905 and 1910.

This was a tremendous achievement, and Jock Stein correctly said that "it won't happen again in my lifetime".

Today was not a great game, played on a bumpy pitch and with East Fife having their own issues of relegation to be avoided, good football was at a premium.

Celtic, in addition, had an important European Cup semi-final against Inter Milan on Wednesday, and were keen therefore to avoid injury.

Respected journalist Cyril Horne, writing in *The Sunday Mail*, wondered whether things might have been different if East Fife had come out and had a "go" from the outset, but is probably correct to state that they "simply didn't have the players to indulge in attacking football" against a team of this calibre.

As it was, Celtic scored three times without reply although Graham Honeyman and Walter Borthwick were both denied by Celtic goalkeeper Evan Williams near the end.

After the game, it was nice to hear the Celtic men saying that all was not yet lost for East Fife in the relegation battle, for although both remaining games were away from home to St Johnstone and Motherwell, neither of these two were unbeatable.

Jock Stein remembered the great days of East Fife, said that the team deserved a bigger support and asked about the welfare of those he had played against twenty years ago.

April 16 2016

Celebrations at Broadwood in 2016

April 16 1927

80,070 people (including a sizeable contingent from Fife) were at Hampden to see East Fife play their first ever Scottish Cup final and only the second Scottish Cup final to involve a Fife team (Raith Rovers having lost to Falkirk in 1913).

East Fife were also the only Second Division team to have reached a final, but today although they fought hard against the mighty Celtic, they were more or less totally outclassed.

And yet they scored first with a Jock Wood header into the King's Park end of the ground. Had they held on to it a little longer, it might have been a different story, but they almost immediately conceded an equaliser through an own goal!

Then John Thomson (late of Wellesley Juniors) pulled off a brilliant save from Davie Edgar, but after that, Celtic took command, and by half time Celtic were ahead after Connolly had released McLean.

After half time Connolly scored himself to make it 3-1 and Celtic now decided that there was little point in humiliating the part timers, and simply played out time.

Tommy McInally, a clown at the best of times, had a barrow load of chances but deliberately put them over the bar — for a laugh! The *Dundee Evening Telegraph* says that McInally "tickled the now happy Celtic choristers with a few of the balloon variety"

This was the first Scottish Cup final to be broadcast live on radio and several enterprising cafes and ice cream shops in Methil capitalised on this by relaying it all to their customers.

April 16 2016

More celebrations in 2016

April 17 1982

While a man called Al Haig, the US Secretary of State, was flying backwards and forwards over the Atlantic in a vain attempt to prevent the Falklands War, football continued.

The poor man was clearly out of his depth and did not seem to grasp the basic truth that the Argentinians had seized these islands and that there would never be peace until they had been turfed out, and he presented a rather comical spectacle of US Diplomacy trying to be nice to everyone and failing miserably.

Far away from these affairs, East Fife were taking on Stenhousemuir in a fixture whose only real significance was whether Stenhousemuir could avoid ending up last in Scotland.

They didn't, as it turned out but today at least at Old Bayview, they put up a fight and East Fife needed a dodgy penalty well sunk by Robin Thomson to win the game.

The weather was OK but the miserable crowd of 356 was an eloquent testimony to the folly of letting a proud team like East Fife lapse into the mediocrity of the Second Division.

It was actually not a bad game, and Martin Caithness had several good chances to put East Fife ahead in the first half. Elsewhere, it looked like Clyde were likely to win the Second Division, and today's 2-0 win for them over Cowdenbeath did them no harm at all.

East Fife had had a frustrating season, never really having recovered from a run of five defeats in a row in the autumn, then a further four in a row in the spring, with the only bright spot at the club at the moment being the emergence of a youngster called Gordon Durie.

The end of the season couldn't come quick enough for some fans.

April 18 1953

It was a curious atmosphere at Celtic Park today with the East Fife fans outnumbered but outshouting the Celtic ones on occasion.

It was a disappointing crowd because Celtic had had a poor season. Their supporters, in any case, were by no means unsympathetic to East Fife, who were challenging for the Championship. The thinking was that if East Fife won the League, it wasn't Rangers!

In addition, most attention was focussed on the England v Scotland game at Wembley, and although 1953 was possibly a bit too early for portable or transistor radios, the Parkhead tannoy kept informing the crowd of the score. (It ended up 2-2).

East Fife really could have done with a victory and should have beaten this lacklustre and half-hearted Celtic side who were lacking Jock Stein, Willie Fernie and John McPhail.

But it was Celtic who went ahead through Jimmy Walsh at the second attempt, and East Fife similarly needed two attempts to score their equaliser. Charlie Fleming crossed to Jimmy Gardiner who headed against goalkeeper John Bonnar but netted the rebound. This was early in the second half and East Fife had loads of time to grab a winner, but somehow or other the Celtic defence held out.

The one point, however, put East Fife to the top of the League, but Rangers and Hibs both had a game in hand, and East Fife had a difficult assignment at Easter Road on Monday.

It was an odd experience to come away from Celtic Park disappointed with "only" a draw, but this poor Celtic team were definitely there for the taking that day!

HIBERNIAN
FOOTBALL CLUB
OFFICIAL PROGRAMME

3ᵈ

No. 25   Friday, 18th April 1958   Kick-off 7.30 p.m.

SCOTTISH LEAGUE
Hibs v East Fife

April 19 1930

For the first time in their history East Fife gained promotion and reached the First Division!

They did this mainly through their own efforts today with a fine 3-0 win over Armadale at Bayview but they also needed neighbours Raith Rovers to beat Albion Rovers.

The Kirkcaldy men did the needful to the tune of 6-2. Their game had kicked off late, because of the late running of the train bringing the Coatbridge men to Kirkcaldy, and therefore East Fife supporters had to wait until they heard the final score before they could celebrate.

The game at Methil was spoiled to a large extent by a swirling wind but Tom Mitchell scored twice and Joe Gowdy once to give the home side a comfortable victory over Armadale.

Gowdy also missed a penalty which would have given him a second goal. It was a great achievement by the home side and they celebrated much, but more sober opinion questioned whether it was a good idea, and how long they could last in the top reaches (not long, as it turned out!).

It was not unknown in the Second Division, before 1930, and indeed subsequently, for teams to be doing well then suddenly "hit a bad run of form" and "inexplicably" let promotion slip.

To the eternal credit of East Fife, they did not do that, but that did not minimise the problem they would have in competing financially, in a time of the worst economic depression since the Industrial Revolution, with the giants of the First Division.

April 19 2008

Adult Ticket for Saturday 19th April, 2018, against Arbroath.

April 19 2008

Showing off the Division Three trophy in 2008

April 20 1953

47,000 were at Easter Road this Holiday Monday to see the home side narrowly defeat East Fife 2-1 in a game which more or less eliminated East Fife from the race for the Scottish League Championship.

Hibs, going for their third successive Scottish League title were a powerful side with their "Famous Five" of Smith, Johnstone, Reilly, Turnbull and Ormond all going strong.

Nevertheless they needed a fair slice of luck as well as some indifferent East Fife finishing to win this game. Hibs scored first through Eddie Turnbull who had picked up a throw-in from Bobby Johnstone, but East Fife equalised when Jackie Stewart seemed to have a few more inches that anyone else to rise above them all and head home.

But then Hibs scored again with a diving header from Willie Ormond to head home a cross from Gordon Smith. The last 20 minutes or so resembled the siege of the Alamo as East Fife threw everything at a Hibs defence which needed help from its "Famous Five" forwards to keep out the Fifers.

The closest East Fife came was when a header rebounded off the bar to Jimmy Bonthrone who had more time than he thought he did, and could have placed the ball in the net rather than blast it over the bar.

In addition referee Mr Brittle might have given a penalty, but the whistles for full time from the Hibs faithful told their own tale.

Rangers won that evening as well, and the League race was now down to two. It was the closest East Fife ever came to winning the Scottish League. But a team from Methil pursuing the big two of Rangers and Hibs all that time?

"Punching above their weight" did not quite cover it!

April 21 1951

East Fife finally saved themselves from any lingering fear of relegation with a 4-1 win over Airdrie at Bayview today.

It was a fine performance on a sunny, albeit slightly windy day with two goals from Ian Gardiner (who should now be considered for the International team, according to *The Courier*) and one each from Davie Duncan and Bobby Black.

It was a good game and led quite a few of the supporters to wonder why this could not have happened a great deal earlier so as to save the fans the worry.

It was a far more clinical performance from East Fife than had been the case of late, with *The Airdrie and Coatbridge Advertiser* very critical of their own team for being short with its pass backs and "the Fife team taking full advantage" thereof.

This day was a very sad day in Scottish football however, for two fans were killed in a train crash in Glasgow en route to the Scottish Cup final, won 1-0 by Celtic.

There were also clear indications that the post-war Labour Government which had done so much to eradicate unnecessary illness and poverty was coming to an end. Ernest Bevin had died a week ago, Stafford Cripps was ill and Aneurin Bevan and Harold Wilson today resigned from the Government in protest at charges being raised for dental care and spectacles in order to pay for the Korean War.

The Government had only a slim majority and would lose the General Election in October 1951.

April 22 1950

East Fife's hopes of landing a Cup double this season (they had already won the League Cup) came to a shuddering halt today in the Hampden rain in the Scottish Cup final when they lost 0-3 to Rangers before a staggering crowd of 118,615.

They had a huge support from Fife with them, and neutral opinion was on their side, but it was simply one of these days when an East Fife supporter can do little other than hold up his hands and say that the better team won.

Rangers had not had a great season, but were now finishing strongly. Today they chose to play their best.

East Fife had to play young Gordon Easson in goal because of an injury to John Niven. It was, apparently, his first ever visit to Hampden and within a minute he had conceded a goal to a header from Rangers Willie Findlay. He then had a fine save from a free-kick early in the second half, but had no answer to the two goals that Willie Thornton scored a few minutes later.

East Fife did not play badly, but in key areas, Rangers were on top. Henry Morris, for example, never really got going against Willie Woodburn, and Charlie Fleming, of whom much was expected, seemed out of touch.

It was the 13th time that Rangers had won the Scottish Cup.

The teams were:

East Fife: Gordon Easson, Willie Laird and Sammy Stewart; Jimmy Philp, Willie Finlay and George Aitken; Bobby Black, Charlie Fleming, Henry Morris, Allan Brown and Davie Duncan.

Rangers: Bobby Brown, George Young and Jock Shaw; Ian McColl, Willie Woodburn and Sammy Cox; Eddie Rutherford, Willie Findlay, Willie Thornton, Jimmy Duncanson and Willie Rae.

Referee: Jack Mowat, Rutherglen.

April 23 1938

Methil was mobilised to go to the Cup final today, and the streets were quiet.

Astonishingly there was no radio broadcast of the game (and yet there had been in 1927!).

News would get through to the Post Office or the offices of the local newspaper, but in any case it was predicted that about 10,000 would be there on trains, buses or cars.

The game was all-ticket, but the crowd was a disappointing 80,091, and although the authorities had said that no-one would be admitted by paying cash, in fact there were a few cash turnstiles.

The weather was fine, and it was a good game, although the teams could not be separated at 1-1. McLeod scored for East Fife, but then McAvoy equalised for Kilmarnock.

East Fife claimed vigorously that following a shoulder charge by Dan McKerrell on goalkeeper Hunter, the ball crossed the line, but referee Hugh Watson of Glasgow demurred.

At the end of the game, managers Davie McLean of East Fife and Jimmy McGrory of Kilmarnock shook hands and looked forward to Wednesday night's replay.

For the East Fife fans there was a sense of anti-climax; things were not helped by the news that Andy Herd, the left half, was injured and probably out of the replay.

The teams were

East Fife: Milton, Laird and Tait; Russell, Sneddon and Herd; Adams, McLeod, McCartney, Millar and McKerrell.

Kilmarnock: Hunter, Fyfe and Milloy; Robertson, Stewart and Ross; Thomson, Reid, Collins, McAvoy and McGrogan.

April 23 1938

April 24 1948

"A pleasant Saturday afternoon atmosphere" at Cliftonhill, Coatbridge was how *The Sunday Post* described this game between the two teams promoted from Division "B", champions East Fife and runners up Albion Rovers.

The Sunday Post also has few qualms about how they will perform next year in the tougher regime of Division "A", for they put on a fine display of football before a crowd of 8,000 who were chivalrous enough to clap East Fife on to the field.

The game itself was a close one, not nearly as one-sided as the 4-1 score line would have suggested. The difference between the two sides was Davie Duncan, whose shooting power impressed everyone ("Dynamite in his boots" was the headline in several newspapers!).

The opinion was expressed that he would be a great asset to Scotland when he made his International debut against Belgium on Wednesday night. He scored two goals himself and sent another two crosses over for Henry Morris to score, Henry beating Albion Rovers centre half Jock Stein with ease.

Thus ended a very successful season for East Fife with the "B" Division won by 11 points over Albion Rovers, and of course the Scottish League Cup won back in November.

They had also scored a massive total of 103 goals in the Scottish League, and had had a reasonably good run for their money in the Scottish Cup as well before losing to Rangers.

On this same day, Hibs more or less won the Scottish League barring some mathematical improbability; Manchester United beat Blackpool 4-2 in the English Cup final at Wembley, with considerable Scottish involvement in the shape of Manager Matt Busby and right winger Jimmy Delaney.

April 25 1931

This was East Fife's last day in the old First Division. 7,000 turned up at Bayview to see Rangers win the League — a surprisingly small attendance in the circumstances, but then again, so many East Fife supporters had given up for the season and in any case the weather was damp and unpleasant.

East Fife had been relegated for a few weeks, but Rangers still had to win today to pip Celtic, who had won the Scottish Cup that season.

Rangers duly did so, winning their fifth League title in a row. In truth, this was not much of a game, for by half-time Rangers were 4-0 up, then visibly eased off in the second half, having no desire to further humiliate the men from Methil.

Bob McPhail scored the first goal, but there was a touch of controversy about the second when the ball did not seem to have crossed the line when it came down from the bar. But there was no doubt about goals three and four, one scored by James "Doc" Marshall and then Sandy Archibald, a Fifer who would in future years become the Manager of Raith Rovers.

The second half provided little entertainment, and the whole atmosphere was one of anti-climax. For the Ibrox fans, it was as well that Rangers won however, for Celtic also won today beating Leith.

For East Fife, this whole season had been a huge disappointment. Frankly they had been outplayed all season, and in a time of general economic uncertainty, the season had been a financial disaster, in spite of one or two large "gates" throughout the season.

April 26 2008

In a curiously anti-climactic way, East Fife's great season of 2007/08 came to an end to-day at Cliftonhill, the home of Albion Rovers.

It was a 2-2 draw in front of 245 spectators (although the *Sky Sports Year Book* says 404).

It was a shame that not more were there to see the end of what could well be regarded as one of the greatest seasons in the club's history, in terms of performances at least.

Granted, the opposition was not great and in that sense the season cannot be compared to the halcyon days of the early 1950s when East Fife held their own against Celtic and Rangers, but for a team to play 36 League games and lose only four — that must be considered a great achievement.

No great progress was made in any of the Cup competitions, and in the League, there was a complex about Stenhousemuir (who beat us twice after we had hammered them 7-0 in September), but other than that, great praise must be given to Dave Baikie's men who went eight games without losing a League goal between September 22 and December 22.

They were never really challenged in the League, and finished 23 points ahead of second placed Stranraer. They wrapped up promotion and the winning of the Division Three championship in the month of March with the trophy being presented last week.

What everyone was aware of, however, was that next season would be a totally different matter, and that in any case, East Fife, with all our history and tradition, really should not be in the lowest tier of Scottish football.

April 26 2008

Bobby Linn in action against Albion Rovers at Cliftonhill

April 27 1938

It is the best night of East Fife's history as they won the Scottish Cup by beating Kilmarnock 4-2 after extra time at Hampden Park.

They became the first team to win the trophy from outside the top tier, and also the first team from Fife to win the "blue riband" of Scottish football.

A crowd of 92,716 watched this game, which kicked off at 6.30 pm and, with extra time, didn't finish until almost 9.00 pm in the gathering gloom.

Both teams were well supported but the bulk of the crowd was made up of Glasgow neutrals who would "adopt" one or other of the teams for the duration of the Cup final.

East Fife were compelled to make one change from the first game. Left half Herd was injured, and John Harvey was recruited from Hearts for his one and only game in East Fife colours. (Incredibly, this was allowed!)

East Fife scored first through Dan McKerrell but were 1-2 down at half-time. Eddie McLeod however equalised by full time, and then the two exhausted teams moved on to extra time.

Within the last 10 minutes, East Fife scored twice through Larry Millar and Dan McKerrell. About 5,000 at the most have travelled from Methil to Hampden, but back home, although there was no commentary on the radio, the Sports News at 10.00pm gave the score, and the team came back to a heroes' reception.

A crowd of about 1,000 were waiting to see the Scottish Cup at Wemyss Castle Station where the players disembarked and then headed to the waiting buses to take them home through crowded streets.

A crowd of 3,000 waited to see them on Wellesley Road, but they went home to Methil by the low road!

It was 2.00 am before the police were able to clear the streets.

The immortal team was:

Milton, Laird and Tait; Russell, Sneddon and Harvey; Adams, McLeod, McCartney, Miller and McKerrell.

April 27 1938

The crowd await the return of their Cup heroes on April 27 1938

April 27 1938

East Fife's Scottish Cup winners, the first team ever to win the Scottish Cup from the Second Division. The team is Back Row: Russell, Laird, Tait, Milton, Harvey, Herd: Front Row: Adams, Millar, McCartney, Sneddon, McLeod and

April 27 1938

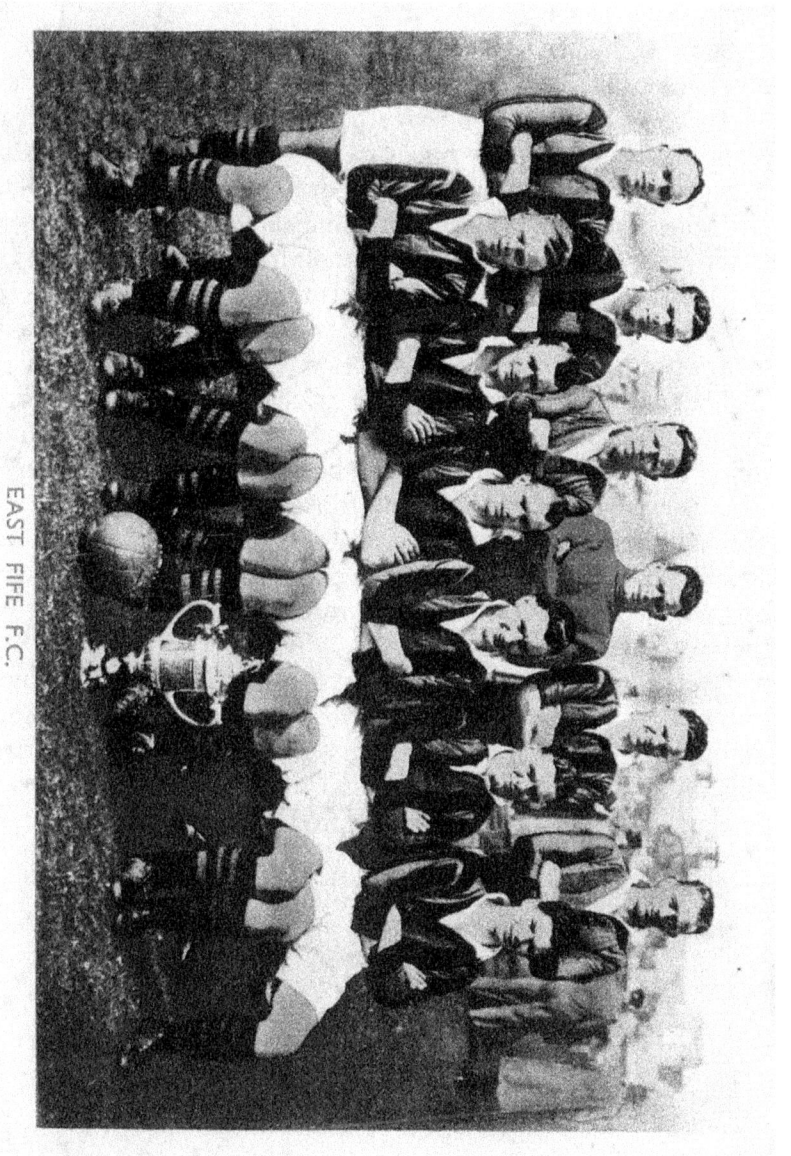

A somewhat primitive colour postcard of the Scottish Cup winners

April 28 1938

The night after the Scottish Cup win, East Fife were (incredibly) in action again, this time to play a League game at Bayview against Forfar Athletic.

Some of the players had stayed overnight in the Beach Hotel, Leven and had not been home but had stayed just to savour the occasion.

Around 5,000 were at Bayview to see an easy 3-0 victory over a Forfar team who shared in the big "gate" and in the delight of the Fifers, particularly when they were given a drink out of the Cup at full time.

(Some of the Forfar players and officials went home boasting to their friends that they had actually had their hands on the Scottish Cup!)

The main attraction for the spectators was of course the Scottish Cup which was on view before the start when a picture was taken of the team with the trophy.

The goals were scored by Adams, McLeod and McCartney, and after the game was over, the team went on to an open topped bus and drove round the whole Levenmouth area before returning to Bayview.

This was for the benefit of all those who had not seen the trophy the night before, when it was too late for youngsters. Much drink was consumed and many supporters were quite happy to admit that they had not been to bed the night before, and that they hadn't been to their work that day either!

An uncomfortable interview perhaps awaited on the Friday — not to mention a rather severe hangover in some cases — but such was the general euphoria over the whole area that it would have been difficult for employers or headmasters to be too harsh on those whose enjoyment of the occasion had teetered towards the extreme.

April 29 1949

By agreement, this game against Hearts was played on the final Friday night of the season, allowing Raith Rovers and Dunfermline (who would be engaged in a game to settle the Second Division title) to have all Fife to themselves on the Saturday.

Tonight's fixture was basically a game of no great importance other than prestige and a desire on the part of East Fife to avenge the hammering inflicted upon them earlier in the season at Tynecastle.

7,000 turned up to see a rather remarkable game in which every single one of East Fife's forward line of Bobby Black, Charlie Fleming, Henry Morris, Douglas Davidson and Davie Duncan scored in a 5-1 victory, and the much vaunted Hearts inside trio of Conn, Bauld and Wardhaugh were unable to make any impact on East Fife's half-back line of Philp, Finlay and Brown.

Hearts' only goal was a Jimmy Wardhaugh penalty, and not everyone agreed with referee Mr Davidson's decision on that one!

Thus ended East Fife's first season in the First Division and it was fair to say that they had impressed everyone and deserved to finish fourth in the League.

As a reward, they were to be taken on a European tour in a few weeks' time. They were thus able to have a day off on the Saturday — and it was indeed a remarkable day of football for Raith Rovers (with several East Fife players seen at the game) beat Dunfermline 4-0 to win the Second Division.

In the First Division, Dundee really should have won the Scottish League but decided to blow up at Falkirk and thus allow Rangers to win a scarcely deserved treble; at Wembley, Wolverhampton Wanderers beat Leicester City to win the English Cup for the first time since 1908.

April 30 2016

This was a curious game of football at New Bayview.

1,360 turned up to see the two Easts of Fife and Stirlingshire confront each other, each with a totally different agenda.

For East Stirlingshire, it turned out to be the last Scottish League game that they would play for some time. They were fated to lose their play-off for re-election and lost out to Edinburgh City.

So it was good-bye to "shirie pirie" even though their fans put up a reasonable show of defiance. But for East Fife it was trophy day.

The Second Division (the lowest tier) had been won a couple of weeks ago with a dull 0-0 draw against Clyde at Broadwood and last week had seen a 0-2 defeat at Berwick. Not exactly form worthy of the champions, and to-day's game was, frankly, a bore with the highlight the countdown to the receiving of the trophy on the podium.

And yet it was a bright, if still cold, day and it was good to see East Fife back out of the bargain basement, and supporters allowed to see any kind of a trophy.

One or two gnarled veterans recalled the great days of Charlie Fleming and George Aitken, but the truth was that there was no real comparison between the 1950s and now.

But the club was at least moving in the right direction, and full marks to Gary Naysmith and his team.

For the record the game was a 1-1 draw with both goals coming early in the second half, Michael McMullin for East Stirlingshire and Kevin Smith for East Fife.

April 30 2016

Jamie Insall shoots in a game against East Stirlingshire

May

East Fife season 1974 75

May 1 1993

It is not often that one can say that Brechin City's away support can come anywhere close to outnumbering any home support, but this seemed to be the case at Bayview today, for the 580 crowd seemed to contain an awful lot of red and white scarves and broad Angus accents, calling each other "min", and asking "Far's the toilets?"

Brechin City were going for promotion (they would eventually squeeze in on goal difference) which was more than could be said for East Fife whose players and supporters gave every sign of having given up for the season.

Indeed Brechin City's record, for all the jokes that were made at their expense, had been markedly better than many teams, East Fife not excepted, over the last decade.

Today East Fife lost 0-2 to a strong but not unbeatable Brechin side, and there was at least some kind of a fightback in the second half with a goal from Beaton.

It had been a miserable season for East Fife, but they now had a strong character in Alex Totten as Manager. He was making the right noises about demanding more commitment from the players, otherwise they would not be re-engaged for next season.

The big question about the club at the moment concerned the future of Bayview. Some were suggesting re-locating to Glenrothes, others talked about moving down to Methil Docks, while the more conservative and historically minded of supporters wondered whether a little redevelopment of Bayview might not be a bad idea.

Standing still, however, was not really an option. Bayview, as it stood, had seen better days. It was a lovely old lady of a stadium, but "old" was the word.

May 2 2015

East Fife confirmed their fourth place in Scottish League Division Two and therefore a place in the play-offs for promotion with a 3-1 win today over Elgin City at New Bayview before a crowd of 697.

It was a good performance to finish off the League season and was much appreciated by the crowd.

Kevin Smith scored twice, and the other was scored by Derek Riordan. Riordan was a much travelled and indeed controversial character who had played mainly for Hibs and Celtic but had joined East Fife in the latter part of this season.

He scored the third goal before Elgin City notched a late and irrelevant goal. Riordan was a Hibee by nature and had a reputation as a trouble maker but his time with the club had been quite trouble free.

The reward was to face Stenhousemuir, who had finished second bottom in Division One in the play-offs. It had been a reasonable good year from East Fife, after a horrendous start involving the loss of the first three games, and another loss of form in the depressingly dark months of December and January.

The League had been won by Albion Rovers this year, a team against whom East Fife had done well, winning twice and drawing once.

It had been an odd year in Scottish football with the Scottish Cup final to be contested by Inverness Caledonian Thistle and Falkirk.

On the other hand, Celtic had won the Scottish Premier League rather easily under the management of a previoulsy unknown Norwegian called Ronnie Deila.

May 2 2015

Action from East Fife and Edinburgh City

May 3 1986

This was a tense nerve-wracking day in Scottish football with East Fife involved at the very end.

They even had a slim, theoretical chance of promotion to the Premier Division themselves — they needed to beat Falkirk and hope other results went their way — and Dave Clarke's men had every reason to kick themselves for their lapses earlier in the season.

Today they travelled to Brockville to play Falkirk before a 6,600 crowd generally believed to be the biggest that Falkirk (or East Fife for that matter) had played before for many years.

The game was delayed ten minutes to allow the crowd in. Hamilton Accies had won the title and deservedly so, but a cluster of teams were involved in the chase for second spot.

Falkirk scored in the first half, and when they scored again early in the second half, it looked as if it were all done and dusted for Falkirk, particularly as their nearest rivals Forfar Athletic were struggling to a draw at Alloa.

Then with seven minutes to go, East Fife pulled one back through McCafferty and then Mitchell scored again almost at the death to give the Brockville supporters a nervous time, but the referee eventually signalled the end and the arrival in the Premier Division of Billy Lamont's Falkirk side.

It was only on the way home that many supporters realised that a late winner might well have done it for East Fife, given the other results.

East Fife were not the only team playing "what if" tonight, for in a far higher profile game, Hearts blew up against Dundee and would have won the League if they had not conceded two late goals to a man called Albert Kidd.

May 4 1974

This was an agonising day for East Fife as they faced relegation from the old First Division, and they couldn't do anything about it.

All East Fife's games had been played, and East Fife were relying upon Hearts to beat Clyde at Tynecastle.

It was not as if this were a great Hearts side in any case and they had clearly given up for the season — no-one wants to break a leg the day before their summer holidays! — but nevertheless Manager Frank Christie went to Tynecastle to support the Jambos.

For East Fife fans it was a question of sitting by the radio to listen to the two Cup finals on that day — Celtic beat Dundee United 3-0, and Liverpool beat Newcastle by the same score — and hope for a score flash from Tynecastle.

They told us the half-time score — 0-0 — but the absence of any "score flashes from Tynecastle" in the second half of those one-sided Cup finals tended to indicate that the score was still 0-0.

And so it was.

The sparse Tynecastle crowd began to evaporate as their feckless favourites failed to break down the Clyde defence, leaving the ground to the small knot of Clyde supporters who began to grow in optimism as the minutes ticked past.

Eventually after the full time interviews of the Cup final, the radio broke the bad news. Without a whimper, East Fife were relegated after three years in the top tier.

The Leagues were to be changed next year, so the chances of East Fife reaching the top 10 Premier League for 1975/76 had now gone.

May 5 2007

By any standards, Stranraer to Methil is a long, long way and as a general rule, East Fife do not take busloads and trainloads down there to support them.

They didn't on this occasion either, but at least the 426 who attended this game did contain a smattering of black and gold clad supporters of East Fife.

The journey back was not quite so tedious as it might have been either, for the weather was OK and at least there was plenty of daylight.

East Fife lost 0-1, but because they had beaten Stranraer so comprehensively 4-1 on the Wednesday night in the first leg, they were now through to the final of the play-offs for the Second Division.

Car radios informed everyone on the way back that the opponents would be Queen's Park rather than Arbroath. The 4-1 score line in the first leg emphatically did not mean that East Fife could take things easily, and Stranraer put up a great fight.

The fact that it was the 65th minute before McGrillen pierced the East Fife defence for the home side made things so much easier for East Fife's defence to hold out and prevent another, potentially disastrous goal.

One has to admire Stranraer in some ways. Their ground is nearer to Northern Ireland than it is to most of Scotland, and there is not such a thing as a derby fixture unless they are in the same Division as Queen of the South.

They are the third oldest surviving club in Scotland behind Queen's Park and Kilmarnock, and are rightly proud of what they have done and continue to do. Pity that they are so remote!

May 5 2007

Stranraer is the venue for this action. A good header, but no goal

May 6 1905

The Fife Cup was played on a League basis this year, and today's 1-1 draw at Stark's Park between Raith Rovers and East Fife helped neither of the two teams, and effectively handed over the Fife Cup to Cowdenbeath.

It was more of a blow to Raith Rovers than to East Fife, a club with lesser pretensions, given that they had not yet celebrated their second birthday!

Football was now going "out of season" for the summer (the cricket season was now in full swing) but there was still a sizeable crowd at Stark's Park to see this game,

East Fife were the better team, so much so that the writer of *The Fife Free Press* is rather surprised that they have not done better in other competitions.

Bernard in goal "had one soft thing chalked against him" while Middlemass, Whyte and Adams did well as did Sandy Russell who had been out for a year.

Two other things happened in football that day — one was the decision to form a Central League, something that would have an impact on East Fife in the future, and the Scottish League decided for the first and only time in its life to have a play-off as Celtic and Rangers had finished on equal points.

Rangers would have won on either goal average or goal difference if either of these methods had been employed, but it was Celtic who won the decider to become Scottish Champions for the fifth time.

Meanwhile in the Far East, it was becoming clear that the efficient Japanese, the allies of Great Britain, were proving too much for the Russians in the Russo-Japanese war.

May 7 1955

The League season was now over, and it was generally agreed that 1954/55 had not been one of East Fife's better seasons in the First Division.

In fact relegation beckoned for a spell, until an impressive late surge made a huge difference.

Today however saw a Fife Cup semi-final game at Stark's Park. Anyone who thought that it would be a pointless friendly was totally wrong, for the 4,000 crowd saw a thrilling encounter.

Raith Rovers were 3-1 up, but East Fife fought back to take the game to extra time in which the Rovers eventually prevailed. It was disappointing. East Fife were now shorn of their better players, notably Charlie Fleming, and Manager Jerry Dawson was still rebuilding the side.

Today was a funny day at Stark's Park and certainly one of the attractions was a man with a "Portobello" radio (the more conventional pronunciation being "portable"!) which was carrying a broadcast of the English Cup final won 3-1 by Newcastle United over Manchester City.

BBC television (there was only one channel in 1955) showed the game live in England, but the Scottish Football Association, in a curious blend of Calvinism, parsimony and bloody-mindedness, decided not to allow it in Scotland.

As a result for the first and only time in history, a Scottish domestic cricket match was shown between Poloc and the West of Scotland!

The Scottish Cup final between Clyde and Celtic had been shown live on BBC a couple of weeks previously, but, when it ended in a draw, the replay was blanked out! Scottish football was clearly very suspicious of television.

May 8 2004

Play-offs were not yet in vogue, and this was a great pity for it meant that second bottom place in the League was relegation, and this was a desperate rear guard action from East Fife to stave it off.

Stenhousemuir had been the whipping boys of the Second Division (the third tier of four) but the fight to avoid second bottom had been an exciting one all season involving Arbroath, Alloa, Forfar, Berwick Rangers and East Fife.

Berwick Rangers and today's visitors Forfar Athletic had more or less saved themselves by now, and indeed it now looked odds on East Fife being the team for the drop.

They could expect few favours from their old friends Forfar Athletic, but at the same time, it must be conceded that for some football players and teams, the summer holidays can start a little earlier if there is no great issue at stake.

Four defeats out of the last six games had clearly made a lot of supporters think that the game was up, for only 448 appeared at New Bayview and they all had that resigned, pained, martyrical look about them.

They saw a poor first half, but then two quick goals from McDonald and McMillan brightened things up for a spell before the lapse into mediocrity once again.

Nevertheless, East Fife won 2-0. In 2004 some of the young whiz-kids in the support could receive texts and were able to spread the word along the stand that Arbroath were losing heavily to Dumbarton.

0-3 was the score there and it meant that East Fife could play their final game next week against doomed Stenhousemuir with a degree of hope, if only Berwick Rangers could beat the Red Lichties as well.

Clutching at straws however!

May 9 1936

The press are all delighted to announce details of the Presentation to Phil Weir, a player looked upon as a local hero who had now played for the club for a staggering 13 years.

During this time he had seen the good and the bad, had experienced promotion and relegation, and of course had been to Hampden in that epic season of 1927 when they reached the final of the Scottish Cup.

He was so well known and so well loved by the supporters that sometimes *The Leven Mail* and *The Courier* refer to him simply as "Philip".

He was honoured at a meeting of supporters in Methil Bowling Green Hall with Mr William Moscrip, President of the club paying tribute to his goal scoring abilities and saying that he was an ideal team man before presenting him with a writing bureau, his wife with a handbag and his son with a bank book containing "the balance of the subscriptions" raised from the grateful supporters.

A toast to East Fife FC was proposed by ex-Provost Taylor and in reply Baillie Gray, on behalf of the club assured supporters that the Directors were imbued with the desire to move further in the footballing world.

Indeed there had been a certain amount of progress this year, for the team had finished sixth in the Second Division as distinct from ninth in 1935.

There was then some social activity with songs from John McArthur, Robert Hay and Alex Stevenson, and a poem by Ben Thomson. Alec McCulloch proposed the vote of thanks.

May 10 2003

Ironically, it was one of the worst games of football ever seen at New Bayview (and worse than a lot played at Old Bayview for that matter!) but Kenny Deuchar's last minute goal was enough to earn East Fife promotion from the lowest tier of the Scottish League.

The opponents were Queen's Park, not one of the better teams in the League it has to be said.

However, they put up stubborn resistance against an East Fife team which lacked finesse but had loads of enthusiasm and commitment and kept belting the ball forward for Deuchar but... so far without success.

The position was that any sort of a win would guarantee promotion, and there was even an outside chance of winning the Championship if Morton and Peterhead drew.

It was the last game of the season, and the "last chance saloon" as the phrase went. Rumours spread (correctly, as it turned out) that Morton were beating Peterhead, so the chances of winning the League had probably gone, but promotion was still a possibility as long as East Fife could score.

Pressure continued to be applied hysterically on that sea end, but Queen's Park seemed to have held out as the referee refused to award a penalty kick.

With hope almost gone, Gordon Love sent over a cross and for once Deuchar was on his own and in a position to nudge the ball over the line. Cue hysteria!

The referee blew for time up almost immediately after that, and although there was not quite any "dancing in the streets of Methil" that night, the supporters left happier than they had been for many a long year.

May 10 2003

Kenny Deuchar is chaired high after promotion is clinched against Queen's Park in 2003

May 11 1921

At a momentous meeting in Glasgow today, it was agreed that a Second Division of the Scottish League should be formed.

It would consist of 20 teams. East Fife thus became members of the Scottish League less than 20 years after their formation in 1903.

This decision followed months of intensive discussions and lobbying with the Central League teams (of which East Fife was one) applying *en masse* for admission to the new Division of the League.

There would be automatic promotion and relegation, normally of two teams either way but in the first season, there would only be one team promoted and three relegated to reduce the number of teams in the First Division to 20 from 22 which was felt to be rather too unwieldy.

The advantage to teams like East Fife was that it gave them a permanent home in a national structure, a place that they were not likely to lose.

There might be a few disadvantages in that there could be some travel to more distant places than had been the case hitherto.

For the moment at least, the Second Division was made up of the Central League teams with a few additions like Forfar, Arbroath, Johnstone and the historic Vale of Leven side who had three times won the Scottish Cup in the 1870s but had now fallen from prominence.

The Scottish League had been more or less forced to incorporate the Central League because of teams like Dunfermline who were rich enough to attract and poach players from Scottish League teams, and the Scottish League teams were unable to do anything about it, for the Central League was unofficial.

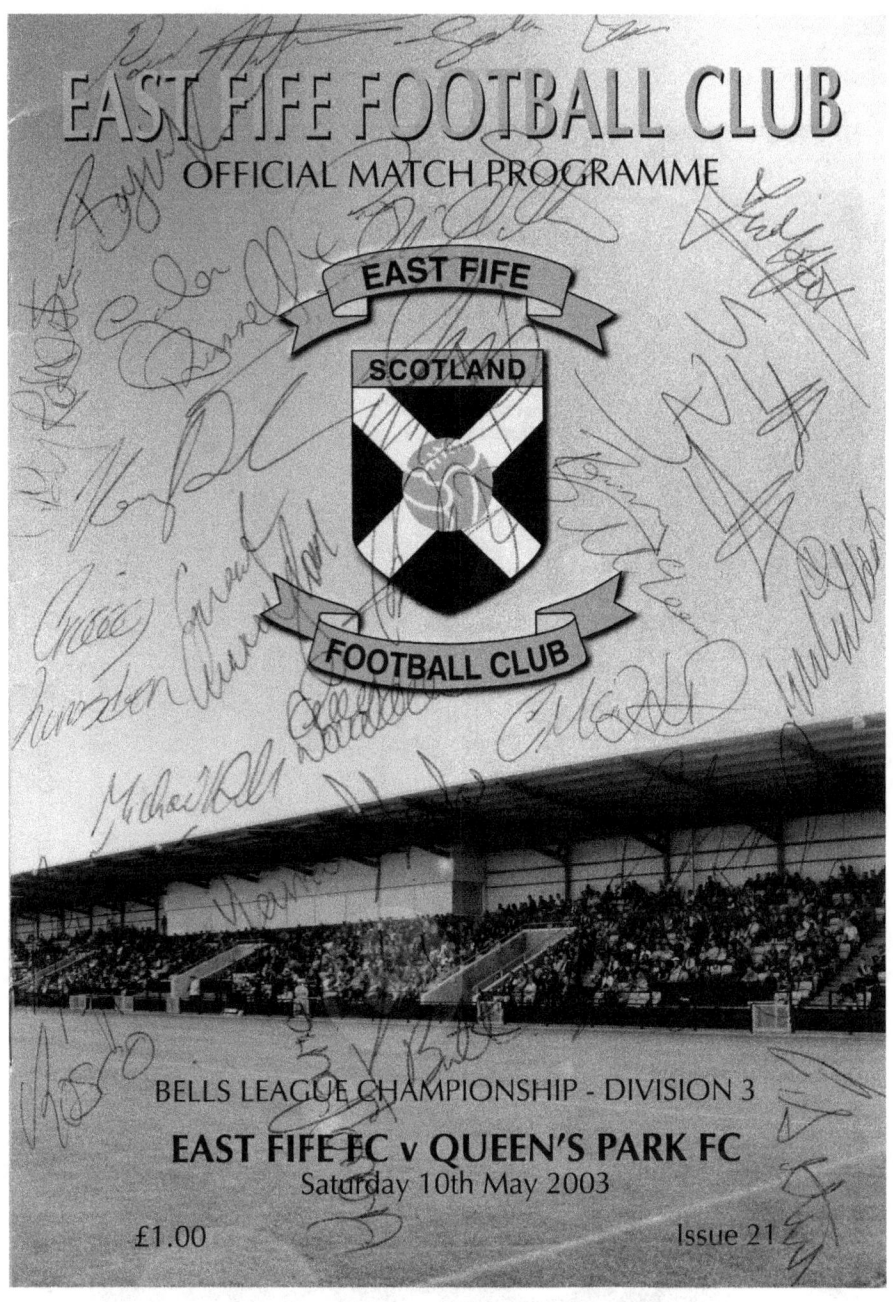

May 12 2007

Stevie Nicholas is on the ball here in the game against Queen's Park

May 12 2007

This was a disappointing day at New Bayview as East Fife lost the final of the Division Two play-off to Queen's Park before a big turn-out of 1625.

East Fife were 4-2 down from the first leg (played at Firhill because Hampden was unavailable) last Wednesday night but they had fought back well after being 3-0 and then 4-1 down, and everyone was confident that this score line could be turned around.

Sadly not so, because East Fife chose to put on one of their worst displays all season and lost 0-3. The trickling of spectators to the exits after Queen's Park scored their second goal was an eloquent testimony to the feelings of disappointment felt by the supporters as the team succumbed to a 7-2 aggregate score line.

East Fife needed an early goal but sadly the early goal came at the other end as Paul Paton struck from about 25 yards. The Fifers then had hard luck on several occasions, but crucially could not make the breakthrough.

The goal in the 75th minute from Alan Trouten off the underside of the bar killed things for Dave Baikie's men. Frankie Carroll then scored more or less on the final whistle.

It was a great triumph for the amateurs (and the honest East Fife supporters would admit that it was well deserved) who now returned to the Second Division for the first time since 2001.

Their Manager, Billy Stark, said that it was the proudest moment in his life, something that meant a lot coming from a man who had won Scottish League and Cup medals with Aberdeen and Celtic. But for East Fife the agony of being in the lower tier continued.

May 13 1926

Today was a strange and sad day in Methil and the surrounding area.

It was the day after the General Strike had been called off, and the drift back to work began — but not the miners.

The strike had been all about the miners refusing to accept a deterioration in their wages and conditions, and the whole Trades Union Congress had backed them to the extent of calling everyone out in support.

But now the Trades Union Congress, perhaps fearing that they had bitten off more than they could chew, backed off leaving the miners to fight on alone. It was claimed that the General Strike passed off with no violence.

This was not 100% true necessarily, but it could have been a great deal worse. It would have been impossible to say with any degree of certainty just how many of East Fife's supporters were miners, but it was certainly a high proportion, and they were now abandoned by their fellow workers, rather destroying the myth of "class solidarity".

Eventually, in circumstances of utmost deprivation and humiliation, the miners were compelled to go back to work in November and to accept what the coal owners offered. Some men were victimised and not offered their jobs back, and there was little that they could do about it. Unrest in the mining industry would now die a death until it returned with renewed ferocity in the 1970s.

There was little doubt however that the General Strike and its aftermath had its effect on East Fife FC, but in a surprising way, for the triumphs of the following season 1926/27 when they reached the final of the Scottish Cup seemed to be the community's way of fighting back.

May 14 1994

It was hardly in the class of the Scottish Cup final victory of 1938, or the three League Cup triumphs of the 1940s and 1950s, but one supposes that this game has to go down as a triumph.

On a nice sunny day at Alloa, East Fife gained a draw (a lucky draw, some said) to finish sixth!

Normally finishing sixth in the Second Division is no cause for celebration but this was the season in which the Leagues were to be redrawn so that the top six in the Second Division would go onto the new Second Division (following this?) while the remaining eight would form the Third Division with two newcomers from the Highlands — Ross County and Inverness Caledonian Thistle.

East Fife's form throughout the season had been far from great — indeed, it was a great deal worse than usual — but they reached the last day knowing that a draw would see them in the second bottom tier for next year.

The game was at Alloa, who needed to win to pip the Fifers, and this seemed to be happening when Kemp scored for them in the first half.

But more or less at the restart Alan Sneddon, that crusty veteran of Celtic and Hibs, scored to level things, and to set up an intriguing second half.

East Fife's defence deserve a great deal of credit for dealing with the increasingly hysterical attacks of the Clackmannanshire men.

The countdown to the final whistle involved a great deal of anxiety but the end of the game saw a mini pitch invasion by young East Fife supporters in the 1,156 crowd to celebrate. It is not often that finishing sixth in any competition triggers the champagne, but this occasion did.

May 15 1982

The crowd was given as 250, but even that looked like an exaggeration.

However they turned up at Links Park, Montrose today to see a fixture which did not really have a great deal going for it.

East Fife ended up seventh in the Second Division (the third tier of three in 1982) and Montrose 10th as a result of this 2-1 win for East Fife, the goals coming from O'Brien and Scott.

The game was played in a relaxed atmosphere with the barking of dogs and the musical box of an ice cream van often heard in the background.

Clyde had won the Second Division in a season which had been characterised by loads of postponements in December and January, and there had been little for East Fife fans to enthuse about other than the emergence of a young star called Gordon Durie who looked as if he could go places.

The season would have been over long ago but for the backlog of fixtures, but there was still exciting football going on elsewhere.

Celtic won the Scottish League by beating St Mirren today, and there was of course the World Cup in Spain to look forward to.

But there were other things happening in the world, notably the Falkland War with the British just about to remove the Argentinians from the islands that they had seized about six weeks ago.

There was a certain amount of worry that this could impact on the World Cup, but at the moment it did not look as if Argentina were likely to play against England, Scotland or Northern Ireland. Meanwhile the world watched and waited.

May 16 1931

It had become the custom for Scotland teams to go on tour to Europe in the month of May.

There had been a tour in 1929, and last year, John Thomson, who used to play for Wellesley Juniors before he moved to Celtic, had earned his Scotland debut in Paris.

It would have to be said that such tours were not always taken seriously by the players and the public, with many players finding reasons to make themselves unavailable for one reason or another.

Celtic, for example, were in America at this time. Nevertheless it was still an honour to be chosen to play for Scotland, and East Fife earned their first ever full International Cap when "Dangerous Dan" Liddle was chosen to fill the left wing berth in the Hohe Warte Stadion, Vienna when Scotland took on Austria.

Austria's football was still rather primitive, in the eyes of the snobby British associations, but today before 45,000 fanatical fans, they beat Scotland 5-0.

At one point, Scotland were reduced to nine men with Dan Liddle and Colin McNab of Dundee injured by savage tackles allowed by a weak Swiss referee, but the defeat was none the less comprehensive.

It was a chastening game for Liddle and fellow Fifer, Jimmy Paterson from Cowdenbeath.

The Austrians were never looked upon as natural friends of Scotland — they had been on the opposite side in the war, and would soon be again in the next war — but they were at least hospitable after the game, and Vienna was a beautiful city.

But there was one young Austrian that everyone kept talking about who was promising to do so much good for his adopted country of Germany and Austria too. Hitler, or something, his name was.

May 17 1948

Davie Duncan was responsible for Scotland's goal this Monday afternoon in Berne as Scotland went down 1-2 to Switzerland.

He had also played in the game at Hampden against Belgium on April 28, and he had scored there.

Scotland were still reeling from their 0-2 defeat at Hampden by England on April 10, and Duncan was one of the changes made.

The game was played in oppressive heat throughout, and if one may believe all that the Scottish Press say, was refereed very badly by an Austrian who was very lenient on "the foreigners". (One must remember, however, that if a country, as in 1948, has just won a major war, it feels entitled to be patronising to everyone else!)

The Swiss had apparently threatened to call the game off if Scotland did not agree to the ball they insisted on, described in *The Courier* as a typical "Continental pimple". In addition, the Austrian referee refused to allow Scotland's trainer to attend to Jock Govan of Hibs. He had been poleaxed and looked as if he were suffering from concussion. George Young, Scotland's captain had to go and get a wet sponge!

Worst of all, the Swiss winner was scored by a man illegally brought on as a substitute!

But Duncan's contribution was effective, crossing from the left for Leslie Johnston of Clyde to score Scotland's only goal.

Meanwhile back home, politicians were calling for an end to the war in Palestine (not a bad idea!) and reporting on how Bradman's Australians, having scored 721 on Saturday, had bowled out Essex twice to win the game by an innings and 451 runs!

May 18 2014

Mascots!

May 18 2014

The pain was intense today at New Bayview this Sunday as East Fife lost out in the second leg of the First Division play-off to Stirling Albion and found themselves consigned to the Second Division (effectively the fourth tier of Scottish football).

Yet, painful though it was, an honest East Fife supporter would have to admit that it was no more than East Fife had deserved over the season, for there had been some awful performances.

They had been lucky to avoid the outright relegation spot (that one went to Arbroath).

In the play-offs they had seemed to rally a little, beating Clyde in an exciting penalty shoot-out, and even coming in to this game having won 2-1 in the first leg at Forthbank.

But this was a nervous performance with chances missed by Scott McBride which would have given East Fife an insuperable lead.

Almost predictably and inevitably, Stirling Albion scored twice in the last quarter of an hour. Even then it was not entirely finished, for an East Fife goal would have taken it to extra time, but Liam Buchanan, on as a substitute could not get the ball past David Crawford in the Stirling goal.

Full time came to the delight of the travelling Binos in the 1,500 crowd, but the despair of the East Fife faithful.

As a general rule, East Fife fans are stoic, unemotional sort of people, but the heads were certainly down that night. The old guys in the support could talk about Charlie Fleming and Henry Morris, but what did a young East Fife supporter have to be happy about?

May 19 2013

David Muir scores at Peterhead

May 19 2013

The distant fields of Balmoor, the home of Peterhead, a good many miles north of Aberdeen and without any railway connection, was where East Fife saved themselves from the bottom tier in the Second Division play off.

They had been equally far away in the semi-final (but in the opposite direction from Berwick Rangers) and had scraped through by the skin of their teeth.

On Wednesday night, the first leg had been a cat and mouse affair at New Bayview.

Today a large crowd of 1855, with a large support from Methil, saw East Fife edge home against Peterhead.

The goal came just after half time from a corner kick knocked in by David Muir. From then on it was end to end stuff with the home side perhaps a little unlucky not to level and take the game to extra time, but the Fifers kept their formation and shape and held out to keep their status in the third tier of Scottish football.

Mind you, they had Scott Durie to thank for more or less everything when he kept out a determined header right at the death. It was only East Fife's third win in their last 21 games, something which said a lot about why they were in this pickle in the first place.

Indeed while no-one wished to do or say anything to deflate the euphoria of the many travelling supporters, it was a somewhat hollow victory and the third tier was not at all the place that East Fife wanted to be.

May 20 1953

Speculation continued to rise that East Fife were about to appoint Willie Thornton of Rangers as their successor to Scot Symon.

Symon had now gone to Preston North End, having led East Fife to their best ever Scottish League performance where they finished third in Division "A".

Charlie Fleming was the only player not to have signed up for next season, but as he enjoyed his game of golf today at Leven, he gave no indication that he was about to depart to England and to the whole host of teams who were interested in securing his services.

Meanwhile tonight a delegation of East Fife Directors and players took a trip to Glasgow to watch the Coronation Cup final. This was in spite of a certain resentment that they had not been invited to take part in this all-British tournament to commemorate the Coronation of Queen Elizabeth which would take place on June 2.

Four Scottish teams and four English teams took part, and if the teams had been chosen on merit, it would have been Rangers, Hibs, East Fife and Hearts. As it turned out, Celtic and Aberdeen were chosen rather than East Fife and Hearts, for the blatant economic reason that the tournament needed Celtic's huge support.

Tonight that huge support were sent into delirium as their team beat Hibs 2-0 before a crowd of 117,000. And yet less than a couple of months ago, East Fife had beaten Celtic 4-1 at Bayview. But tonight was a tremendous night for the green and whites and no-one could take it away from them.

May 21 2017

This Sunday was the "Last Of The Grass" with entertainment for fans available at Bayview priced £15.00.

The reason for this was that as from tomorrow a new artificial, all weather pitch was to be installed on New Bayview.

While many of the older generation were heard to turn in their graves at the thought of football not being played on grass, the truth of the matter was that artificial pitches did save clubs loads of money in the winter in that they minimised the amount of games that would be lost to bad weather.

For a smaller club, a postponement was a disaster in that money spent on programmes, hospitality and pies was wasted and the game had to be re-arranged some midweek when it was more difficult to attract fans.

So in spite of a few complaints and qualms about the increase in injuries for players, the decision was taken to install a new 3G pitch to be completed by July 14.

There were of course various types of all-weather pitches, and this one was meant to be one of the better ones. The project was funded by Fifers For The Community, a charity which had managed to source various grants etc. and it was of course hoped that the community could get the benefit of this new enterprise.

It was another example of how football was changing and now East Fife had, sadly but inevitably, taken another step away from the old days. But the players themselves seemed happy about things, although many of the spectators deplored the move away from grass.

More ominously the bigger clubs were making noises about being unhappy with things, even though several Premier League clubs now had an all-weather pitch.

May 22 1957

"These were the days, my friend" Mary Hopkins would sing a decade later, but May 1957 was a great month for Scotland and a contextual reminder that the horrors of Scotland in the early 21st century may yet just be a temporary factor in the rich tapestry of the history of Scotland.

Admittedly Scotland had lost to England at Wembley in 1957 — but only very narrowly 2-1 — but then in May they beat Spain 4-2 at Hampden in the World Cup qualifying section, then Switzerland in Basle also in the World Cup. Now tonight in Stuttgart, they beat West Germany 3-1 in a Friendly.

West Germany were, of course, the World Cup holders since 1954 and this was a great triumph for Scotland, although a newspaper reporter made the unfortunate comment that "this was the first time that Scotland had beaten Germany since the War!"

Two goals were scored by Bobby Collins of Celtic — "the wee barra", as he was called — and the other by Dundonian Jackie Mudie who played for Blackpool.

The only sad thing about all this as far as East Fife supporters were concerned was that no East Fife player was even close nowadays to being called up for Scotland.

Hopes were still being expressed though that Charlie Fleming, now of Sunderland, might yet be invited to don the Scotland jersey for the second time, but "Legs", although still playing well and banging in the goals for the Wearsiders, was now nearly 30 and like many an Anglo-Scot, was not really high on the list of the Selectors' priorities.

May 23 1939

The football season had finished a month ago, but there seemed to be no lack of action.

The Daily Record carries a story about plans to reconstruct the Scottish Leagues (sounds familiar to modern eyes, doesn't it?). The idea, according to Davie Meiklejohn, ex-Rangers and Scotland and now an excellent journalist, was to reduce the First Division from 20 teams to 18 while keeping 18 in the Second Division.

This idea did not find a great deal of favour with East Fife and other aspirants to promotion (East Fife had finished third in the 1938/39 season) for the obvious reason that it lessened their chances, not necessarily of gaining promotion but of remaining in the First Division if they did so.

Davie McLean, East Fife's Manager, was quite outspoken in his opposition. But the same newspaper also tells about East Fife's new signing, Willie Fleming from Falkirk. Apparently, they had been watching him for three years until they were convinced that he had rid himself of his injury problems.

Meanwhile East Fife had apparently decided to shelve their plans to extend their stand, build dressing rooms underneath and to build up the terracing on the north side.

They had intended to use the £10,000 from the Scottish Cup triumph of 1938, but the ground improvements would have cost a great deal more than that.

In any case, there was another factor entering any calculations in 1939. Hitler had now seized Czechoslovakia and was making designs on Poland. Britain and France had decided that enough was enough, and that any attempt on Poland would mean war.

It looked as if it was coming.

May 24 1931

"Dangerous Dan" Liddle once again earned a cap for Scotland on their summer tour, and this time he was on the winning side as Scotland beat Switzerland 3-2 at the Parc des Charmilles, Geneva.

This game raised a few eyebrows in Scotland, for it was played on a Sunday.

In 1931 that would certainly not have been allowed in Scotland — even cricket and golf were frowned upon if played on what was erroneously called the Sabbath — but the attitude of the SFA seems to have been along the lines of "when in Rome, do as the Romans do".

In any case, there was a certain irony about the Church of Scotland which had based itself on men like John Knox and John Calvin opposing a football match played in Geneva, a city very much linked to John Calvin!

Scotland had been badly beaten in the last two games of this tour, but this game restored a little pride. Jimmy Easson of Portsmouth and Willie Boyd of Clyde put Scotland ahead in the first half, but then the Swiss scored two to equalise before Andy Love of Aberdeen settled it for Scotland.

Liddle is hardly mentioned in newspaper reports, from which we can possibly infer that he did not have a great game. He certainly never played for Scotland again, the left wing place reverting to the great Alan Morton of Rangers when the domestic Internationals began again the following season.

It was nevertheless a great experience for Dan Liddle, but he had now to return to the grim realities of Second Division football.

May 25 2013

East Fife Football Club

CELEBRATION DINNER

Saturday 25th May 2013

Buckhaven Community Centre

*"Celebrating 75 years since winning
The Scottish Cup and 110 years
Since the club was formed"*

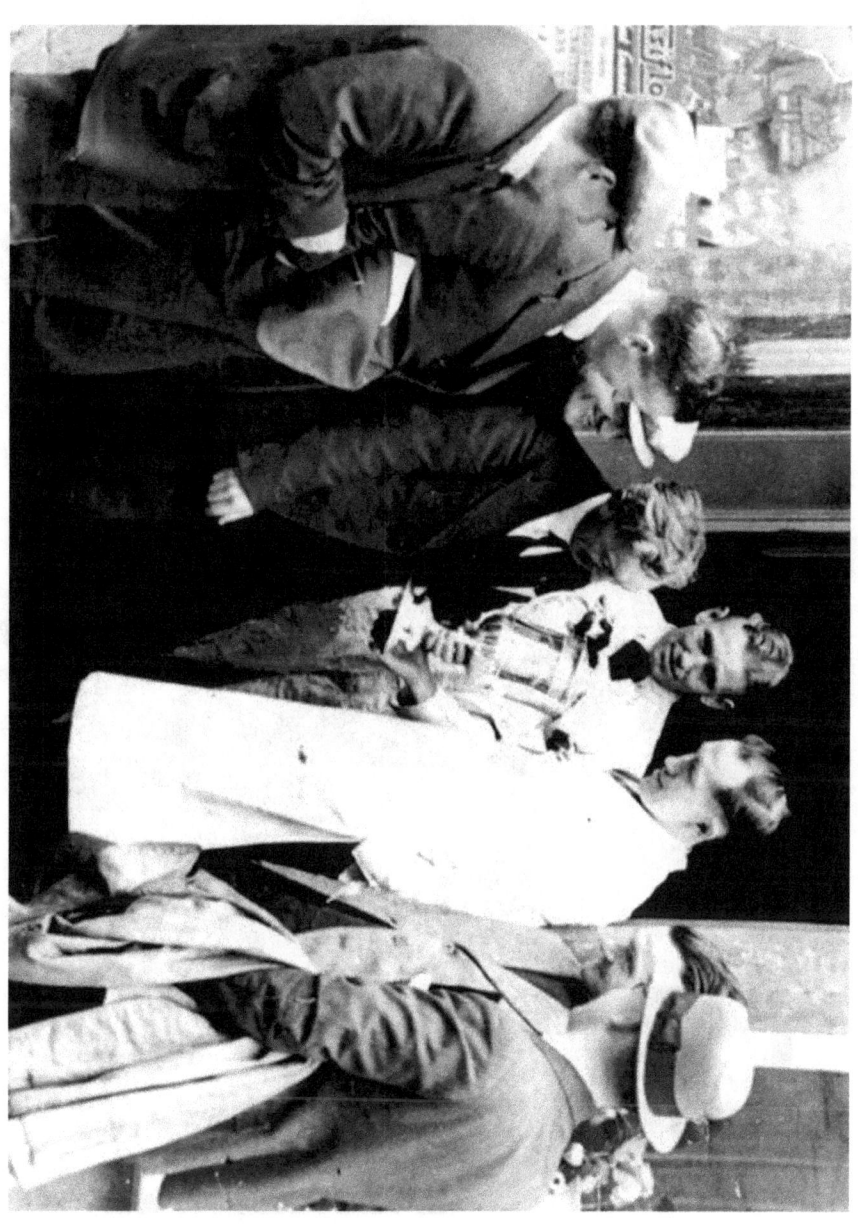
Methil residents admire the Scottish Cup in 1938

Scottish Cup on display in 1938

May 25 1967

There was no direct connection with East Fife as far as anyone could establish, but East Fife supporters were nevertheless able to join in and share in Scottish football's greatest ever day as Celtic beat Inter Milan 2-1 to win the European Cup for the first and only time.

What made the victory all the sweeter was that Celtic won the trophy before any English team had done so. Like everywhere else in Scotland, Methil, Buckhaven and Leven were all ghost towns between the hours of 5.30 pm and 7.30 pm.

Everyone clustered round flickering black and white TVs at home and in pubs before the explosion of relief and joy at the full time whistle.

The concession of an early penalty had made life difficult for Celtic, but this side had loads of character and simply overwhelmed Inter Milan with a great display of attacking Scottish football at its best.

It was remarkable too how many East Fife supporters who had never been to Parkhead in their lives suddenly confessed to a soft spot for the green and whites on the grounds that they had once seen Charlie Tully or Jimmy McGrory at Bayview!

Still, everyone needs something to shout about and be happy about, and the afterglow of victory affected all of Scotland the rest of the summer.

Yet, less than three years previously, on September 9 1964, East Fife had beaten Celtic 2-0 at Bayview in the League Cup, and the two Celtic goal scorers in Lisbon, Stevie Chalmers and Tommy Gemmell had been in that side, as indeed had Jimmy Johnstone!

May 26 1938

Success, as always, has its price.

A slight puncture in the balloon of euphoria which had landed in Levenmouth for the past month was detected today with reports that right half Davie Russell was on his way to Sheffield Wednesday for a reported fee of £2,000, a not inconsiderable amount in 1938, equivalent to over £130,000 today.

"The Rambler" writing in *The Dundee Evening Telegraph* tries unconvincingly to imply that he ("the Rambler") was privy to the transfer negotiations and tells everyone sagely that Russell would earn three times as much in Sheffield as he would at East Fife.

East Fife supporters were disappointed to see the departure of the Dundee-born right half who had played 92 times for the club, but one suspects that the Directors were a little less so, for the money was keeping rolling in.

Negotiations took place in an Edinburgh hotel and everyone departed happily, not least Russell himself who was to be married a week come Friday, and his signing-on fee and cut of the transfer fee were handy little bonuses.

He had been a great player for the club, and would do well for Sheffield Wednesday next season, but then of course war came along and disrupted things.

In May 1938, Hitler was now making ominous signs of aggression towards Czechoslovakia. Many people pointed out that the obvious thing for the British Government to do was to sign a treaty with the Soviet Union, but this of course was unpalatable for a Conservative Government.

In later years Russell became Manager of Bury and Tranmere Rovers.

May 27 1955

The meeting of the Scottish League today broke up in disarray, with a further meeting to be called on June 17.

This was the day after the 1955 General Election, and the meeting was held with the radios in the background reporting an increased majority for the Conservative Government of Anthony Eden.

Locally it was predictable with the Conservatives winning the constituency called East Fife, and Labour winning Kirkcaldy, but what was a lot less predictable was what next year's Scottish League set-up was going to look like.

Berwick Rangers had proposed an 18 team First Division and a 19 team Second Division. There was an obvious disadvantage that a Second Division with an odd number would mean a team having a day off every week.

On the other hand, as far as East Fife were concerned, an 18 team First Division as distinct from the current 16 team First Division would mean extra security for their now perilous toehold in the First Division.

The other proposal was from the Scottish League themselves, namely that the Second Division should be split up and would incorporate some of the current "C" Division clubs.

East Fife's reserves played in the "C" Division, but East Fife and several others had already resigned from that Division. Berwick's motion was the one put to the vote. It beat the status quo, but failed to gain a two thirds majority, and therefore the status quo of two 16 team Leagues seemed to prevail.

The uncertainty about the "C" Division threw everything into confusion, and basically, no-one was any the wiser!

May 28 1925

Today in Lochgelly was born George Aitken, sometimes called "Dod" and arguably East Fife's best ever player and part of the immortal half back line of Philp, Finlay and Aitken.

His other clubs were Third Lanark and Sunderland and he spent the last few years of his career as a coach with Watford.

He won five Scottish caps when he was with East Fife and another three when he was with Sunderland. He also won Scottish League Cup medals in 1947/48 and 1949/50, and was generally looked upon as one of the better players of his day.

He joined the club in 1943 and originally played only on a part-time basis while his day job was that of a miner, this being a time when coal was very much in demand for the war effort and later for the post-war recovery of the nation.

His debut International was the famous 3-1 victory over England at Wembley on April 9 1949, the first time that England had lost a game since World War II.

Although this game is often referred to as "Cowan's Wembley" because of the excellence of Morton goalkeeper Jimmy Cowan, this is not to minimise the work of George Aitken, who neutralised the potentially very difficult Stan Mortensen of Blackpool. Billy Steel, Jimmy Mason and Laurie Reilly scored the goals.

Aitken was on the winning side in all the five Scotland games he played as an East Fife player, and even as a Sunderland player, he lost only once in his final International game against England in 1954.

His departure from East Fife was messy, but he was always looked upon with much affection by East Fife and Scotland supporters.

He died in January 2003.

May 29 1936

The AGM of the Shareholders was held tonight in the Bowling Green Hall in Methil.

Chairman William Moscrip reported a profit of £340. That was the good news.

The bad news was that transfers of players had brought in £936 and that if it had not been for that, the club would have been every much in the red.

He complained about the activities of larger clubs (he did not name names) saying that they were very willing to poach East Fife players, and could afford to pay men £4 or £5 per week, something that was simply out of the question as far as East Fife were concerned.

Promotion had not been achieved this year and the club had gone out of the Scottish Cup at the first time of asking, losing to Rangers at Ibrox. Although that game had yielded a good "gate", their defeat had prevented them from earning more in other games.

Manager David McLean then stressed that there had been successes this season as well — they had beaten Dunfermline 3-0 in the final of the Wemyss Cup, and Joe Cowan, recently of Celtic and Raith Rovers, had scored 29 goals this season.

Mr McLean was grateful for the support the team had received, but he had one small complaint about the amount of barracking that he heard during the course of a game.

Surely it was better, he argued, to encourage the players when they were going through a bad patch, rather than submit them to such filth and abuse. Support would be much appreciated.

May 30 1923

The Courier today carried a story that a former East Fife player was among those suspended for match-fixing at a Bury v Coventry City fixture in 1920.

In what appears to have been a major criminal attempt to arrange the result of a game, several Directors and players were given life bans including a man from Cardenden called John Allen.

John Allen had been born in Cardenden and played first for a junior football team called Bowhill Thistle. He then was picked up by Hibs, but when he didn't quite make the grade there, he joined East Fife in 1913 and played some games at left back, before Bury bought him more or less on the eve of the war.

War time regulations precluded full time football, so he returned to his native Fife to work as a miner and to play for East Fife on a Saturday afternoon. At the end of the war, he returned to Bury.

Recently he had been married and acquired a restaurant business in Wolverhampton, but this scandal would obviously affect that.

Also banned was a former Dundee player called George Chaplin, inevitably in the 1920s nicknamed "Charlie".

Match-fixing was a fairly common occurrence in the 1920s (one hopes that it does not happen now!) and the draconian punishments handed out by the English FA were an attempt to stamp it out.

No evidence has been found to link Allen with any match-fixing in his time with East Fife, but it would be a brave and perhaps naïve person who would say that it never happened.

May 31 1967

In the same way as Methil had closed down a week ago so that everyone could watch Celtic win the European Cup, a similar thing happened tonight when Rangers played Bayern Munich in the final of the European Cup Winners Cup.

Feelings towards Rangers were more ambivalent. It would, of course, have been virtually impossible for anyone of the Roman Catholic religion to support Rangers, given their blatant, although unstated, policy of religious discrimination, now in the "swinging sixties" coming under more attack.

On the other hand it would have been a lovely thing for Scottish football if both European Cups could be won by Scottish clubs in the same season.

There was also in Methil a residual love for Scot Symon, the man who had created the great East Fife side of the late 1940s and early 1950s, and who was now the Manager of Rangers, having led them to great domestic glories as well.

Always a very dignified and even august, well-dressed sort of a man — never a tracksuit Manager, nor one who threw tantrums at referees when he didn't get his own way — Symon himself was always very grateful to East Fife for the start that they had given him in his managerial career.

For these reasons, there was a slight inclination towards supporting Rangers on this particular night, but sadly it did not work out for the Ibrox men who lost out unluckily in extra time.

Rangers found this result hard to cope with, given Celtic's success the previous week, and Scot Symon's days at Ibrox were now numbered.

June

East Fife July 2009.
Back row, from left: Dave Westwood, Scott Thomson, Robert Campbell, Stewart Baillie, Andrew Stobie, Michael Brown, Jonny Smart, Jordyn Sheerin, Gordon Forrest. Middle (standing): Scott Crabbe, Jim Stevenson, Eugene Clarke, Alex Blyth, Darren Thomson, Aaron Conway, Guy Kerr, John Ovenstone, David Muir, Shaun Fagan, Stuart Cargill, Brian McNeill, David Marshall, David Stevenson, Jim Corstorphine. Front: Michael Bruce, Goran Stanic, Paul Nugent, Sid Collumbine, Stevie Crawford, John Sharp, Bobby Linn, Lloyd Young, Johnny MacRae.

June 1 1946

A charity game between Old Crocks and Durie Select was played today at Bayview in aid of funds for the Wemyss Memorial Hospital.

The National Health Service was very much on the drawing board, but it wouldn't come to fruition for another couple of years yet, so any donation of funds was most welcome.

As it turned out, a crowd of 2,000 turned up to pay one shilling each for admission and to fill the various cans and buckets all round the ground.

There were at least two attractions. One was the ever popular Tommy Adams acting as referee, and the other was the appearance of the great Alec James, one time Wembley Wizard and Arsenal, for whom he had a glittering career.

But his first senior team was Raith Rovers, and quite a few of those who used to worship him at Stark's Park made their way along the coast to see him again. He claimed that this was the first time he had ever played at Bayview.

Another star playing for the Old Crocks was goalkeeper Tom Hamilton, one time of Rangers who had played in their famous Scottish Cup final of 1928, and had played for Scotland against England at Wembley in 1932.

The Durie Select was mainly made up of local juniors, and not surprisingly they were considerably faster than the Old Crocks, but the boys of the old brigade did not lack skill, and in any case some skilful refereeing by Tommy Adams who turned a "Nelson eye" to a few things, made sure that the game ended 3-3.

June 2 1953

It was "chilly for June" as the saying went.

A cold east wind blowing, rain never far away, everyone wearing raincoats and hats — yet it was meant to be a joyous day.

It was the Coronation of Queen Elizabeth II (although Scottish people rightly maintained that she should be Queen Elizabeth I as Scotland had never had an Elizabeth as Queen before!)

A bit of an anti-climax in Methil. A few parades and loads of flags and bunting, but sadly no Queen, as it was all happening in London, although a very few were able to see it on the new medium of television.

A lot of cynicism about the gross inequalities of Buckingham Palace and Methil Docks, but yet there was some sort of improvement in society as well.

Unemployment had gone, rationing was on its last legs, prosperity was in the air and the National Health Service (you could now see the Doctor for free!) was beginning to make a difference.

On the football front, East Fife had nearly won the Scottish League, and although Scot Symon was going to be with Preston North End next year, there were still loads of good players and a whole new football season to look forward to.

Pity it was another couple of months away, but today was a public holiday. Time to enjoy ourselves, and we could always at least talk about the football including the sad news about the death of Alec James of the baggy pants, who had once played for Raith Rovers.

June 3 1949

Today East Fife's players arrived home after a very successful tour of Sweden and Denmark in which they had played three games and won them all, one in Sweden against a Stockholm XI and two in Denmark in Odense.

More importantly they had spread the gospel of Scottish football and won friends. It had also helped the team spirit of the players, all of whom were firm in their desire to go back abroad again next year.

The Danes also promised to send a team to Methil for a return game. The team, away since May 18, had disembarked at Harwich yesterday before being takento the White City in London to see the British, Empire and European Title Boxing Match in which Bruce Woodcock beat Freddie Mills.

This was a treat paid for by the Directors for what they had done to enhance the name of East Fife. The Chairman, three Directors and Manager Scot Symon were also taken to see round the House of Commons, but that particular invitation does not seem to have been extended to the players!

Scottish football was generally held in high esteem on the continent in 1949, and Scottish teams were usually made very welcome with the Odense Chairman being quoted as saying that "East Fife play the kind of football we delight to watch. If we are beaten, that does not matter".

The players would now all have a well-deserved holiday and would not need to come back to Bayview until the middle or the end of July for training. But it was one of these close-seasons that were filled with eager anticipation for August.

June 4 1904

East Fife today received a bad blow when they failed to gain admission to the Northern League at a meeting held in the Athletic Rooms, Seagate, Dundee under the Chairmanship of Mr P Baxter of St Johnstone.

The procedure was complex. In the first place, the two lowest placed teams in the League, Forfar Athletic and Lochee, had to seek re-election.

Then there was a motion to increase the number of teams in the League from 12 to either 13 or 14. Clearly an increase to 14 would have been more beneficial to East Fife in that it would have given them more chance, but the vote was to increase the number to only 13.

This seems strange to modern ears because it meant that, of necessity, at least one team would be idle every Saturday, but the counter argument was that many teams were interested in other competitions as well or indeed playing friendlies.

But then a motion from Cowdenbeath and Stenhousemuir proposed replacing Forfar Athletic and Lochee by Kirkcaldy United and East of Fife (sic).

The removal of the influential Forfar Athletic was never likely to gain a great deal of favour, and the motion fell. So, there remained only the vote for the one extra place and three candidates, Aberdeen Bon Accord, East Fife and Kirkcaldy United.

Bon Accord failed to get any votes (presumably because they were an unknown quantity and distant in any case), and the "unknown quantity" factor may also have counted against East Fife (who had only been in existence for a year) and the vote went for Kirkcaldy United who, after all, represented a more densely populated area than East Fife.

June 5 1905

Today the morning newspapers, in particular, *The Courier*, carried the extraordinarily welcome news that East Fife had been admitted to the Northern League.

East Fife had been lobbying hard for this move for some considerable time, in particular subjecting that crucial character, James Black of Forfar Athletic (nominally Secretary but *de facto* dictator of the Northern League) to a charm offensive, pointing out the attractions of having East Fife in the Northern League.

Black, for his part, was no fool, and had been worried that two Fife teams Lochgelly United and Dunfermline Athletic might be prevailed upon to join the new Central League.

Cowdenbeath had had their application for the Scottish League accepted, and Stenhousemuir wished to try somewhere more local to themselves, having found the travelling to places like Aberdeen and Forfar a bit tedious and expensive.

In addition, Black was determined to reduce the size of the League from 13 to 12, and realised that he could do this by voting in only one team rather than two.

It thus came about that three teams applied — Aberdeen Bon Accord, East Fife and Hearts of Beath — but only one would be successful. Black and the East Fife delegates worked hard, and no-one could resist the blandishments of the determined but charming Black, so East Fife were elected to join Aberdeen and Dundee Reserves, Lochee United, Forfar Athletic, St Johnstone, Dundee Wanderers, Kirkcaldy United and Montrose.

That made ten, and the two who might have defected, Dunfermline Athletic and Lochgelly, saw East Fife there and decided to stay. It was a great night for East Fife and James Black who had wangled things to get the answer he wanted!

June 6 1914

The Courier today reported the bad news that East Fife had not been admitted to the Second Division of the Scottish League for next season.

This was a result of a vote taken at the AGM of the Scottish League in Glasgow. There was a certain amount of optimism in the air when the motion of Celtic and Third Lanark was carried to the effect that the Second Division should be increased from 12 to 14 for season 1914/15.

The procedure was complicated, however. In the first place it was decided that there would be no relegation from the First Division, so the bottom two teams of the First Division — St Mirren and Dumbarton — should stay where they were, and that Cowdenbeath (last year's winners of the Second Division) would not be promoted.

But there were now seven teams applying for three positions in the Scottish League Second Division — Vale of Leven and Johnstone who had to seek re-election, and East Fife, Lochgelly, Forfar Athletic, Clydebank and Bathgate.

There were four votes but East Fife and Forfar Athletic failed to get past the first vote, and were eliminated, but there was a certain amount of good news for Fife in that Lochgelly were admitted.

This was bad news for East Fife, but there was still the Central League, and of course the advantage of the Central League was that it did not travelling to grounds like Arthurlie and Abercorn in the West of Scotland.

In any case, although no-one knew it at the time, things were going to change rapidly and radically for the whole world.

An Archduke was assassinated at the end of June 1914, but it is worth noting that newspapers for today contained not the slightest hint that there was going to be any trouble in Europe

June 7 1945

John McArthur, the Chairman of East Fife, was today heavily involved in the re-construction of the Scottish League for season 1945/46. Summer 1945 was a strange time.

On the one hand, the European War was over, but on the other, so many soldiers were still overseas, and in any case, the war in the far-east was still raging.

This meant that 1945/46 could not really be an official season, but on the other hand, now that travel restrictions were being eased and petrol more plentiful, there was no reason why there couldn't be a national League of sorts, rather than the regional Leagues which had been in existence during the war.

Mr McArthur was one of the North-Eastern League representatives at the meeting to re-form the Scottish League with the very difficult task of deciding which teams were to be in Division One and which in Division Two of the new Scottish League.

It was also agreed that, 1945/46 being an unofficial season, there would be no promotion or relegation between the two Divisions. The discussions were tortuous, and no-one really was sure which criteria were used.

East Fife found themselves in the "B" Division of 14 teams along with the other three Fife teams of Cowdenbeath, Dunfermline Athletic and Raith Rovers, the two Dundee teams, Arbroath, Airdrie, Ayr United, St Johnstone, Albion Rovers, Alloa, Dumbarton, and Stenhousemuir.

No-one was entirely happy about all that, but then again, you cannot please everyone; it was a patch-up temporary situation in any case.

June 8 1933

Times were hard in the Fife coalfield, and this compelled Mr Moscrip, the Chairman of East Fife, to announce sadly that only six players were being retained for the next season, along with John McCurley, who had not made the grade with Newcastle United and had been loaned out to East Fife, who were now hoping to make his transfer complete.

The season just gone by had not been great, and there had been a noticeable tailing off of attendances towards the end of the season.

To a large extent it was the economic depression to blame, but also to blame were some of the lacklustre performances that had been seen, and the fans had been campaigning for a long time for the club to rid itself of its "deadwood".

One of those on the open to transfer list was Arthur McGachie. He had been a great goal scorer for the club in the past and it was sad to see him go, and even sadder when Dunfermline and Cowdenbeath later picked him up.

That belts were having to be tightened still further came with the announcement that the wages paid would have to be "more realistic".

The truth was that there was not a great deal of money to be made out of the game in 1933.

Clubs like Arsenal and Rangers enjoyed "the wealth of Croesus" according to one journalist, but for the other clubs, it was a struggle for survival.

Yet, no-one could doubt that passion for the game that was still engendered. Even during the summer when no games were being played, it was still the main topic of conversation in workshop, mine and mill, not to mention the school playground.

June 9 1982

The death was announced today of Dan Liddle, commonly known as "Dangerous Dan", East Fife's first ever Scotland Internationalist and generally regarded as one of the best left wingers in the game.

He would have earned more Scotland caps, one felt, if he had not come at the same time as other great left wingers like Alan Morton of Rangers, Alec Troup of Dundee and Everton and Adam McLean of Celtic.

As it was, all his caps were won on the foreign tour of 1931, after he had been able to show off his talents in the otherwise disastrous season of 1930/31 when East Fife were in the First Division.

The tour itself was a half-hearted sort of affair and far from successful on the playing front, and it is a shame that Dan never won a domestic cap, particularly against England.

The return to the Second Division in 1931/32 meant that Dan was no longer in the limelight.

At the end of that season, he was transferred to Leicester City for whom he played until 1946, before finishing his career with Mansfield Town. He did not return to Scotland very often and lived in Wigston, Leicestershire.

He was born in Bo'ness in 1912, and played junior football for Wallyford Bluebell before joining East Fife in 1929 when the club was showing signs of ambition by wanting promotion.

Liddle was very instrumental in the club's gaining of that goal in 1930, and as well as being called "Dangerous Dan", he was also called "Eric", a flattering comparison to Eric Liddle, the famous Scottish athlete of the 1924 Olympic Games.

June 10 1938

This Friday night was a great night for Scottish football.

Scotland v England games were of course a source of great interest and enthusiasm until the 1970s, but it was remarkable how seldom club teams from Scotland played a team from England in any sort of quasi-serious competition.

But this was the Empire Exhibition Trophy in which four Scottish teams took on four English teams with all the games played at Ibrox, that venue being chosen because of its proximity to Bellahouston Park where the Empire Exhibition was held.

It was all, of course, British propaganda designed to boost morale as a counterblast to the vulgar and strident noises coming from Germany.

East Fife, as Scottish Cup holders might have felt that they should have been invited to join the competition, but then again they were still a small provincial team from a poor mining area in Fife, well away from the big city and still undeniably in the Second Division.

Nevertheless, there was great interest in this competition, particularly tonight in the final which was broadcast on the radio with a commentary from Rex Kingsley of *The Sunday Mail*.

The final was between Celtic and Everton, and Celtic had one Fifer playing for them in Chick Geatons of Lochgelly.

It was a tense game but to the delight of all Scotland, Celtic eventually won through in extra time, the only goal of the game coming from Johnny Crum, who famously ran to the supporters and performed an impromptu Highland Fling — somewhat primitive in comparison with modern celebrations, but remarkable for the time!

June 11 1927

Ahead of the AGM next Thursday, East Fife announced a profit of £319 14 shillings and 7 pence — a very healthy position considering the economic uncertainty all around.

The position is even better than that for there are also a couple of transfers which took place after the "books were closed" at the end of the season.

The reason for this healthy position was not difficult to work out, and it came from their Scottish Cup run and in particular their share in the huge Hampden gate of the Scottish Cup final.

Had that not happened, the picture would have been a great deal bleaker, and credit was paid to the club for what they had done for their beleaguered community, still struggling to cope with the aftermath of last summer's industrial disputes.

Curiously, the ground and stand receipts of £3,065 was almost exactly matched by the payment of wages to players which was £3,025. Although the position was healthy (there had also been a slight profit last season) the Treasurer suggested that there was no need for complacency, and of course it all depended on results on the field.

Manager David McLean had seemed to have gathered together a useful squad, and another run in the Scottish Cup would be welcome.

The club also had to reckon with the fact that as Raith Rovers had been promoted again to the First Division, there would be no money spinning "derby" fixtures in the Scottish League next year. But the solution lay mainly in the hands of the players.

June 12 1944

The news from France continued to be good, and although one had to be very wary of believing any kind or news in war-time lest it be propaganda or quite simply lies, it did seem that some sort of bridgehead had been established in Normandy, and that advances were being made across France.

It was still however an anxious time for the many mothers and wives, for precedents in the 20th century at Dunkirk and the Somme had not been encouraging.

Meanwhile, although East Fife's season had long finished, there was still the Summer Cup in which Raith Rovers were involved and it was always possible to take a vicarious interest in them.

There was also a great deal of junior football still going on. Meanwhile Douglas Young, who had stood as the Scottish Nationalist candidate in a by-election for Kirkcaldy Burghs in February, had an interesting and eventful day today.

In the morning he had been sentenced to three months imprisonment for failing to obey an order by the National Service Officer to present himself for an interview (to be conscripted), but at night the local branch of the Scottish National Party had selected him as their Prospective Candidate for the next General Election.

Young, an interesting character, who became Lecturer in Greek and St Andrews University, had already been "inside" for refusing to do National Service. His argument seems to have been that this was England's war and not Scotland's, but his stance, admirable as it was in some ways, did not do him any great favours at a time when the country was fighting for its life.

June 13 1938

While most of Fife was basking in the summer sunshine and the recollections of the Scottish Cup victory of April (and quite a few were also still talking about Celtic's triumph in the all-Britain Empire Exhibition Cup a few days ago) a discordant note was struck with the appearance of Nemesis (the Greek Goddess of Revenge) at a meeting of the Fife Education Committee.

Apparently some teachers had deserted their pupils to attend the Raith Rovers v East Fife Scottish Cup quarter final replay on Wednesday March 23!

And the list included a few head teachers!

And that was not counting the vast amount of pupils!

It was even rumoured that the Director of Education himself had not been at his desk that afternoon!

Councillor William Walker of Cupar fulminated and demanded that the names of the teachers be made public. "If we are not going to have supervision of some kind by the furnishing of names, we are not going to have any control at all."

But the authorities "played things with a straight bat that would have done credit to Wally Hammond" (England's best batsman in 1938), for Provost Leith of Burntisland stated that the Staffing Committee had all the facts before them and agreed to take no action.

This was surely the best course to follow, for the affair was now almost three months ago, and it had only concerned a half-day. But in any case, it was a great game, and which East Fife supporter would have wanted to miss it? Even Raith Rovers supporters sympathised!

June 14 1919

Slowly things were beginning to return to normal.

Most of the soldiers had been demobbed and were home, although there were still a few in the Middle East, and in Russia where another war was going on between "Red" Russians and "White" Russians with Britain on the side of the "Whites".

The Peace Conference which had started in January at Versailles was almost concluded and the Treaty would be signed soon.

In football, it had been announced that season 1919/20 would be a full season with a Scottish Cup and full Internationals, something which had not been seen since 1914.

The Fife Football Association was to resume activities next season and the draw for the Fife Cup brought Raith Rovers to East Fife with the winners to play Dunfermline Athletic.

The Wemyss Cup draw paired East Fife with the winners of Raith Rovers and Lochgelly.

Mr Robertson, the Secretary of East Fife announced that he had signed six players for the new season — James, Fisher and David from Dunfermline Athletic, Neish and Stewart from Raith Rovers and Malcolm from Hearts.

He expected to build up one of the strongest teams in the short history of the club. In the meantime, much sporting interest was being aroused by the imminent arrival of the Australians to play Scotland at cricket in Edinburgh in early July, although it was not the full Australian team — only the Australian Imperial Forces XI, consisting of men who had served in the war and had not yet gone home.

All these things helped people to take their minds off the horrors of what had gone before.

June 15 1920

Friction between the Central League and other organisations was likely to increase by the news that East Fife's Manager David McLean was interested in the services of Lieutenant W Cobban DCM, who last season played for Dunfermline.

The snag (if that was the appropriate term) was that Cobban was actually on the books of Raith Rovers and that Raith Rovers were wanting a transfer fee of £100 for him.

But as neither East Fife not Dunfermline Athletic were at this time Scottish League clubs, there was nothing that Raith Rovers could do to insist on a fee.

It was reported that East Fife had offered substantial terms for Cobban's services. This anomaly was one of the reasons why pressure was growing on the Scottish League to start a Second Division of the League (as had existed before the war) and to make it bigger so that it would include teams like East Fife and Dunfermline who, after all, covered and represented reasonable sized communities which deserved Scottish League football.

The Second Division would of course come to pass in 1921/22, but in the meantime such anomalies remained. A better known and higher profile case involved Dunfermline and the famous centre forward Andrew Nesbit Wilson, who scored goals galore for Scotland while playing for Dunfermline Athletic in seasons 1919/20 and 1920/21.

When Dunfermline joined the Scottish League, he was obliged to return to play for Middlesbrough, for whom he was registered. As for Lieutenant W Cobban, nothing further seems to have happened as far as East Fife were concerned.

June 16 1926

With the mines still at a virtual standstill (although the General Strike had collapsed ignominiously a month ago) and the area still suffering dreadful poverty and deprivation as a result, it was good to see that at least one institution in the area was in the black.

This was East Fife FC who were proud to announce that they had made a credit balance over the last year of £136 16 shillings and 5 pence. That was the good news.

The bad news was that this was only due to the £1,355 that they had received in transfer fees for various players. Players' wages were a major item — £2,617 — and that was not quite balanced by the £2,572 raised by entrance money.

There were other items of expenditure, for example the "guarantee" money that had to be made up for away teams if not enough money was raised at the "gate" at any particular game.

This was not an easy time for quite a few football clubs with several teams clearly struggling. The team had done well enough finishing fourth in the League but the loss to Bo'ness in the Scottish Cup as early as January had been a bad blow, in that the team could always benefit from a good Cup run.

Indeed the draw "Bo'ness away from home" was a nightmare tie — in that there was no money to be got out of it, and the likelihood was a defeat, and no further chance of money. But if ever the team could achieve promotion to the First Division . . .

June 17 1933

Tommy Boyce, East Fife's goalkeeper, was reported today to be lying in the Adamson Hospital, Cupar with a fractured left leg sustained in a motor bicycle accident near Milton of Balgonie.

This was clearly a major blow to his career. Motor bicycle accidents were hardly unusual in 1933, for the motor bike was a very common method of transport in the 1930s, being considerably more economic than the motor car, something that was clearly out of the pocket of working class families in the 1930s.

The economic depression was continuing, even though the National Government with Ramsay MacDonald only a nominal Prime Minister of what was in fact a Conservative Government had been in power for almost two years now.

There seemed little that anyone could do about unemployment, and what was not unconnected with the worldwide economic depression were the events in Germany.

The new Chancellor seemed intent on abolishing and dismantling the democratic way of life of the Weimar Republic, persecuting minorities like his Jewish community and, worst of all, showing clear signs of ignoring the Treaty of Versailles and of wishing to "have another go", as the saying went.

He was a curious little character as well, and still a subject of ridicule in British newspapers. No doubt all these matters were a source of some interest to Tommy Boyce as he recuperated from his accident in his hospital in Cupar.

But the weather was decent, and most East Fife supporters were looking forward to the new season. The past couple of seasons had been acceptable, but "another go" at the First Division seemed desirable!

June 18 1982

This was the night that for a brief period, Scotland could consider themselves to be the best team in the world.

All Methil and indeed the rest of Scotland ignored the fine weather this Friday night and clustered round a TV set to see the game in Seville between Scotland and Brazil.

There was an East Fife connection, as well, albeit in the future, for Steve Archibald would one day become the Manager of East Fife. Scotland had already beaten New Zealand 5-2, and had a reasonable team and a very good Manager in Jock Stein.

The heat was intense in Seville, and the atmosphere was brilliant with the supporters of both nations who absolutely loved their football and despised the hooliganism and criminality of other nations.

The Falklands War had just finished as well with the surrender of the Argentinians, and the air of euphoria was tangible. And then Scotland went ahead with a goal from the edge of the box scored by Dave Narey of Dundee United — and this was the goal that Jimmy Hill described with breath-taking stupidity as a "toe poke". For the next 15 minutes or so, Scotland felt that victory was in sight, not only tonight over Brazil but even in the World Cup itself!

Sadly, it could not last. Brazil equalised through Zico before half time, went ahead through Oscar immediately after half-time and Scotland obeyed the unwritten laws of football, and subsided piteously.

Yet sober reflection stressed that this was Brazil, a country which had already won the World Cup three times. Scotland could hold their heads up, at least.

June 19 1954

This was a catastrophic day in the annals of Scottish football, and sadly, one has to admit that there was an East Fife connection.

It was the day that Scotland went down 0-7 to Uruguay in the 1954 World Cup finals in Switzerland, and, horror of horrors, it was shown on the infant medium of TV.

They had already lost 0-1 to Austria and the Manager Andy Beattie had resigned. Scotland only took 13 players, failed to provide any training gear for their players, and the shirts they wore in the game were thick, heavy ones which were suitable for Scotland in November, but not the heat of Switzerland in midsummer.

You couldn't have made it up! It came as a traumatic blow for Scotland, for whom the idea that British football was the best in the world died hard. England similarly found it hard to cope with, and for a long time after that "foreign" and "continental" were almost dirty words in the context of British football. Somehow or another, what foreigners played was "not real football".

Today, with Scotland several goals down and players almost choking in the heat, the cries of encouragement from the side lines were along the lines of "Come On Scotland! Get stuck in!"

The East Fife connection was of course Allan Brown, now playing for Blackpool. Other East Fife men like Henry Morris, Charlie Fleming and George Aitken (now with Sunderland) did well to miss this shambles.

For TV viewers, a great deal less than 10% of the population watching the tiny screen, this was an awful experience.

June 20 1940

John McArthur, Chairman on East Fife today gave notice of a motion that he was submitting to the SFA for discussion at their meeting on July 24.

The motion read "In view of the grave national emergency, competitive football at all grades shall be discontinued for the duration of the war, or until such time as a resumption may be considered desirable in the best interests of the country"

By any standards it was a drastic and draconian measure, but no-one could deny that the country of Great Britain was in as much peril as it had been at any other time in its history.

The Army had sustained a colossal defeat at Dunkirk (however much propaganda tried to emphasise that this was a great rescue of the British Expeditionary Force by the Royal Navy and the "little boats") and on this very day France capitulated to the Germans, leaving Great Britain and its Empire alone, with the very lukewarm moral backing of the USA.

The three strong points seemed to be the undefeated Royal Navy, the untested RAF and a new, dynamic but not yet entirely well-loved Prime Minister in Winston Churchill. Whatever happened however, the problem was not going to go away any time soon, and Mr McArthur's motion therefore made some sort of sense.

On the other hand, there was always the propaganda aspect of the game in that something was needed to boost people's spirits in the same way that cinema became even more popular in wartime because it tried to keep everyone happy. Football had continued in some sort of a way in the Great War, and it might be an idea to keep it going, if possible. It was an issue that was hotly discussed.

June 21 1922

Midsummer Day 1922 and the weather was glorious.

The Sporting Gossip column of *The Dundee Evening Telegraph* was concerned that team building for the new season is a rather slow process with only six players signed for next season, although East Fife Directors have been quoted as admitting an interest in quite a few local Juniors, notably Ferguson of Leslie Hearts, and it is rumoured that Gray of Dalkeith Thistle, who was attracting the attention of Dundee, may well go to Bayview instead.

East Fife were considered to be a good destination for Juniors. In their first season in the Scottish League Second Division, they were in the extraordinary position of being half way up the League with 38 points form 38 games, having won 15, lost 15 and drawn 8.

It was a fairly unusual statistic and tolerably satisfactory, but everyone in Methil was aware that they would have a long way to go to catch Raith Rovers who had actually finished third in the First Division, behind champions Celtic and runners up Rangers. They clearly had a good Manager in James Logan.

In the meantime concern was being expressed about Prime Minister Lloyd George and in particular the repeated scandals about the apparent selling of knighthoods and other honours.

He was a man whom one either loved or hated. No great love for him was found in mining areas, but on the other hand he was the man who had won the war, and those who had ever heard him speak were in no doubt about his rhetorical ability. But his Coalition Government was dependent on Conservative support and it was becoming clearer that that this support was weakening.

June 22 1931

East Fife were on their knees in 1931.

After the joy of promotion in 1930, there had been the season of 1930/31 where it had been clear from an early stage that they were simply not good enough for the First Division, yet surprisingly for a team that finished last, there had been eight victories, so things were not 100% bad.

Nevertheless it was a sobering, chastening experience for the Fifers. Some players had gone at the end of the season, and Mr McLean, now back in harness after his ill-advised sojourn with Bristol Rovers was spending his summer rebuilding the team.

Today he was honing in on two potential recruits for next season. One was Owen Feenie who hailed from Kinglassie, but had been with Dundee for the last couple of seasons but without ever breaking through into the first team.

He had been spotted when he played for Denbeath Star a couple of seasons ago. He was six feet, sturdy and played wing half. Another wing half also came to McLean's attention. This was a fellow called John Hamilton. McLean had had eyes on him for some time, having been interested in him when he played for Penicuik and he had tried to persuade him to go to Bristol, but the youngster preferred to stay in Scotland.

But now he jumped at the chance of senior football. The East Fife team was now more or less complete for season 1931/32, apart from a recognised centre forward, but McLean was confident that he could persuade Arthur McGachie to accept the reduced terms on offer for Second Division for next season.

June 23 1998

Ex-East Fife player Gordon Durie had the misfortune to play for Scotland against Morocco in what turned out to be Scotland's last game in the World Cup finals for well over 20 years.

Durie, commonly known as Juke Box Jury, was born in Paisley but started his career with East Fife before moving on to Hibs, Chelsea, Tottenham Hotspur and Rangers.

This game was played in St Etienne in France, and it was one of those classic Scottish games when Scotland had some sort of a chance but failed to produce the goods when required, and it was all the harder to take because Scotland had not up till now played at all badly.

It was generally agreed that a 1-2 defeat to Brazil in the opening game of the tournament was no disaster, and it was followed by a hard fought 1-1 draw with Norway. A defeat of little known Morocco, not renowned as one of the best teams in the world would be enough to earn Scotland qualification to the next phase.

Sadly Scotland did not turn up and went down 0-3 in what can only be described as an awful performance for which no excuses were really possible. Not for the first time in our lives did we stare at our TV screens wondering why Scotland had such a death wish about them.

Elementary errors were made to concede goals, Craig Burley was sent off and it was yet another collectors' item of the Scottish self-destruction complex. Durie was hardly ever seen, was substituted near the end and never played for Scotland again.

June 24 1929

East Fife's AGM reported a loss of £112, but the Directors thought that this was acceptable "considering the district conditions".

The club were in a better state than most clubs in the Second Division, who were similarly struggling. President Taylor reported that takings from the terracing were the same as last year, but he felt that the stand was not as well patronised as it might have been.

Transfer fees were not as much as previously, and there certainly would not be very much money to buy in players. On the playing side, the team had held its own in Division Two but there were the frightening examples of Arthurlie and Bathgate, both of whom had had to resign from the League this season.

The solution, Mr Taylor felt, was to build up a team from local players on the grounds that they would not need too much in the way of travelling expenses and would in any case have a greater loyalty to the club.

Far too many players from the local area and the local junior teams were being enticed to leave the area to play for other teams. He suggested that local junior teams should have the "freedom of Bayview" for training purposes, and this was agreed.

The meeting finished amicably and the two Directors who had to retire were re-elected. At the Directors' Meeting after the AGM, Mr Taylor was re-elected President and Mr Moscrip the vice-President. Hopes were expressed that season 1929/30 might see an upsurge in the form of the team.

June 25 1946

The AGM of the Shareholders announced that East Fife had made a profit of over £1,000 in season 1945/46.

After this unofficial season — because there were so many players still in the forces — season 1946/47 was to be a full one with Internationals, a Scottish Cup and a new competition called the Scottish League Cup.

East Fife were to be in Division "B". Mr McArthur was re-elected Chairman. Mr McArthur effectively did everything in the club in spite of serious health problems and an attempt last year to hand over the running of the club to someone else.

Mr Pearson and Mr Hamilton were re-elected Directors. Mr McArthur announced that he had signed two Dundonians from Dundee Violet, both of them proven goal scorers, one called Henry Morris and another called Douglas Davidson.

Both had been demobbed earlier this year, Morris had scored 27 goals since May and Davidson had recently scored 5 against Dundee Harp.

On a less happy note, John Sneddon, who had been sent off in a game v Kilmarnock, was fined £5 and banned for one month, so would be unavailable for the whole month of August.

Season tickets were set at £2.00 for ground and stand, while ladies and juniors were allowed to purchase them for £1 5 shillings.

There would only be 14 teams in Division "B", hence 13 home games, and there would also be three home games in the Scottish League Cup. Much enthusiasm was expressed about the imminence of the new season. It was another sign that the War was at last over, and that things were returning to normal.

June 26 1935

The case of David Linton, the outside left of Denbeath Star, was discussed at the meetings of both the Scottish League and the SFA today.

It appears that the youngster had foolishly signed for both East Fife and for Dundee, unaware that what he was doing was illegal.

Apparently he had signed for Dundee first, which seemed to give Dundee a strong claim on the player, but it was decided to set up a special sub-committee of representatives of the Scottish League and the SFA along with Tom Crawley, the Chairman of the Scottish Junior Football Association to discuss the matter.

Other things discussed today included a suggestion that the price for admission to Second Division matches should be reduced from seven pence to six pence, now that "entertainment tax" surcharged had been remitted.

Dates for Cup ties and for International matches were also agreed, and Mr Moscrip of East Fife was elected to the Emergency and Finance Committee.

Outside of football, the economic depression was passing but still the unemployment level was far too high, a point made by the Labour Opposition to the National Government, now led by Stanley Baldwin after the aged and ailing Ramsay MacDonald had given up as Prime Minister.

Only a fool however would not be worried about the International situation: at this precise moment in time, Italy was squaring up to Abyssinia. This looked to the rest of the world like sheer bullying, however much Mussolini, still admired in many quarters in Britain and the USA, pretended otherwise.

June 27 1903

The Committee of the Northern League met at the Athletic Rooms, Dundee this Saturday morning to discuss an appeal from East Fife (or East of Fife, as some people wanted them to be named).

East Fife were not yet technically in existence in that they had not yet staged a fixture (and would not do so until August 15), and they did not as yet have a ground, so it was hardly surprising that the Northern League had turned them down at the AGM at Arbroath on June 6.

But with commendable determination and obstinacy the founding fathers of East Fife tried again. It was not as silly an idea as one would have thought because the other teams were aware of the wide area that East Fife would represent, but there were still a few questions to ask about the new club.

Secretary James Black of Forfar Athletic read out a letter of appeal from East Fife. Mr McEwan of Dundee pointed out that he thought that the AGM may have made a mistake in turning down this clearly ambitious club, but felt that the Committee could not really go against the AGM.

At this point, the Chairman, Mr Peter Baxter of St Johnstone, ruled that East Fife's appeal could not be entertained. The 12 teams in the Northern League were to be Aberdeen, Arbroath, Cowdenbeath, Dundee A, Dundee Wanderers, Dunfermline Athletic, Forfar Athletic, Lochee, Lochgelly, Montrose, St Johnstone and Stenhousemuir and the fixtures were now agreed and released.

This was a disappointment to the nascent East Fife, but there was a certain feeling that their day might come.

June 28 1914

It was a lovely summer Sunday.

The Church, for all its repression and blatant support of the rich against the poor (contrary to the apparent message of Christianity) by solidly backing the coal owners against the miners in 1912, had at least achieved one thing for the working man, and that was that everyone in 1914, had a day off on Sunday.

So the mines and the docks were closed with only absolutely essential services allowed on the "Sabbath" as it was erroneously called.

After Church, it was time for a walk along the beach or up a hill — as long as no-one enjoyed themselves! Certainly no football would be allowed, although it was difficult to stop kids from kicking a ball about on a Sunday.

So what did people talk about? Suffragettes, and were women to be allowed to vote? Was this necessary, and how could it possibly excuse the blowing up of post boxes or vandalising of works of art? Ireland? Would Ireland at last get Home Rule? And how would these Orangemen in the north cope with that? Labour problems? Would the mines be out on strike again as they had been in 1912?

In football, East Fife, refused admission to the Scottish League this year, but next year surely they would get in, particularly if they could do well in the Scottish Qualifying Cup.

All these things would exercise the mind on the Sunday stroll. The following morning's newspapers however would carry a story about some Archduke being murdered by fanatics in the Balkans, but what did that have to do with us?

June 29 1944

If there are any benefits of a war, it is that football is still played in summer!

Although East Fife had stopped for the summer, Clyde and Morton were due to play each other at Hampden in the Summer Cup, and Waverley of *The Daily Record* was doing his best to keep the interest going.

He also carried a story that Alec Smith who had "guested" for East Fife in season 1942/43 and got a few goals for them had been given a free transfer by Motherwell and was looking for another club.

Possibly East Fife might care to think of taking him on a slightly more permanent basis? In 1944, of course, it was not anything like as simple as that because every player had to do some war related work before he was allowed to play on a Saturday afternoon.

But hopes were beginning to rise that the war might end soon. Italy had almost entirely been recaptured — Rome was certainly in Allied hands — and the news from France was consistently good.

It was clear that a strong bridgehead had been established and that Allied troops were pouring in to aid the liberation of France. Hope was even expressed that Germany might negotiate before the Allies landed on German soil, but that seemed to be ruled out by the "unconditional surrender" demands of the Allies.

Meanwhile back home, although rationing was in force, people's standard of living had, paradoxically, risen in war time. The reason was obvious in that everyone had a job and everyone felt wanted. It was still however a very anxious time for those who had husbands, fathers or sons in Italy, France or the High Seas.

June 30 1926

This time would normally be looked upon as a happy time with the school holidays and people thinking of going away at least on a day trip.

Although holiday places like Blackpool and Rothesay were now approaching their heyday, foreign holidays were undreamed of and would remain that way for most of the population for the next 40 years. In any case, this year was grim.

The mines were on strike and had been for a couple of months, as the miners resisted the attempts of the mine owners to coerce the miners into accepting longer hours and lower wages. The miners, now deserted by the Trades Union Congress, who had given in after only 10 days in May, were on their own.

Predictably demonised by the right-wing press who kept telling everyone that the miners would be happily back working of it weren't for their leaders like AJ Cook, the miners of East Fife and everywhere else however did what they always did. They stuck together and looked after each other.

The lovely midsummer weather possibly mitigated for a spell the effects of the poverty felt by the community, but hardship would bite really hard by the autumn when the miners would be forced back on the owners' terms.

But today was a day for walks and rambles — as long as it did not cost money — and as long as someone had a football, they could play that game endlessly and look forward to the start of the season to see their beloved black and golds.

The Bayview Pie Hut

Index

A

Aberdeen 29, 57, 75, 79, 80, 91, 97, 141, 143, 146, 160, 167, 168, 170, 181, 190, 221, 288, 289, 295, 326, 331, 332, 333, 337, 352, 353, 365, 367, 395, 404, 410, 411, 416, 463, 472, 473, 477, 494, 495, 517
Aberdeen Bon Accord 190, 221, 494, 495
Aberdeen Press and Journal, The 331
Aberhill end viii, 321, 355, 363
Adam, -- (Montrose) 304
Adams, Tommy 2, 29, 44, 45, 93, 100, 112, 129, 132, 136, 143, 144, 168, 186, 199, 219, 253, 262, 267, 271, 296, 299, 314, 336, 349, 350, 361, 374, 380, 415, 430, 436, 438, 440, 454, 491
Adamson, John 258
Agnew, Scott 118
Aikman, Archie (Falkirk) 199
Ainslie Park 10
Airdrie 60, 68, 97, 110, 134, 141, 182, 201, 241, 279, 297, 329, 349, 380, 428, 497
Airdrie and Coatbridge Advertiser, The 428
Aitken, George 33, 57, 65, 73, 82, 95, 96, 117, 133, 139, 143, 152, 153, 154, 186, 192, 199, 201, 211, 214, 217, 219, 230, 234, 280, 282, 292, 333, 334, 349, 350, 358, 360, 383, 429, 442, 484, 509
Albion Rovers 56, 60, 61, 133, 157, 201, 231, 267, 294, 374, 383, 394, 396, 406, 409, 413, 424, 432, 434, 435, 448, 497
Alexandria 285
Alison, -- (Falkirk) 199
Allan, A 250
Allen, John 486
Alloa 58, 78, 89, 96, 130, 144, 173, 176, 219, 243, 265, 353, 358, 380, 403, 450, 456, 465, 497
Allum, Ross (Spartans) 10
Anderson, Alan (Hearts) 364
Anderson, Harry (Raith Rovers) 356
Annan Athletic 327, 401
Annfield 207, 256
Arbroath 44, 58, 95, 171, 176, 190, 215, 221, 231, 232, 242, 273, 383, 392, 393, 401, 411, 425, 452, 456, 460, 470, 497, 517
Arbroath Herald, The 242, 392
Archibald, Steve 75, 113, 170, 235, 381, 433, 508
Armadale 115, 176, 203, 413, 424
Armistice Day 208, 212
Armstrong, Warwick, cricketer 8
Arsenal 170, 224, 379, 491, 498
Arthurlie 366, 496, 514
Asquith, Herbert, MP 249, 250, 324, 373, 378
astroturf 30
Auchterderran 33
Austin, Nathan 41, 269
Austria 296, 387, 467, 509
Ayr United 137, 138, 208, 236, 247, 267, 297, 332, 370, 375, 396, 497

523

B

Baikie, Dave 434, 463
Baird, Hugh (Airdrie) 329
Baird, John (Falkirk, Raith Rovers) 40, 48
Baird, Sammy (Rangers) 238
Bairns *see Falkirk*
Baldwin, Stanley, politician 249, 516
Balmoor 472
Banjo, David (Arbroath) 231, 232
Barr, Robert 138, 231
Barrett, Peter 193, 285, 366
Batchelor, Tommy (Raith Rovers) 113
Bath City 19, 171
Bathgate 46, 89, 92, 176, 373, 409, 496, 514
Bauld, Willie (Hearts) 158, 441
Bawbee She Kyles 280
Baxter, Bill, manager, 270
Baxter, Jim (Raith Rovers) 123
Baxter, Peter (St. Johnstone) 494, 517
Bayern Munich 487
Bayview vi, viii, 1, 2, 9, 13, 20, 22, 26, 35, 36, 40, 46, 48, 56, 60, 66, 69, 70, 71, 77, 82, 84, 89, 91, 95, 98, 100, 102, 103, 109, 111, 112, 113, 118, 120, 123, 126, 127, 130, 135, 136, 138, 139, 140, 141, 146, 153, 155, 156, 170, 171, 178, 180, 188, 189, 194, 199, 203, 205, 206, 210, 215, 217, 218, 219, 221, 224, 225, 227, 230, 234, 241, 242, 243, 245, 253, 256, 257, 259, 260, 262, 263, 264, 265, 266, 267, 271, 275, 280, 281, 282, 284, 285, 291, 292, 294, 295, 296, 298, 300, 301, 303, 304, 305, 309, 310, 311, 312, 315, 318, 325, 326, 330, 332, 335, 337, 338, 340, 349, 353, 354, 356, 361, 362, 363, 364, 365, 370, 373, 376, 378, 379, 382, 383, 384, 386, 387, 389, 392, 393, 395, 401, 403, 406, 410, 411, 413, 416, 417, 421, 424, 428, 433, 440, 442, 447, 448, 456, 458, 463, 470, 472, 473, 474, 481, 491, 493, 511, 514, 521
Bayview Pie Hut 521
Beath 46, 113, 495
Beatles 65
Beaton,-- (Brechin City) 447
Beattie, Andy manager 339
Beattie, Frank (Kilmarnock) 509
Beckham, David (Manchester United) 75
Bell, Andy (Raith Rovers) 113
Bellahouston Park 500
Bellslea Park 29
Bennett, Alex (St Mirren) 206
Benzie, -- referee 214
Bernard, John 92, 103, 208, 248, 255, 271, 291, 298, 317, 324, 356, 369, 394, 405, 413, 454
Berwick 96, 140, 230, 285, 313, 348, 442, 456, 472, 483
Berwick Advertiser, The 348
Bevan, Aneurin, politician 12, 428
Beveridge, -- 34
Bevin Boy 19
Birnie, Councillor 258
Birrell,(Cowdenbeath) 353
Black, Bobby 8, 82, 84, 132, 136, 192, 252, 258, 259, 312, 391, 399, 428, 429, 441
Black, James (Forfar Athletic) 363, 495, 517
Black and Golds 57, 391
Blackburn Rovers 34
Blackley, John (Hibs) 281
Blackpool 25, 432, 475, 484, 509, 520
Blairhall 19, 171, 246
Blairhall Colliery 19
Bo'ness 176, 213, 249, 260, 499, 506
Boghead 127, 349, 351, 362, 374
Bogie, James (Raith Rovers) 279
Bohemian 322
Bolt, Bobby (Falkirk) 199

Bonnar, Johnnie (Arbroath, Celtic) 312, 383, 422
Bonthrone, Jimmy 65, 75, 77, 94, 95, 117, 126, 133, 134, 139, 141, 159, 166, 177, 185, 207, 211, 230, 241, 264, 283, 293, 329, 332, 337, 339, 352, 358, 362, 404, 427
Borough Briggs 401
Borthwick, Walter 190, 198, 339, 340, 341, 364, 417
Bowhill Juniors 46
Bowhill Rovers 33
Bowhill Thistle 486
Boyce, Tommy 507
Boyd, Willie (Clyde) 477
Bradford City 265
Bradman, Don, cricketer 12, 18, 468
Brant, Harry (Albion Rovers) 406
Brash, Alex (Forfar Athletic, Raith Rovers) 300
Brazil 508, 513
Brechin City 140, 155, 245, 262, 396, 447
British Expeditionary Force 92, 510
Brittle, Willie, referee 339, 427
Broadwood 222, 223, 418, 442
Brockville 160, 177, 334, 416, 450
Brodie (Cowdenbeath) 265
Brodie -- 313, 398
Broomhall 46
Brora Rangers 302, 303
Broughty Anchorage 44
Brown, Allan 73, 84, 111, 112, 136, 139, 176, 192, 231, 240, 257, 280, 372, 396, 429, 441, 509
Brown, Bobby (Rangers) 162, 284
Brown, Craig (Aberdeen) 288
Brown, Ian 389
Brown, Michael 490
Brown, Ross 287
Brown, Willie, (Airdrie) 329
Brown,-- 331
Browning (Vale of Leven) 285

Brownlie, John (Hibs) 281
Broxburn 115, 176
Bruce, Jock (Forfar Athletic) 295
Bruce, Michael 490
Brunton, James 258
Buchan, Willie (Celtic) 355
Buchanan, Jock (Rangers) 406
Buchanan, Liam 187, 470
Buchanan (Clyde) 263
Buchanan, Peter (Queen's Park) 367
Buckhaven 1, 13, 103, 111, 158, 298, 481
Buckhaven Co-operative Society 13
Buckhaven High School 111, 158
Buckley, Paddy (Aberdeen) 91, 337
Buddies see St Mirren
Buick, Jim (Arbroath) 221
Bully Wee see Clyde
Burley, Craig (Scotland) 513
Burnley 192
Burns, Robert poet 31, 188, 236, 309
Burntisland Shipyard 304
Burt, Paul 245, 266
Burton -- 89, 240, 243
Bury 482, 486
Busby, Matt (Manchester United) 432

C

Café Val D'Or 167
Cahill, Patrick 115, 316, 317
Cairns -- 198
Caithness, Martin 266, 421
Calvin, John, religious figure
Cameron, -- 142
Cameron, -- (Forfar Athletic) 413
Campbell, Dick (Arbroath) 273, 401
Campbell, James, administrator 17, 258
Campbell, Robert 490
Campbell -- (Motherwell) 313
Campbell – (Morton) 321
Canavan, -- 168

Cannonball *see Fleming, Charlie*
Cant, Andy 89, 243, 265
Cany, Jimmy (Arbroath) 171, 190
Cappielow 141, 159, 235, 321, 351, 358, 375
Carbone Carbasoque 2
Cardenden 103, 195, 486
Cardiff City 29
Carpentier, Georges, boxer 8
Carrie, Bob (Falkirk) 334
Carroll, Frank 93
Carroll, -- 463
Carruthers,-- (Edinburgh City) 253
Carruthers -- referee 253, 272, 279
Carver, Willie 44
Casciani, Pat 18, 271
Cathkin 325, 334
Celtic 2, 3, 17, 40, 43, 46, 53, 57, 68, 73, 77, 80, 82, 91, 97, 103, 105, 109, 113, 120, 123, 125, 127, 130, 131, 133, 135, 153, 156, 170, 177, 180, 189, 190, 201, 202, 211, 214, 217, 233, 235, 238, 241, 259, 263, 264, 268, 280, 281, 283, 288, 291, 292, 293, 294, 295, 298, 304, 305, 311, 312, 313, 314, 318, 321, 332, 334, 339, 340, 341, 342, 343, 345, 346, 349, 353, 355, 356, 362, 363, 366, 374, 375, 383, 384, 389, 390, 391, 392, 393, 395, 396, 404, 410, 411, 416, 417, 419, 422, 428, 433, 434, 448, 451, 454, 455, 463, 465, 466, 467, 473, 475, 481, 485, 487, 496, 499, 500, 503, 511
Centenary 54
Central League 53, 89, 92, 176, 356, 373, 378, 454, 460, 495, 496, 505
Chalmers, Steve (Celtic) 89, 131, 481
Chamberlain, Neville, PM 304
Chaplin, Charlie, comedian 285, 486
Charles , Ray, (Queen of the South) 389
Cheetham,-- (Armadale) 115
Chelsea 85, 513

Chisholm, Gordon 138
Chisholm, -- (Armadale) 115
Christie, George 65, 120, 133, 140, 185, 224, 254, 451
Churchill, Winston, politician 37, 143, 361, 510
City Park 253
Clarke, Dave 160, 198, 450, 490
Cliftonhill 157, 201, 432, 434, 435
Clyde 33, 57, 131, 156, 170, 181, 222, 223, 233, 263, 311, 327, 337, 358, 393, 401, 421, 442, 451, 455, 466, 468, 470, 477, 519
Clydebank 69, 70, 171, 174, 193, 254, 496
Clydeholm 193
Coatbridge 2, 60, 424, 428, 432
Cobban , Lieutenant W, soldier 505
Coleman, David commentator 36
Collie, Stuart (Forfar Athletic) 363
Collins, Bobby (Celtic) 77, 312, 475
Collins, -- (Kilmarnock) 430
Colville, Harry (Dunfermline) 189
Commonwealth Games 245
Conn, Alfie (Hearts) 181, 441
Cook, Andrew (Raith Rovers) 128
Cook, Barry (referee) 231
Cook AJ (miners' leader) 520
Copeland, Ernie (Raith Rovers) 134
Copland, Jackie (Dundee United) 390
Corstorphine, Jim 106, 490
Courier, The see Dundee Courier
Cowan, Joe 113, 253, 262, 271, 272, 279, 314, 336, 355, 368, 485
Cowan, Jimmy (Morton), 153, 159, 246, 484
Cowdenbeath 1, 12, 39, 73, 111, 121, 203, 260, 265, 292, 304, 314, 329, 353, 379, 380, 392, 393, 412, 421, 454, 467, 494, 495, 496, 497, 498, 517
Cowie, Doug (Raith Rovers manager) 117
Cox, Sammy 57, 153, 185, 264, 429
Craigmyle, Peter, referee 168

Crail 1
Crawford, Steve 185, 225, 470, 490
Crawley, Tom administrator 516
Crockett, Bert, referee 292
Cromar, R (Queen's Park) 362
Cropley, Alex (Hibs) 281
Crozier, Joe 272, 311
Crum, John (Celtic) 500
Cullis, Stan (Wolves) 186
Cumbernauld 233
Cumming, John (Hearts) 158
Cupar 25, 503, 507
Curran, John 97, 178, 185, 224, 263, 293, 395
Currie, Dom 88, 89, 118, 143, 203, 231, 233, 240, 260, 353
Czechoslovakia 296, 380, 476, 482

D

Dailey, Doug 135, 160, 268
Daily Record, The 476, 519
Dale, -- referee 309
Dalglish, Kenny 340, 342
Dalkeith Thistle 511
Dallas, Andrew referee 230
Daly, Jon 188
Dalymount Park 322, 323
Dalziel, Henry MP 324
Dalziel, Gordon (Raith Rovers) 235
Dangerous Dan 229, 467, 477, 499
Dark Blues *see Vale of Leven*
Davidson, Bobby, referee 441, 134
Davidson, Douglas, 84, 143, 144, 168, 186, 199, 219, 309, 374, 441, 515
Davidson, Jackie 134, 199, 349, 407
Davis, Harold (Rangers) 57, 238
Dawson, Jerry (Falkirk and manager) 33, 68, 141, 185, 186, 199, 238, 455
Deans, Dixie (Celtic) 180, 313, 340
Deila, Ronnie (Celtic) 448
Delaney, Jimmy (Manchester United) 432

Dempsey, Jack boxer 8
Denbeath Star 46, 512, 516
Denmark 493
Dens Park 26, 167, 190, 252, 345, 354
Deuchar, Kenny 458, 459
Deutschland Uber Alles 47
Dewar, George 71, 102, 121, 123, 133, 204, 230, 236, 321, 324, 332, 333, 360, 370, 398
Dick, Kenny (Forfar) 105
Dingwall 118, 411
Divers, John (Celtic) 233
Division "A" 432
Division "B" 67, 141, 192, 267, 349, 361, 374, 383, 432, 497, 515
Division "B" Supplementary League 67
Division "C" 483
Division One 18, 58, 60, 177, 188, 237, 247, 294, 307, 396, 448, 497
Division Three trophy 426
Division Two 10, 18, 56, 92, 140, 155, 170, 173, 193, 231, 236, 256, 275, 353, 370, 396, 401, 448, 463, 497, 514
Docherty Mark 273
Donnelly, Frank 120, 131, 321, 333, 352, 360
Dons *see Aberdeen*
Doonhamers *see Queen of the South*
Dorward -- (Kirkcaldy United) 356
Dougan, Patrick 335
Douglas Park 204, 229
Douglas, J W H T , cricketer 8
Downie, Billy 271
Dublin 188, 322, 323, 379
Ducal Toon 229
Duchart, Alex 264
Dudgeon Park 303
Duggan, Chris 274, 344
Dumbarton 42, 95, 96, 127, 182, 257, 349, 351, 362, 370, 374, 393, 410, 456, 496, 497
Dumfries 71, 280, 386

Duncan, Davie 15, 82, 84, 100, 101, 111, 127, 143, 157, 160, 167, 168, 178, 191, 192, 199, 200, 201, 214, 217, 241, 259, 267, 309, 312, 329, 334, 338, 349, 350, 361, 372, 374, 407, 428, 429, 432, 441, 468
Dundee 14, 16, 23, 26, 27, 29, 34, 42, 80, 141, 146, 167, 169, 176, 190, 201, 203, 205, 234, 252, 283, 291, 292, 294, 310, 311, 325, 326, 337, 339, 353, 354, 373, 390, 393, 407, 409, 415, 419, 441, 450, 451, 467, 482, 486, 494, 495, 497, 499, 508, 511, 512, 515, 516, 517
Dundee A 517
Dundee City 169
Dundee Courier, The 80, 82, 87, 92, 111, 126, 129, 134, 144, 153, 156, 157, 167, 169, 175, 176, 186, 192, 199, 203, 205, 208, 227, 229, 237, 242, 247, 250, 253, 258, 262, 265, 271, 280, 291, 314, 331, 361, 373, 375, 405, 409, 428, 457, 468, 486, 495, 496
Dundee Evening Telegraph, The 205, 419, 482, 511
Dundee Harp 515
Dundee Hibernian 169
Dundee Reserves 495
Dundee United 16, 146, 169, 294, 310, 339, 390, 407, 409, 415, 451, 508
Dundee Violet 167, 515
Dundee Wanderers 495, 517
Dunfermline Athletic 1, 7, 31, 32, 34, 46, 71, 111, 115, 126, 136, 144, 162, 168, 175, 189, 191, 192, 195, 203, 212, 224, 227, 270, 295, 296, 304, 309, 315, 321, 329, 331, 364, 378, 441, 460, 485, 495, 497, 498, 504, 505, 517
Dunfermline Athletic Juniors 46
Dunlop, Ross 60
Dunnikier Colliery 46
Dunsire — (Forfar Athletic) 363
Dunterlie Park 366

Durie, Gordon 62, 85, 86, 345, 421, 466, 472, 491, 513
Durie Select 491
Dyet -- (King's Park) 369

E

Easson, Gordon 429
Easson, Jimmy (Portsmouth) 477
East End Park 175, 195, 212, 345
East Fife *passim*
East Fife Juniors 46
East Fife Limited Liability Company 39
East Kilbride 233
East of Fife 8, 17, 80, 121, 494, 517
East of Scotland League 10
East Stirlingshire 23, 87, 96, 171, 254, 338, 370, 377, 380, 442, 443
Easter Road 68, 77, 318, 330, 422, 427
Eastern League 23, 203, 213, 250, 497
Eden, Anthony PM 57, 368, 483
Edgar, Peter 115, 265, 366, 419
Edinburgh 10, 15, 23, 39, 91, 165, 213, 245, 253, 271, 290, 296, 348, 368, 379, 394, 415, 442, 449, 482, 504
Edinburgh City 253, 442, 449
Edwards, Alex (Hibs) 281
Elgin City 228, 269, 327, 401, 448
Elie 1, 14
Emery, Don 29, 91, 166, 185, 384
Empire Exhibition Trophy 500
ESC Clydebank 254
European Cup 207, 417, 481, 487
European Cup Winners Cup 487
Evans, Bobby (Celtic) 153, 395
Evening Telegraph, The see *Dundee Evening Telegraph, The*
Evening Times, The (Glasgow) 126, 135, 236, 238, 339, 351, 389
Everton 499, 500
Eyemouth 292, 293

F

Falconer -- 353
Falkirk 34, 40, 41, 71, 143, 160, 167, 176, 177, 181, 185, 186, 199, 237, 263, 330, 334, 362, 366, 371, 380, 391, 395, 412, 415, 419, 441, 448, 450, 476
Falkirk Herald, The 371
Falkland, Fife 36, 403, 466
Falklands War 421, 508
Fallon, John (Celtic) 120, 131
Farm, George, manager 65
Faultless, Charles (referee) 304
Feenie, Owen 512
Ferguson, Sir Alex 60, 75, 146, 206, 511
Fernie, Willie (Celtic) 109, 422
Ferranti Thistle 245
Ferry, Mark 61
Fiddes, Jimmy (Falkirk) 199
Fife County Council 25
Fife County League 46
Fife Cup 106, 210, 412, 454, 455, 504
Fife Football Association 504
Fife Free Press, The 210, 257, 279, 356, 454
Fifeshire Junior League 46
Fifeshire League 175
Fifie (Tay Ferry) 167
Findlay, Willie (Rangers) 429
Finlay, Willie 15, 33, 57, 73, 97, 166, 185, 186, 192, 199, 214, 283, 350 416, 429, 441, 484
Finlayson, -- 198, 307
Firhill 98, 135, 411, 463
Firs Park 380
First Division 12, 14, 18, 60, 95, 103, 112, 123, 132, 157, 160, 169, 173, 178, 190, 204, 206, 208, 222, 224, 229, 236, 247, 256, 265, 270, 286, 291, 292, 294, 296, 301, 306, 311, 325, 331, 352, 354, 364, 367, 371, 372, 375, 380, 389, 390, 391, 393, 394, 401, 405, 409, 410, 411, 424, 433, 441, 451, 455, 460, 470, 476, 483, 496, 499, 501, 506, 507, 511, 512
First Minister 35, 313
Fisher, -- 504
Fitchie, Tommy (Arsenal) 379
Fitzpatrick, Tony (St Mirren) 206
Flanagan, Nathan 59
Fleming, Charlie 2, 3, 19, 29, 73, 79, 82, 89, 90, 91, 97, 100, 112, 126, 134, 139, 141, 147, 156, 159, 162, 165, 166, 171, 178, 181, 184, 185, 192, 207, 211, 235, 241, 246, 252, 259, 263, 270, 282, 329, 334, 337, 362, 383, 384, 399, 404, 407, 408, 410, 416, 422, 429, 441, 442, 455, 470, 473, 475, 476, 509
Forfar Athletic 36, 42, 55, 58, 87, 105, 118, 124, 131, 132, 133, 136, 176, 179, 182, 215, 222, 225, 226, 248, 270, 290, 295, 297, 300, 305, 355, 358, 363, 369, 386, 396, 401, 403, 413, 415, 440, 450, 456, 460, 494, 495, 496, 517
Forfar Dispatch, The 132
Forfar West End 133
Forthbank 129, 176, 256, 269, 369, 470
Forthill Athletic 44
Fraser, Gary (Montrose) 327
Fraser, Neale, tennis player 9
Fraserburgh 29
Freuchie 16
Frickleton, Sammy 256
Frye - (Queen of the South) 71
Furtado, Willis 286, 287

G

Gabriel, Jimmy 248, 363, 386
Gallacher, Patsy (Celtic) 121, 199, 259, 329, 346, 376
Gardiner, James Ian 97, 159, 165, 178, 185, 241, 263, 283, 284, 337, 357, 384, 404, 416, 422, 428

Gardiner, John 313
Garth, -- 406
Gayfield 95, 190, 215, 273, 274, 392, 401, 402
Gear, Johnny 15
Geatons, Charlie (Celtic) 298, 500
Gemmell, Tommy (Celtic) 178, 481
General Strike 3, 193, 464, 506
Gerrie, -- (Dundee) 252
Gibb, -- (Partick Thistle) 185, 221
Gibson, Willie (Hearts) 376
Gilchrist, Ian 313, 398
Gilfillan, Jock 331
Gillies, Willie 256, 272
Gilpin, Jimmy (Raith Rovers) 117
Gilshan, -- (Ayr United) 236
Gilzean, Alan (Dundee, Tottenham Hotspur) 26
Glasgow 17, 24, 35, 39, 44, 46, 53, 66, 77, 96, 123, 126, 127, 135, 140, 167, 182, 189, 192, 211, 213, 233, 236, 238, 257, 263, 272, 273, 285, 292, 293, 300, 301, 309, 313, 314, 315, 325, 334, 335, 339, 340, 346, 362, 367, 369, 372, 374, 375, 376, 386, 393, 395, 405, 428, 430, 436, 460, 473, 496
Glasgow Herald, The 77, 300, 325, 340, 367, 376
Glasgow Perthshire 44
Glasgow Rangers 1, 3, 34, 43, 46, 57, 62, 64, 72, 73, 85, 96, 98, 102, 109, 113, 117, 120, 123, 127, 136, 140, 141, 143, 153, 156, 162, 166, 167, 177, 185, 186, 187, 188, 193, 199, 204, 217, 230, 234, 238, 241, 246, 255, 264, 271, 283, 284, 285, 293, 302, 303, 304, 309, 313, 314, 326, 329, 337, 348, 349, 350, 354, 363, 366, 372, 374, 376, 384, 386, 389, 390, 392, 393, 399, 403, 404, 406, 410, 411, 413, 416, 422, 427, 429, 432, 433, 434, 441, 454, 456, 472, 473, 476, 477, 483, 485, 487, 491, 498, 499, 511, 513

Glebe Park 155, 360
Glencraig Celtic 46
Gleneagles 370
Glenrothes 1, 35, 447
Gloucestershire 12
Gold, David (Arbroath) 15, 273
Gordon, Ben 28, 31
Gordon, Jimmy (Dunfermline Athletic) 212
Gorman, Davie 64, 160, 180, 198
Govan, Jock (Hibs) 468
Gowdy, Joe 18, 103, 406, 413, 424
Grant, Peter (Falkirk) 40, 41
Grant, -- (referee) 129, 290
Gray, Matt (Third Lanark) 325
Gray, -- (Baillie) 457
Gray, -- 95
Great Britain 2, 4, 8, 155, 203, 249, 288, 296, 401, 454, 510
Great War 46, 205, 212, 265, 353, 510
Greenock Morton 140, 159, 208, 230
Gretna 114
Grove, -- (Partick Thistle) 391
Guild, Alan 70, 133, 172, 173, 275, 398

H

Haddock, Harry (Clyde) 233, 263
Haig, Douglas (Fieldmarshal) 7
Haig, Al (US politician) 421
Halliday, -- (Thornhill) 305
Hamill, Jamie (Stranraer) 58
Hamilton Academical 204, 229, 233, 292, 353, 374, 383, 450
Hamilton, George (Aberdeen) 337
Hamiton, John 512
Hamilton, Ronnie (Kilmarnock) 352
Hamilton, Ross (Stenhousemuir) 149
Hamilton, Tom (Rangers) 491
Hamilton, -- (Morton) 159
Hamilton, -- (St Mirren) 306
Hamilton --, director 515
Hampden Park 9, 77, 109, 126, 162,

165, 166, 173, 181, 185, 186, 190, 192, 199, 211, 225, 234, 247, 335, 367, 375, 378, 406, 407, 413, 419, 429, 436, 457, 463, 468, 475, 501, 519
Hanlon --, Stranraer 354
Harkness, Jack, journalist 100
Harris, Tony, dentist 29
Harvey – (Stranraer) 266,
Harvey, John 436, 438
Hather, Jackie (Aberdeen) 91, 337
Haughney, Mike (Celtic) 211
Hay, David (Celtic) 345, 457
Haywood, Norman (Raith Rovers) 387
Headingley 18
Hearts 2, 17, 46, 57, 80, 84, 100, 102, 111, 141, 143, 144, 155, 158, 159, 164, 181, 238, 241, 264, 293, 294, 329, 347, 361, 364, 376, 379, 404, 410, 411, 436, 441, 450, 451, 473, 495, 504, 511
Hearts of Beath 46, 495
Hearts Reserves 80
Heggarty, Kevin 160, 180
Hemmings, Kane (Dundee) 26
Henderson, Arthur, politician 25
Henderson, Alex, miner 121
Henderson, Jimmy 253, 296
Henderson, -- (Dunfermline Athletic) 192
Henderson, -- (Falkirk) 199
Henderson, -- (Dundee Hibs) 205
Herbert, -- 375
Herd, Andy 387, 430, 436, 438
Herd, G (Queen's Park) 362
Herriot, Jim (Dunfermline Atheltic) 281
Hibernian 23, 33, 34, 68, 77, 85, 91, 98, 112, 122, 136, 141, 153, 159, 166, 169, 178, 203, 205, 207, 210, 241, 246, 259, 281, 293, 318, 330, 337, 345, 349, 368, 373, 375, 379, 384, 404, 409, 410, 412, 422, 423, 427, 432, 448, 465, 468, 473, 486, 513
Higgins, John (Celtic) 211
Highland League 29, 303, 336, 354

Hill, – (Stenhousemuir) 93
Hill, Hugh 98
Hill, Frank (Forfar Athletic) 295
Hill, Jimmy, commentator 508
Hislop. Steve 226
Hitler, Adolf 44, 93, 129, 182, 262, 296, 368, 380, 387, 467, 476, 482
Hohe Warte Stadion 467
Holland 369
Honest Men 138
Honeyman, Graham 160, 198, 306, 417
Hood, Harry (Clyde, Celtic) 180, 340, 393
Hope, -- 305
Horne, Andrew 242, 324, 392
Horne, Cyril, journalist 417
Houston, Robert 17
Howie, Hugh (Hibs) 166
Howitt, -- (Partick Thistle) 185
Hughes, Joe 198, 281, 390
Hughes, John 120
Humphries, Wilson (Motherwell) 293
Hunter, Paul 66
Hunter, -- 157
Hunter, -- Kilmarnock 430
Hunter, -- Motherwell 313

I

Ibrox 62, 63, 85, 98, 104, 193, 234, 235, 238, 243, 254, 255, 306, 314, 372, 375, 384, 396, 399, 433, 485, 487, 500
Insall, Jamie 443
Inter Milan 417, 481
Inverkeithing Juniors 46
Inverleith 378
Inverness Caledonian 40, 336, 355, 448, 465
Inverness Caledonian Thistle 40, 336, 448, 465
Inverness Thistle 336
Ireland 3, 23, 118, 153, 156, 158, 159, 169, 378, 390, 452, 466, 518

J

Jackson, Jakie (Partick Thistle) 301
Jackson, John (Dumbarton) 257
Jackson, -- referee 91
James, Alex (Raith Rovers, Arsenal) 491, 492
Jamieson, Sean 231
Johnston, Leslie (Clyde) 468
Johnstone. Jimmy (Celtic) 23, 24, 35, 73, 78, 142, 144, 180, 192, 214, 232, 268, 417, 427, 460, 481, 494, 495, 496, 497, 517
Joyner, Francis (Raith Rovers) 381

K

Kane, Chris 302, 303
Keane, Roy (Manchester United) 75
Keith, -- (Raith Rovers) 82
Kelly, -- 87, 401
Kelly, – (Ayr United) 267
Kelly, – (Northern Ireland)
Kelly, Archie (Motherwell) 143, 207, 293
Kelly, Bernie (Raith Rovers) 134
Kelty Rangers 46
Kennedy, -- (Dumbarton) 127
Kennedy, Jim (Celtic) 131`,
Kennedy, Stuart (Forfar Athletic) 300
Kerr, Guy 490
Kerr, Jason 60, 327, 401
Kerr, Jerry, manager 415
Kerr, -- 89
Kerr, Andy, (Partick Thistle) 185
Kilbowie Park 193, 254
Kilbride, referee 142
Kilgour, David (Forfar Athletic) 248, 413
Kilmarnock 34, 35, 157, 165, 177, 210, 213, 266, 297, 317, 321, 326, 332, 339, 352, 362, 367, 375, 395, 406, 407, 430, 431, 436, 452, 515

King's Park 84, 115, 129, 176, 207, 369, 378, 419
Kinglassie 109, 512
Kingseat Juniors 18, 46
Kinnear, Davie (Dunfermline Athletic) 309
Kinnear, Harry 206, 364, 376
Kinnell, -- (Dunfermline Athletic) 309
Kinsella, Jimmy 190, 398
Kirkcaldy 1, 7, 13, 16, 33, 46, 53, 84, 103, 117, 155, 167, 176, 181, 186, 210, 212, 235, 257, 263, 279, 280, 282, 298, 324, 335, 346, 356, 381, 387, 412, 424, 483, 494, 495, 502
Kirkcaldy United 7, 53, 176, 210, 324, 335, 356, 494, 495
Kirkwood, -- 181
Kirkwood, John 290
Kirriemuir Pipe Band 132
Knox, Archie (St Mirren) 306
Kruzycki, Andrew 105, 131
Kyle – 257

L

Laird, Willie 192, 199, 309, 429, 430, 436, 438
Laker, Jim, cricketer 57
Lamont, Mark 61
Lamont, Billy (Falkirk)
Lamont,-- (Albion Rovers) 294, 450
Larbert 109, 286
Law, Denis (Manchester United) 47
Lawlor, Johnny (Stirling Albion) 313
Lawson – (Aberdeen) 326
League Challenge Cup 40, 55, 60, 118, 322
League Cup 3, 10, 14, 24, 26, 29, 31, 34, 36, 42, 43, 48, 55, 56, 57, 58, 60, 62, 65, 66, 67, 68, 71, 73, 77, 82, 84, 91, 95, 96, 97, 98, 100, 102, 105, 109, 111, 117, 118, 120, 123, 126, 132,

133, 134, 135, 136, 139, 140, 141, 143, 144, 155, 162, 165, 166, 167, 168, 170, 177, 181, 183, 184, 185, 186, 189, 190, 191, 192, 199, 200, 204, 207, 211, 235, 238, 241, 252, 259, 264, 288, 293, 315, 321, 334, 349, 361, 399, 407, 416, 429, 432, 465, 481, 484, 515
Ledgerwood, Tommy (Partick Thistle) 185
"Legs" see Fleming, Charlie
Leicester City 441, 499
Leishman, Robert 264
Leith, James, Provost of Burntisland 503
Leith Athletic 87, 248, 272, 368, 383, 386
Lennox, Bobby (Celtic) 180
Leslie Hearts 46, 511
Leven 1, 17, 44, 46, 53, 123, 229, 258, 271, 272, 282, 285, 301, 311, 336, 356, 392, 440, 457, 460, 473, 481, 496
Leven Advertiser, The 271, 272, 311
Leven Mail, The 44, 229, 301, 356, 392, 457
Leven Thistle 17
Levenmouth 1, 3, 17, 47, 80, 130, 158, 227, 247, 309, 345, 355, 368, 412, 440, 482
Liddle, Danny 103, 113, 229, 291, 386, 413, 467, 477, 499
Links Park 102, 327, 466
Linn, Bobby 48, 225, 435, 490
Linwood, Alec (Morton) 141
Lister, Jim (Forfar Atheltic) 42
Liston, referee 109
Livingston 60, 194, 245
Livingstone, W., referee 372
Lloyd George, politician 250, 353, 373, 511
Lochee 494, 495, 517
Lochgelly 176, 250, 298, 412, 484, 495, 496, 500, 504, 517
Lochore and Crosshill United 46

Logan, James (Raith Rovers) 7, 511
Logan, -- (Stranraer) 275
Love, Andy (Aberdeen) 477
Love, Gordon 458
Love, John 376
Love Street 206, 306, 363
Lowery, Ted 290, 297
Lowland League 10
Loxton, Sam cricketer 12
Loy, Rory (Dundee) 26
Luke, Billy 97
Lynch, Johnny (St Mirren) 178

Mac/Mc

Macartney -- 93
McArthur, John 14, 37, 162, 163, 186, 297, 457, 497, 510, 515
McAusland, Kyle (Ayr United) 138
McBeth -- 221
McBride, (Scott) 231, 470
McBride, -- 240
McCaig, Charlie 102
McCallum, R (Bobby) (Motherwell) 313
McCallum, Willie (Motherwell) 313
McCann, Bert (Motherwell) 264
McCartney, Bob 182, 253, 271, 296, 363, 380, 387, 430, 436, 438, 440
McClair, Brian (Manchester United) 75
McCloy, Peter (Motherwell) 313
McCoist, Ally (Rangers) 85, 98
McColl, Ian (Rangers) 429
McColl, R S (Queen's Park) 335
McCormack, -- (Leith Athletic) 272
McCreary, -- (East Stirlingshire) 338
McCulloch, Lee (Rangers) 62
McCulloch, --, administrator 457
McCurley, Jock 103, 208, 498
McDiarmid Park 24
MacDonald, G., referee 111
McDonald, Greig 377, 456

MacDonald, Ramsay, PM 25, 115, 157, 507, 516
McDowell, Donnie (St Mirren) 206
McEwan, -- (Dundee) 517
McFeat,-- (Dumbarton) 374
McGachie, Arthur 18, 103, 195, 221, 237, 248, 257, 375, 406, 409, 413, 498, 512
McGann, -- 313, 398
McGarr, Ernie 340, 342, 351
McGarrity, John 162, 192
McGarvey, Frank (St Mirren, Celtic) 206, 345
McGeechan, -- 406
McGillivray, -- (Leith Atheletic) 87
McGinlay, Brian, referee 66
McGowan, Bob (Rangers) 255
McGowan,-- (Partick Thistle) 185
McGraw, Alan (Morton) 321
McGregor, -- (Albion Rovers) 201
McGrillen, -- (Stenhousemuir) 452
McGrogan, Felix (Raith Rovers) 65, 430
McGrory, Jimmy (Celtic) 103, 291, 295, 298, 355, 384, 430, 481
McGuigan, -- (Ayr United) 267
McHugh, Bob (Falkirk) 40
McInally, Arthur (Alloa Athletic) 130
McInally, Jackie (Kilmarnock) 352
McInally, Tommy (Celtic) 346, 419
McInnes, Joe (Third Lanark) 325
McIntosh, Leighton (Arbroath) 273
McIvor, -- 160
MacKay, James, miner 121
MacKay, Dave (Hearts) 158
MacKay, -- referee 182
MacKay, -- 193
MacKay, N (Queen's Park) 367
MacKay, Donald (Dundee United) 390
McKay, Stuart 155
McKee, -- 142
McKenzie, Keith (Queen's Park) 66,
McKenzie, Johnny (Partick Thistle) 185
Mackenzie -- (Inverness Caledonian) 336
McKerrell, Dan 93, 380, 414, 415, 430, 436, 438
McLaren, Billy 364
McLaren, Jackie (Raith Rovers) 113
McLaughlin, Joe (Raith Rovers) 82
McLean, Adam (Celtic) 419, 499
McLean, David, manager 44, 272, 314 363, 381, 430, 476, 485, 501. 505, 512
McLean, David (Forfar Athletic) 295, 413
McLean, Jim (Dundee United) 390
McLean, -- (Dunfermline Athletic) 192
McLean – (Queen of the South) 71
McLeish, Henry 35, 38, 173, 313, 398
McLennan, Danny 97, 185, 219, 267, 283
McLeod, Eddie 253, 271, 279, 296, 336, 381, 430, 436, 438, 440
McMahon, -- 262
McManus, Paul 26, 137, 145, 146
McMeekin, -- (Arthurlie) 366
McMillan, Harold, Prime Minister 117, 329
McMillan, Ian (Airdrie) 329
McMillan, -- 456
McMillan, -- (Ayr United) 396
McMinn, Tony 11
McMullin, Michael (East Stirlingshire) 442
McNeill, Billy (Celtic) 131, 173, 490
McNiff, Martin (Clyde) 222
McParland, Davie (Partick Thistle) 315
McPhail, Billy (Clyde, Celtic) 77, 109, 263
McPhail, Bob (Airdrie, Rangers) 255, 329, 433
McPhail, John (Celtic) 73, 384, 422
McPhee, Billy 198, 281, 306, 320, 340
McPhie, -- (Falkirk) 199
McQuade -- 198
McSeveney, Willie (Motherwell) 264

McSevich—(Aberdeen) 326
McStay, Paul (Celtic) 66
McTavish, John 346
McTurk—(Queen of the South) 71

M

Magennis, Josh (Aberdeen) 288
Magpies 348
Maguire, Chris (Aberdeen) 288
Mailer — (Dunfermline Athletic) 224
Malcolm, Craig (Stranraer) 55
Malcolm, -- (Hearts) 504
Maley, Willie (Celtic) 298, 346
Malloy, -- (Arthurlie) 366
Manchester City 192, 455
Manchester United 75, 262, 432
Mansfield Town 499
Marine Gardens 253, 368, 386, 394
Marshall, David 490
Marshall, James "Doc" (Rangers) 255, 433
Marshall, -- (Leith) 394
Martin, Fred (Aberdeen) 416
Martin, Scott 274
Martis, John 160, 198, 313
Mason, James, golfer 53,
Mason, Jimmy (Third Lanark) 153, 484
Masson, Terry (Montrose) 327
Matthew, Andy 97, 165, 166, 185, 211, 238, 337, 362
Maule, Johnny (Raith Rovers) 82
Maxton, James, politician 25
Mayes, -- (Clyde) 311
Mazana-Marinez (Stenhousemuir) 286
Mbuyi-Mutombo (Partick Thistle) 118
Meadowbank 245, 276
Meiklejohn, Davie (Rangers) 234, 255, 476
Merenghi, -- (Stranraer) 55
Methil 1, 2, 25, 29, 36, 53, 65, 68, 93, 105, 110, 111, 112, 126, 135, 153, 171, 173, 177, 180, 182, 186, 195, 210, 212, 213, 219, 229, 233, 237, 241, 242, 252, 253, 254, 255, 265, 267, 271, 279, 280, 294, 311, 326, 335, 337, 339, 346, 348, 352, 355, 366, 381, 412, 419, 424, 427, 430, 433, 436, 447, 452, 457, 458, 464, 472, 479, 481, 485, 487, 492, 493, 508, 511
Michael Colliery 46, 121
Middlesbrough 505
Milburn Park 285
Mill Park 92, 373
Millar, Larry 182, 381, 415, 430, 436, 438
Miller, Bertie 198, 306, 307, 313, 398
Miller, Davie 266
Milne, -- 380
Milton, Jimmy 430, 436, 438, 507
Milton of Balgonie 507
Miners' Strike 3, 18, 391
Mitchell, John (Forfar Athletic) 300
Mitchell, Tom 386, 413, 424
Mitchell, J M , politician 25
Mochan, Neil (Celtic) 77, 211, 238, 395
Moffat, Andy 240, 260
Moffat , Barrie 155, 215
Moffat, Michael (Ayr United) 138
Moffat, --, goalkeeper 227
Moffatt, -- (Motherwell) 313
Mole, Jamie (Raith Rovers) 48
Montrose 65, 71, 102, 171, 209, 243, 304, 325, 327, 328, 349, 369, 466, 495, 517
Morecambe, Eric, comedian 36
Morgan, James 16
Morocco 513
Morris, Henry 3, 12, 15, 65, 82, 87, 95, 96, 100, 111, 117, 132, 133, 136, 144, 151, 152, 153, 156, 167, 168, 192, 199, 201, 217, 219, 230, 234, 235, 252, 259, 267, 270, 292, 309, 334, 338, 358, 372, 374, 383, 385, 399, 407, 429, 432, 441, 470, 509, 515
Morrison, Harry, miner 121
Morrison, -- 87,

Mortensen, Stan, (England) 332, 484
Morton 140, 141, 153, 159, 171, 208, 230, 235, 246, 255, 271, 275, 292, 304, 321, 325, 329, 349, 351, 358, 375, 393, 458, 477, 484, 499, 519
Moscrip, William, director 457, 485, 498, 514, 516
Motherwell 44, 71, 141, 165, 264, 268, 293, 303, 313, 375, 410, 417, 519
Mowat, Jack, referee 159, 166, 429
Moyes, David 18
Mudie, -- 219
Mudie, Jackie (Blackpool), 475
Muir, David 63, 471, 472, 490
Muir, Willie 26
Muirton Park 142, 217
Munro, Andy (Forfar Athletic) 42
Munro, David, referee, 303
Murray, Bill (Sunderland) manager 282
Murray, Jimmy (Hearts) 158
Murray, Maxie (Rangers) 238
Murray, -- 285
Murray, -- (Motherwell) 313
Murray, -- (Alloa) 403
Mussolini, Benito, dictator 44, 129, 516
Myles, George, golfer 53

N

Nairn, Davie 257, 305
Nangle, John 80, 81
Napier, Charlie (Celtic) 103, 298
Narey, Dave (Dundee United) 508
Nasser, Gamal Abdel, dictator 57
National Coal Board 3
National Health Service 12, 252, 491, 492
Naysmith, Gary 60, 327, 402, 442
Neil, -- 240
Neish, Jimmy 353
Neish, Jock 89, 157, 169, 240, 243, 249, 265, 353, 504
Neish, Tom 89

New Bayview 1, 2, 20, 22, 35, 36, 40, 60, 118, 138, 146, 188, 215, 217, 225, 303, 401, 442, 448, 456, 458, 463, 470, 472, 474
Newcastle United 192, 455, 498
Newman 230, 256, 262
Newton Park 213, 249
Nibloe, Joe (Kilmarnock) 297
Nicholas, Charlie (Clyde) 170
Nicholas, Stevie 473
Nisbit, -- referee 348
Nithsdale Wanderers 243
Niven, John 34, 132, 143, 186, 199, 201, 234, 334, 338, 349, 372, 399, 429
Northcroft, Mike referee 42
Northern Ireland 153, 156, 158, 159, 390, 452, 466
Northern League 17, 80, 175, 242, 324, 494, 495, 517
Number 1 Pit 195

O

O'Brien, Paul (Queen's Park) 66
O'Brien, George (Dunfermline Athletic) 224
O'Brien --- 466
O'Connor, Derek 116
O'Hara, Kevin 286
O'Neill, Joe (Aberdeen) 91
O'Neill, -- (Vale of Leven) 285
Ochilview 146, 371, 372, 405
Odense 493
Old Crocks 491
Orion 80
Ormond, Willie (Hibs) 68, 427
Orr, Tommy (Morton) 159
Overton, Kirkcaldy 210

P

Page, Jonathan 222, 223
Paisley 206, 306, 375, 513
Palmerston 71, 91, 386

Paris 24, 144, 467
Parker, Bobby (Hearts) 111
Pars *see Dunfermline Athletic*
Partick Thistle 29, 98, 112, 118, 135, 166, 178, 183, 185, 189, 216, 234, 301, 304, 315, 321, 325, 357, 366, 386, 391, 399, 411, 413
Paterson, George (Dunfermline Athletic) 195
Paterson, Jimmy (Cowdenbeath) 467
Paterson, -- 295
Paterson, -- (Ayr United) 236
Pathhead 210, 356
Paton, George 143
Paton, Johnny (Celtic) 214
Paton, Paul (Queen's Park) 463
Patterson, "Pasha" 391
Peacock, Bertie (Celtic) 73
Pearson, Tom, chairman 403, 515
Peebles, George (Dunfermline Athletic) 189
Peggie, Jimmy 210, 412
Penicuik 512
Penman, Willie (Raith Rovers) 82
Penman Cup 93, 147, 378, 379
Perrie, -- (Forfar Athletic) 132
Peterhead 31, 42, 60, 458, 471, 472
Phillips, John 272
Phillips, Hugh, referee 315
Philp, Jim 33, 57, 192, 199, 214, 217, 219, 220, 349, 350, 361, 383, 429, 441, 484
Pinkerton, -- (St Bernards) 296
Pittenweem 1
Pittodrie 97, 283, 288, 289, 326, 332, 353
Plumb, Angus 181, 189, 211, 339, 395, 410
Poland 110, 147, 173, 476
Pollock, Jamie 138
Polmont 142, 213
Poloc 455
Porteous, -- (Armadale) 115
Powderhall 15, 253

Pratt, Archie 272, 311
Premier Division 24, 256, 318, 351, 450
Premier League 24, 35, 40, 118, 286, 318, 376, 448, 451, 474
Prentice, Bobby (Hearts) 376
Preston North End 33, 185, 246, 473, 492
Princess Margaret 181
Printy, -- 160
Probables v Possibles 44
Purdon, RR, County Assessor. 25

Q

Queen of the South 65, 71, 85, 91, 146, 153, 245, 280, 305, 386, 389, 394, 399, 411, 416, 452
Queen's Park 66, 71, 100, 177, 211, 247, 315, 335, 338, 350, 362, 367, 373, 401, 452, 458, 459, 462, 463
Quinn, Pat 135, 180, 198, 306, 340, 406, 411
Quinn, -- (Albion Rovers) 406
Quinn,-- referee 229

R

Rae, Alex 313, 354
Rae, Willie (Rangers) 429
Raith Rovers 1, 4, 7, 33, 48, 53, 58, 65, 66, 71, 82, 84, 95, 111, 113, 116, 117, 118, 123, 133, 134, 139, 140, 147, 170, 171, 177, 190, 203, 210, 222, 235, 257, 263, 264, 270, 275, 279, 280, 283, 296, 300, 304, 305, 307, 308, 315, 329, 330, 332, 339, 356, 362, 372, 379, 381, 382, 387, 389, 395, 411, 419, 424, 433, 441, 454, 455, 485, 491, 492, 497, 501, 502, 503, 504, 505, 511
Ramsay, Bob (Forfar Athletic) 363
Rankin, Stan (Morton) 351
Rarity, James 248, 301, 369

Recreation Grounds 392
Recreation Park 78, 173, 250, 358
Red Lichties 221, 231, 456
Redpath, Willie (Motherwell) 293
Reid, Bobby (Raith Rovers) 117
Reid, George (Kilmarnock) 430
Reilly, Lawrie (Hibs) 153, 166, 189, 224, 265, 427, 484
Renfrew Juniors 34
Rest of the UK 246
Rice, Peter (St Mirren) 178
Ring, Tommy (Clyde) 233, 263
Riordan, Derek 448
Roberts, -- 348, 392
Robertson, George (Kilmarnock) 430
Robertson, Jocky (Third Lanark) 325
Robertson, Scott (Stranraer) 55
Robertson, Wattie 89, 203, 240
Robertson, -- referee 405
Robertson, -- secretary 504
Robinson, Scott 286
Rodger, Jim 333
Rodger, -- (Forfar Athletic) 132
Rodi, Joe 44, 304
Rolland, Andy (Cowdenbeath) 121
Rolland --, Chairman 39
Ross, Bobby 333
Ross, Sammy (Kilmarnock) 430
Ross, -- 89, 240, 373
Ross County 118, 354, 411, 465
Rosslyn Juniors 46
Rosyth Recreation 46
Rough, Alan (Partick Thistle) 135
Russell, Bobby 295, 366
Russell, Davie 271, 279, 430, 436, 438, 482
Russell, Sandy 454
Rutherford, Drew 206
Rutherford, Willie 173
Rutherford, Eddie (Rangers) 429
Ryan, Vincent (Celtic) 211

S

St Andrews 1, 502
St Bernards 271, 296, 394, 400, 414, 415
St Johnstone 23, 24, 73, 142, 144, 268, 417, 494, 495, 497, 517
St Mirren 83, 100, 112, 178, 181, 190, 206, 207, 238, 306, 315, 326, 349, 363, 375, 396, 404, 410, 466, 496
Scarff, Peter (Celtic) 103, 291, 298
Scotland 3, 4, 9, 10, 35, 36, 47, 57, 58, 68, 85, 118, 121, 140, 151, 152, 153, 156, 158, 159, 170, 171, 173, 193, 195, 201, 203, 207, 233, 241, 243, 246, 254, 255, 263, 264, 265, 268, 281, 282, 283, 294, 295, 297, 300, 303, 305, 309, 313, 321, 325, 326, 338, 340, 345, 356, 378, 379, 391, 395, 404, 405, 407, 412, 421, 422, 432, 452, 455, 466, 467, 468, 475, 476, 477, 481, 484, 491, 492, 496, 499, 500, 502, 504, 505, 508, 509, 512, 513
Scotland v England 9, 140, 378, 407, 500
Scotsman, The 291, 368, 415
Scott, Bobby 336
Scott, George 129, 245, 262, 272, 363
Scott, Gordon 300, 466
Scott, Sir Walter 14
Scott, -- 210
Scottish Amateur Golf Championship 53
Scottish Cup 3, 4, 10, 24, 29, 33, 34, 39, 40, 43, 57, 91, 108, 118, 127, 146, 157, 165, 170, 177, 182, 186, 208, 222, 225, 241, 260, 264, 266, 269, 270, 271, 272, 285, 288, 291, 292, 293, 294, 297, 298, 300, 301, 303, 304, 305, 306, 307, 309, 310, 311, 312, 315, 318, 321, 325, 326, 327, 329, 330, 331, 332, 333, 335, 336, 338, 339, 345, 346, 349, 350, 352, 353, 354, 355, 361, 362, 363, 365, 366, 367, 370,

372, 373, 374, 375, 376, 381, 382, 384, 386, 387, 388, 391, 392, 393, 395, 399, 400, 403, 404, 406, 413, 414, 415, 416, 419, 428, 429, 432, 433, 436, 438, 439, 440, 448, 455, 457, 460, 464, 465, 476, 479, 480, 485, 491, 500, 501, 503, 504, 506, 515

Scottish Football Association (SFA) 14, 207, 403, 477, 510, 516

Scottish Junior Football Association 516

Scottish League 2, 8, 10, 14, 23, 26, 29, 31, 34, 36, 42, 43, 46, 48, 56, 58, 62, 66, 67, 71, 77, 89, 92, 96, 97, 98, 100, 111, 118, 120, 123, 126, 127, 130, 132, 134, 135, 136, 140, 141, 143, 144, 158, 162, 165, 166, 168, 170, 173, 176, 177, 181, 185, 186, 188, 189, 190, 191, 192, 193, 199, 200, 203, 204, 205, 207, 210, 211, 214, 222, 237, 238, 241, 243, 245, 252, 254, 260, 263, 279, 283, 285, 288, 292, 293, 294, 307, 314, 315, 321, 322, 326, 346, 349, 352, 353, 361, 379, 384, 391, 404, 407, 409, 410, 412, 413, 416, 427, 432, 441, 442, 448, 454, 458, 460, 463, 466, 473, 483, 484, 492, 495, 496, 497, 501, 505, 511, 515, 516, 518

Scottish League Cup 14, 26, 29, 31, 34, 36, 42, 43, 48, 56, 58, 62, 66, 67, 71, 77, 97, 98, 100, 111, 118, 120, 123, 126, 132, 134, 135, 136, 141, 143, 144, 162, 165, 166, 168, 170, 177, 181, 185, 186, 189, 190, 191, 192, 199, 200, 204, 207, 211, 238, 241, 252, 288, 293, 315, 321, 349, 361, 407, 432, 484, 515

Scottish Qualifying Cup 8, 39, 240, 243, 260, 346, 348, 366, 518

Scottish Sun, The 85

Second Division 3, 12, 23, 33, 46, 60, 68, 71, 87, 89, 96, 106, 108, 113, 117, 127, 130, 138, 140, 171, 204, 219, 222, 230, 233, 245, 247, 248, 254, 256, 265, 269, 270, 271, 279, 285, 292, 294, 313, 314, 315, 321, 327, 330, 332, 351, 353, 354, 358, 366, 368, 372, 379, 380, 387, 391, 393, 394, 409, 410, 411, 419, 421, 424, 438, 441, 442, 452, 456, 457, 460, 463, 465, 466, 470, 472, 476, 477, 483, 496, 499, 500, 505, 511, 512, 514, 516

Second World War 4, 29, 84, 129, 132, 253

Seith, Bobby (Hearts) 364

Sharkey, -- 301, 409

Sharp, John 490

Sharp, Willie (Partick Thistle)

Sharpe, Lee (Manchester United) 75

Shaw, Jock (Rangers) 429

Shawfield 156, 233, 263

Sheffield United 31

Shields, Dene 62, 128

Shielfield Park 96

Shire *see East Stirlingshire*

Simpson, Billy (Rangers) 156

Simpson, Jimmy (Rangers) 350

Simpson, Ronnie (Queen's Park) 350

Simpson, Wallis, socialite 262

Sinclair, Davie (Ayr United) 138

Skene, Ralph 7

Skivington, -- (Alloa) 219

Sky Sports Year Book 434

Sloan, Robert 225

Smart, Jonathan 146, 490

Smeaton, -- 338

Smith, Alec 519

Smith, Darren (Stirling Albion) 269

Smith, Gordon (Hibs) 68, 246, 427

Smith, Harold 123

Smith, Jimmy (Rangers) 314

Smith, John (Forfar Athletic), 136

Smith, Johnson, miner 121

Smith, Kevin 26, 40, 55, 60, 222, 442, 448

Smith, Matt (Kilmarnock) 297

Smith, Sam (Forfar Atheletic), 136

Sneddon, John 253, 430, 436, 438, 515
Sneddon, Alan (Hibs) 465
Somerset Park 236, 344, 396
Somme 7, 502
Sons of the Rock *see Dumbarton*
Souness, Graeme (Rangers) 98
Soutar, Doug 307, 313
Southern League Cup 168
Spain 3, 44, 182, 262, 296, 387, 466, 475
Spartans 10, 11
Spiders *see Queen's Park*
Sporting Post, The 87
Stair Park 55, 58, 266
Stanton, Pat (Hibs) 281
Stark, Billy (St Mirren, Queen's Park) 206, 463
Stark's Park 48, 49, 65, 71, 95, 117, 134, 155, 275, 279, 379, 381, 387, 388, 412, 454, 455, 491
Station Park 42, 105, 124, 131, 132, 136, 182, 248, 270, 290, 295, 297, 320
Steel, Billy (Dundee) 153, 484
Steele, John 272, 311
Steele, -- (Clyde) 233
Stein, Jock (Celtic) 97, 180, 201, 340, 417, 422, 432, 508
Stenhousemuir 25, 87, 93, 118, 146, 176, 243, 286, 330, 371, 372, 396, 405, 407, 413, 421, 434, 448, 456, 494, 495, 497, 517
Steven, -- (Airdrieonians) 110
Stewart, Hal (Morton) 321
Stewart, Ian 321, 325, 358, 370, 393
Stewart, Jackie 185, 211, 337, 339, 384, 395, 410, 427
Stewart, John (Kilmarnock) 430
Stewart, Peter 330
Stewart, Sammy 57, 68, 89, 95, 97, 100, 105, 111, 120, 158, 162, 167, 185, 192, 199, 240, 315, 320, 339, 416, 429
Still,-- (Dunfermline Athletic) 168
Stirling Albion 84, 129, 207, 244, 256, 269, 395, 407, 410, 470
Stirrat, Ron 95, 320, 333, 360, 393
Stockbridge 271, 415
Stockdale, Doug (Raith Rovers) 139
Stockholm XI 493
Stranraer 55, 58, 59, 119, 266, 275, 292, 300, 303, 354, 434, 452, 453
Struth, Bill (Rangers) 73, 234, 255
Suez 57, 189, 211, 403
Sunday Mail, The 417, 500
Sunday Post, The 73, 89, 100, 112, 127, 153, 168, 201, 219, 259, 285, 295, 350, 361, 372, 432
Sunderland 19, 31, 126, 171, 181, 282, 393, 410, 475, 484, 509
Sunter, -- (Forfar Athletic) 132
Supplementary Round 105
Swan, -- (Dundee Hibs) 169
Sweden 493
Swindon Town 29, 166
Switzerland 468, 475, 477, 509
Syme, W M , referee 158, 389
Symon, Scot 14, 33, 67, 73, 95, 143, 167, 185, 192, 199, 234, 238, 259, 261, 334, 407, 473, 487, 492, 493

T

Tade, Gregory 48
Tait, Bobby 430, 436, 438
Tait, James, miner 121
Tannadice 169, 294, 390, 407, 409
Tay Road Bridge 167
Taylor, Andrew, miner 121,
Taylor, Paul 389
Taylor, -- president 457, 514
Telfer, Willie (St Mirren, Rangers) 101, 238
Telford Street 336
Third Lanark 25, 82, 130, 153, 213, 292, 325, 334, 370, 394, 404, 410, 484, 496

Thom, Gary 188
Thomson, Alec (Celtic) 103, 298
Thomson, Andrew, miner 121
Thomson, Ben, supporter 457
Thomson, Benny (Kilmarnock) 430
Thomson, Bertie (Celtic) 291, 298
Thomson, Craig 24
Thomson, Darren 490
Thomson, John (Celtic) 113, 142, 195, 291, 298, 419, 467
Thomson, Philip, miner 121
Thomson, Robin 245, 421
Thomson, Scott 490
Thorburn ,-- 356
Thornhill 305
Thornton, Willie (Rangers) 283, 429, 473
Tierney, Cornelius (Celtic) 103
Tod, Andy (Forfar Athletic) 225
Torbet, John (Partick Thistle) 301
Totten, Alex, manager 56, 447
Tottenham Hotspur 17, 513
Town Hall Park 17
Trades Union Congress (TUC) 464, 520
Tran, -- 320
Tranmere Rovers 482
Troup, Alec (Forfar Atheltic) 271, 499
Trouten, Alan (Queen's Park) 463
Trowbridge Town 19
Tryst 146
Tully, Charlie (Celtic) 109, 156, 211, 214, 259, 312, 384, 481
Turnbull, Eddie (Hibs) 68, 367, 427
Twaddle, Kevin (Ayr United) 137
Tynecastle 28, 143, 158, 159, 164, 166, 181, 186, 294, 361, 376, 391, 414, 415, 441, 451

U

Ure, Ian (Dundee, Arsenal) 26
Urquhart, John (Raith Rovers) 181
Uruguay 509

V

Vale of Leven 285, 460, 496
Venters, Alec (Rangers) 314
Vernon, Scott (Aberdeen) 288
Victoria 80, 411
Vienna 467
Vincent, James (Dundee) 26

W

Waddell, Andy 105, 120, 121, 131, 230, 275, 307, 398
Waddell, Bobby 398
Waddell, Willie (Rangers) 153, 162, 283, 332, 352
Wales 118, 193, 195, 246, 356
Walker, Jimmy 140, 173, 230, 236, 292, 313, 333, 360
Walker, Jimmy (Partick Thistle) 185, 399
Walker, Paul 146
Walker, William, councillor 503
Walker, -- 363
Walker, --, referee, 210
Wallace, Ryan, 60
Wallace, Gordon (Raith Rovers) 171
Wallace, Lee (Rangers) 62
Wallyford Bluebell 499
Walsh, Jimmy (Celtic) 395, 422
Wardhaugh, Jimmy (Hearts) 111, 158, 441
Wardlaw, Gareth 86
Warrender, -- 243
Warriors 371, 372
Watson, Hugh, referee 430
Watt, Hamish (Forfar Athletic) 105
Watt, -- 313, 354
Watters, Jimmy (Hearts) 57
Wearside 19, 282
Webb, Willie, referee 167, 192, 257, 374
Webster Tyre Company 29

Weir, Philip 18, 87, 127, 130, 195, 208, 212, 248, 249, 251, 255, 257, 291, 295, 297, 305, 316, 331, 353, 363, 369, 371, 386, 406, 413, 457
Wellesley Juniors 46, 113, 298, 419, 436, 467
Wellesley Road 436
Wellesley Road turnstiles xiv
Wells O' Wearie, The 255
Wembley 47, 100, 257, 395, 405, 422, 432, 441, 475, 484, 491
Wembley Wizards 257
Wemyss 44, 121, 130, 250, 346, 436, 485, 491, 504
Wemyss Castle Station 436
Wemyss Memorial Hospital 44, 491
West Fife League 46
West Germany 47, 475
West of Scotland 455, 496
Wharton, Tom, referee 35, 189, 362
White, -- (Ayr United) 267
Whiteford, -- (Motherwell) 313
Whitelaw, John (Raith Rovers) 279, 381
Whiteside, -- (Raith Rovers) 307
Whyte, --, 454
Whyte, -- (Dunfermline) 192
Whyte, -- (Falkirk) 199,
Wilkie, Kyle 27, 269, 327, 328
Wilkie, -- 147, 304
Williams, Evan (Celtic) 417
Williamson, Colin (Brora Rangers) 303
Williamson, --318
Wilson, Andrew Nesbit (Dunfermline Athletic) 505
Wilson, Davie (Rangers) 123
Wilson, Harold, Prime Minister 256, 354, 428
Wilson, John 247, 291, 298
Wilson, Kyle 32,
Wilson, George 240, 260
Wilson, -- referee 236
Winchester, Ernie (Aberdeen) 332
Winning, George 44

Wishaw Juniors 331
Wolverhampton Wanderers 192, 441
Wood, Jock 175, 193, 305, 326, 331, 366, 391, 419
Woodburn, Willie (Rangers) 153, 429
Woods, Chris (Rangers) 98
Woolwich Arsenal 379
World Cup 47, 140, 173, 466, 475, 508, 509, 513
Wright, Alex (Partick Thistle) 185
Wright, Drey (St Johnstone) 24
Wright, Tommy 224, 282, 410
Wright, Tommy (St Johnstone) 24

Y

Yardley, George 233, 320
Yoker 193
Yorston, Harry (Aberdeen) 337
Young, Alec (Hearts) 158, 181
Young, Andy (Raith Rovers) 134
Young, Archie (Dunfermline Athletic) 195
Young, Darren 11, 24, 31, 60, 222
Young, Douglas, politician 502
Young, George (Rangers) 153, 246, 283, 284, 429, 468
Young, Jake 105, 120, 270, 320, 333, 352, 360
Young, Lloyd 49, 124, 490
Young, Quinton "Cutty" 376
Younger, Tommy (Hibs) 166

Years

1903 1, 4, 17, 80, 81, 125, 175, 210, 227, 258, 326, 460, 517
1904 213, 494
1905 242, 417, 454, 495
1906 324, 379
1907 6, 210
1908 412, 441, 522
1909 348, 392

1910 311, 335, 373, 417
1911 43
1912 39, 311, 378, 499, 518
1913 53, 176, 177, 419, 486
1914 47, 53, 92, 110, 356, 496, 504, 518
1915 23
1916 7, 250
1917 203, 412
1918 13, 110, 212
1919 504, 505
1920 52, 157, 240, 260, 297, 366, 486, 505
1921 8, 46, 89, 130, 205, 243, 265, 301, 346, 391, 460, 505
1922 205, 212, 353, 375, 511
1923 130, 157, 169, 249, 265, 285, 316, 317, 409, 486
1924 115, 127, 157, 329, 499
1925 25, 409, 484
1926 3, 18, 19, 33, 193, 363, 391, 464, 506, 520
1927 3, 19, 108, 151, 272, 304, 305, 311, 326, 331, 366, 391, 419, 430, 457, 501
1928 221, 257, 295, 491
1929 248, 297, 301, 406, 409, 467, 499, 514
1930 18, 103, 208, 229, 237, 247, 255, 272, 363, 369, 371, 386, 394, 405, 407, 413, 424, 499, 512
1930s ii, 507
1931 113, 142, 193, 195, 291, 298, 375, 433, 467, 477, 499, 512
1932 290, 297, 491
1933 87, 498, 507
1934 44, 272, 363, 371
1935 129, 271, 311, 457, 516
1936 15, 44, 262, 271, 314, 368, 457, 485
1937 182, 253, 336, 355
1938 4, 186, 279, 296, 309, 361, 365, 381, 382, 387, 388, 400, 414, 415, 430, 431, 436, 437, 438, 439, 440, 465, 476, 479, 480, 482, 500, 503
1939 47, 93, 110, 147, 222, 304, 380, 403, 476
1940s 2, 48, 267, 270, 465, 487
1942 519
1943 16, 34, 484
1944 186, 502, 519
1945 3, 12, 37, 207, 497, 515
1946 16, 33, 144, 168, 201, 219, 491, 499, 515
1947 3, 14, 19, 34, 67, 143, 167, 185, 186, 199, 200, 267, 309, 325, 338, 350, 361, 484
1947/48 3, 14, 34, 67, 185, 484
1948 12, 29, 100, 101, 112, 164, 214, 349, 374, 383, 407, 410, 432, 468
1949 3, 14, 31, 34, 43, 84, 111, 132, 136, 151, 152, 153, 161, 162, 163, 191, 192, 234, 252, 259, 441, 484, 493
1949/50 3, 31, 34, 43, 484
1950 43, 73, 82, 139, 165, 280, 312, 334, 372, 399, 429
1950s 2, 19, 48, 96, 165, 171, 188, 233, 270, 315, 389, 434, 442, 465, 487
1951 10, 34, 159, 178, 241, 246, 283, 312, 428
1952 15, 29, 34, 165, 263, 283, 284, 293
1953 3, 29, 79, 97, 126, 134, 135, 156, 165, 166, 183, 184, 185, 207, 315, 329, 337, 357, 384, 404, 422, 427, 473, 492
1953/54 3, 135, 315
1954 91, 141, 165, 416, 455, 475, 484, 509
1955 19, 54, 181, 224, 253, 282, 395, 410, 455, 483
1956 9, 29, 33, 57, 72, 109, 189, 211, 330, 362, 403
1957 33, 68, 77, 158, 177, 238, 264, 339, 362, 475
1958 9, 33, 173, 265, 268, 282, 411, 423
1959 29
1960 9, 173, 244, 315, 320

543

1960s 35, 96, 171, 270, 332
1961 204, 233, 270
1962 71, 102, 294, 396
1963 95, 117, 123, 230, 321, 325, 332, 370
1964 65, 105, 120, 131, 236, 254, 292, 321, 332, 358, 360, 367, 393, 481
1965 96, 133, 173, 332, 333, 352, 367
1966 47, 95, 140, 171, 275, 353, 354
1967 47, 121, 190, 275, 303, 313, 325, 398, 481, 487
1968 38, 69, 70, 122, 270
1969 270
1970 174, 245, 307, 308
1971 198, 268, 306, 411
1972 135, 160, 180, 281, 364, 390, 417
1973 202, 340, 341, 342, 343
1974 116, 245, 256, 351, 446, 451
1975 76, 216, 318, 351, 451
1976 206
1977 376
1981 215, 266, 275, 278
1982 179, 245, 300, 403, 421, 466, 499, 508
1983 99, 170, 347
1984 64, 318, 345
1986 98, 450
1988 389
1989 66, 170
1990 389
1991 310
1993 56, 447
1994 56, 66, 235, 276, 336, 465
1995 74, 75, 146, 170, 245, 288
1996 83
1997 19
1998 1, 20, 21, 22, 194, 215, 217, 513
1999 35, 155
2000 294
2001 35, 463
2002 114, 209
2003 458, 459, 461, 484
2004 456
2007 145, 146, 434, 452, 453, 462, 463
2008 128, 218, 344, 377, 425, 426, 434, 435
2009 490
2010 48, 49, 78, 124, 225, 226, 288
2011 225, 288, 289
2012 62, 63, 85, 86, 137, 138, 188, 231, 232
2013 104, 187, 188, 471, 472, 478
2014 24, 33, 55, 469, 470
2015 40, 41, 269, 448, 449
2016 26, 27, 42, 60, 61, 85, 106, 119, 327, 328, 401, 402, 418, 420, 442, 443
2017 10, 11, 28, 30, 31, 32, 58, 59, 222, 223, 273, 274, 286, 287, 474
2018 24, 36, 118, 302, 303, 325, 425

www.ingramcontent.com/pod-product-compliance
Lightning Source LLC
Chambersburg PA
CBHW071732150426
43191CB00010B/1544